# North–South Knowledge Networks

## Towards equitable collaboration between academics, donors and universities

Edited by Tor Halvorsen
and Jorun Nossum

AFRICAN
MINDS

Published in 2016 by

African Minds
4 Eccleston Place, Somerset West, 7130, Cape Town, South Africa
info@africanminds.org.za
www.africanminds.org.za

and

UIB Global
PO Box 7800
5020 Bergen
http://www.uib.no/en/research/global

ISBNs
9781928331308 PRINT
9781928331315 e-Book
978192833-322 e-Pub

Copies of this book are available for free download at
www.africanminds.org.za and http://www.uib.no/en/research/global

ORDERS
For orders from Africa:
African Minds
Email: info@africanminds.org.za

For orders from outside Africa:
African Books Collective
PO Box 721, Oxford OX1 9EN, UK
Email: orders@africanbookscollective.com

# Contents

# Preface

*Tor Halvorsen and Jorun Nossum*

This book emerged out of a workshop held at the University of Bergen in June 2015 with participants from a number of the projects within the Norwegian Higher Education and Development (NORHED) programme. A number of other academics who are interested in how development aid can promote higher education and research have also contributed to the book.

The topic of academic collaboration between South and North is not new. However, during the workshop it became clear that, as the academic world becomes more and more marked by competition, it is time to rethink academic collaboration, in relation to what space it can claim in programmes such as NORHED's.

In our call for papers to be presented at the workshop, we indicated that the NORHED programme builds on ideas about true knowledge societies being based on the notion of gift societies that can operate at national and international (or post-national) level.

To quote our call for papers, we hoped to bring together academics who

> choose to collaborate across borders and boundaries in the interests of improving knowledge as we wish and think best.

We use publications from wherever we can get them, and publish what we know openly. We stand on one another's shoulders, and we all contribute. The well-known 'regulars' on curriculums all over the world are so because they build on the undercurrent of researchers. Lesser-known research-ers appear in the often very long lists of references of articles or books. Thus, the academic community is like a gift-society, where we constantly exchange bits and pieces of knowledge, or create networks for a more systematic structuring of these gift-relations for the benefit of all.

Our call for papers however also noted that

this gift-society is however easily distorted. It is influenced by competitive forces from the outside and misplaced social ambitions on the inside. These undermine and transform the gift-relations on which academic knowledge-production depends. Today, this can be observed in the ways universities are being transformed for competition. Knowledge resources increasingly become tools for promoting this competition. The academic honour that was earlier driving the exchanges of knowledge (gifts), and which constitute a *raison d'être for all academic work,* is transformed into organisational resources for promotion of one's own position. What deter-mines this position is reputation gained from external evaluations, external rating, systems of ranking, and all kinds of citation and other measurable quantities of produc-tion. Rankings seem to be more discussed by professors than their latest books. Resources are spent on the so-called 'best', who are isolated in centres of excellence where they are una-ble to live up to their gift commitments. This takes an extra toll on the 'next-best', to the degree that they may vanish: the pool of knowledge diminishes. In such a scenario, univer-sities develop strategies to enhance reputation, important in external evaluations, which give access to resources. Within these strategies, collaboration with universities that may

improve one's perceived standing in society becomes important. Collaboration must be justified as a tool for better
positioning oneself in competition for resources. Such strategic choices contradict the gifts exchanged between academics
in open public space.

Many of these thoughts are elaborated on in the first chapter by Göran
Hydén, in which he develops a taxonomy of types of academic collaboration. Hydén shows that this is a complex world, with many competing
models. Hydén also offers a number of suggestions as to how such
programmes should work today, and explains why he favours the re-in-
statement of gift-society types of exchange, arguing that 'higher
education and research in low-income countries needs continued support but on terms that are different from the standard approaches
adopted by the OECD donor cartel in the past' (this volume: p.30).

In Chapter 2, the focus shifts to South Africa's Square Kilometre
Array (SKA), a bilateral astronomy project. John Higgins shows how
government officials justified this huge and costly project, not in terms
of the opportunities it provides to extend and enlarge academic knowledge worldwide, but with reference to the practical spin-offs and
benefits that can be capitalised on in the competitive academic world.
Thus, the proper links between theory and the empirical world, which
should underpin such huge projects, have been lost. Higgins explains
why current higher education policy is limiting and damaging, both in
South Africa, and across the world, and why the relationship between
curiosity and innovation must be reaffirmed and encouraged.

In Chapters 3 to 6, higher education in Uganda is in the spotlight. In
Chapter 3, Eren Zink shows how social identities and job prospects
strongly influence how Ugandan PhD students navigate international
academic landscapes. Having studied how a variety of programmes
move people around as they seek to gain their PhDs, he shows how
so-called sandwich programmes enable PhD candidates to maintain
their status at home, while gaining exposure to international research
institutions and networks.

In Chapter 4, ABK Kasozi discusses the scarcity of research in
Ugandan universities, the role of donors in setting research agendas,

and the danger that this represents to the integrity of academics and universities. Acknowledging that funding is crucial, Kasozi argues that donor programmes should be directed towards the building of solid partnerships between academics at the micro level, thus strengthening both disciplines and faculties. In many ways, Kasozi supports the ideas behind the NORHED programme, insisting that when knowledge develops within relations of mutual exchange, both parties are better able to understand one another and are then more likely to find ways to work around the problems generated by globalisation to their mutual benefit.

In Chapter 5, Mahmood Mamdani, based on his experience at Makerere University and of numerous donor programmes, invites discussion about the role of the state in governing public universities. He is critical of how the Ugandan government legitimises its tight rein on the university, controlling its leadership structure yet failing to fund or manage the institution adequately. Pointing out what donor money and international collaboration *can't* do, he highlights some of the issues his own research institute has faced in building research capacity and postgraduate training. As he observes, more important than how much money an institution has, is how its money gets used.

In Chapter 6, Maria Musoke and Ane Landøy present an example of how relations between university libraries can enhance the quality of these crucial departments. In many ways, this collaboration can serve as a model for wider academic co-operation, and shows how productive a *mutual* exchange of resources and expertise can be.

In Chapter 7, Johnson Muchunguzi Ishengoma moves us to Tanzania. His concerns are of a more general kind: how the contemporary development-aid framework enables donors and Northern research institutions to impose their values on research agendas globally, and on North-South research collaborations in particular. Like NORHED, Ishengoma is critical of overly simplistic ideas about capacity building, and points out that far more is at stake – whose knowledge counts, and what should be researched, for example. He questions the power asymmetries inherent in much donor-funded research, and outlines what he sees as characteristics of effective North–South collaboration.

Recounting an incident of brutal repression at the University of Malawi, Joe Mlenga describes in Chapter 8 how the state seeks to control all knowledge development, fearing that its own power will be undermined by independent research and teaching. As Mlenga notes, the risks are high for those promoting academic freedom, but without it, no institution can really claim to be a university.

In Chapter 9, Fadwa Taha and Anders Bjørkelo take the case of Sudan to show how strict state and ideological control of higher education has undermined universities, academic research, curriculum content and much international networking. The authors see the future of tertiary education in Sudan as bleak, and their chapter serves as a reminder that any overly simplistic 'decolonisation programme' can lead to a stripping away of knowledge, to the great detriment of the local and the wider worlds.

Ishtiaq Jamil and Sk Tawfique M Haque debate the complicated relations between the 'donor North' and 'recipient South' in Chapter 10, highlighting the conflicts between the altruism of academic co-operation and the strategic interests of state and economic actors. Based on years of their own of experience with several projects, the authors offer a well-grounded argument in favour of academic co-operation, showing that it can be beneficial for all parties, and offer all partners access to new knowledge that is relevant to their own contexts, as well as to the global challenges we face. Post-colonial domination can thus be transformed into post-colonial learning that is entirely new. The authors suggest a number of ways of organising North–South interactions so as to make collaborations more rewarding for all.

In Chapter 11, Jorun Nossum draws on her experience of North–South collaborations in the higher education and research sector to discuss the challenge of creating equal partnerships. Noting that many donors seem to be giving up on trying to strengthen institutions in lower-income countries, and now prefer to drive aid exclusively via Northern institutions, Nossum considers how academic collaboration can be organised to secure high(er)-quality linkages between academics in, for example, Norway and East Africa. She insists that it is possible, albeit far from easy, to unite donor and academic interests to the benefit of both, and ultimately also to the benefit of the world's least-resourced communities.

In the final chapter, Tor Halvorsen argues that universities are entering a new phase of development that has the potential to transform relations between academics in the South and the North. Explaining why the massive environmental challenges facing the world require the building of 'universities of democracy', Halvorsen argues that the aim of universities must be to build knowledge exchanges and strengthen the academic community in ways that undermine neoliberalism's already crumbling hegemony and destroy the dominance of the 'knowledge economy' in universities and research agendas.

Taken together, the chapters in this book attempt to contribute to the debate about how development aid can and should be a tool for improving knowledge societies, based on a 'gift-oriented' understanding of how academics can work together. We invite readers to take up the discussion in their own institutions, pointing out how donor programmes such as NORHED can contribute to improving collaborations and capacity development among researchers.

The NORHED programme, as Nossum shows in Chapter 11, emerged after a long process of trial and error. Various Norwegian actors have a long history of co-operation with universities in the South. The University of Bergen, for example, recently celebrated its 50-year-old relationship with the University of Khartoum. Several inter-governmental and development-aid programmes have evolved out of this and other experiences with academics in developing countries, creating a financial base for long-term research and teaching collaborations between universities in Norway and a number of countries in the South (see Hydén, this volume).

In 1999, Norway's Ministry of Foreign Affairs developed a strategy for offering higher education support to developing countries while working closely with the Norwegian academic community. The research and education ministries have supported similar initiatives, and the university sector has gradually come to value North–South collaborations for contributing to and improving their internationalisation strategies. The Research Council of Norway has, over the years, supported projects with the explicit purpose of strengthening collaborative research with universities in the South.

The NORHED programme builds on all of this, but also represents something new. Firstly, it has taken the bold step of putting actors in the South in the driving seat – finally putting into practice an idea that has been discussed in development circles for decades. In terms of project content, administration and budgets, the so-called Southern partners are in control. In principle, the partner in Norway is (re)-funded by their Southern partner/s.

Secondly, the units of collaboration are universities themselves, and within these, the academics propose their own projects. Project leaders thus emerge from within the academic environment, define their own needs, and contribute, ideally at least, to strengthening academic knowledge and resources within the institution they are affiliated to. Funding is not directed specifically towards the governance and general development of the sector, but instead seeks to grow institutions by strengthening education quality and research, and the relationship between them.

Thirdly, the NORHED programme provides a framework that is based on input from the South as well as from actors in Norway. Above all, this framework values and seeks to promote what is too easily forgotten in contemporary times: the link between teaching and research. NORHED's focus is on the quality of scholarship and academic work, particularly in masters and PhD programmes. This is based on the view that universities cannot improve unless the candidates that these universities educate can make the most of their research opportunities, and thereby ensure the development of high-quality research staff.

Capacity building is defined as supporting those who enter universities so that they can use their time and talent to push themselves as much as possible. This too presupposes the engagement and a high level of skill among their professors. Research collaborations supported by NORHED makes it possible for researchers to fully dedicate themselves to their studies, and ensures that they are trained by scholars who are themselves active researchers with international credibility. The support given to emerging academics invites and encourages them to constantly expand and traverse the borders of academic knowledge.

It follows from this that the NORHED programme acknowledges the status and autonomy of the academic community. Its support validates the notion that academic knowledge matters, and that the voices of scholars are worth hearing. The hope is that the programme will be able to strengthen links between academics and society and that the professors and their students will be able to provide evidence-based advice to those who ask, but also, and much more importantly, reach those who do not ask and do not want to hear. Again, the programme seeks to promote respect in society for scholarship, and particularly of the critical kind that presupposes academic freedom.

Fundamental to the framework is the concept that knowledge is socially embedded in three ways; that is, how you educate, what you educate and who you educate matters. Historically, all over the world, this embeddedness has prioritised the male world. This will gradually change at universities to the degree that parity is achieved between the genders. In Norway, for example, labour-market and educational reforms, combined with strong women's movements, have transformed how knowledge is gathered and communicated, who has access to universities, and what is taught to ensure and promote gender equality. In most countries, gender bias towards men reproduces itself in politics and culture, and the world of work generally offers few incentives to change this. Women's liberation movements are resisted. The most crucial agent of change in this context is the re-embedding of knowledge and the academic sector in programmes that are sensitive to issues of gender and identity. Prioritising the recruitment of women is obviously a basic precondition for projects supported by NORHED. Thus, instead of just reflecting social values, the NORHED programme is aware that universities are institutions of culture and belonging, with significant social influence and impact, and aims to contribute to the ability of universities to strengthen value systems. If universities are to play this role, their independence and academic freedom must be unquestionable.

Like most education, one of the aims of the programme is to help create a more skilled workforce. However, this is not based on a narrow idea of utility-based qualifications, but rather on reflective knowledge, ensuring that education for work and education for democracy go together.

Compared to a number of other donor programmes NORHED's goals build on ideas about development rarely seen today. Other programmes have, for example, *political* goals such as building better leaders, *functional* goals relating to promoting economic growth, *pedagogical* goals producing better students or *social* goals of spreading enlightenment and promoting middle-class values.

Instead, the NORHED programme seems to be based on a more organic idea. By accepting that knowledge is embedded within a social context, NORHED projects aim to shape this context through the ways in which staff are recruited, how research problems are defined and prioritised, etc. It is also accepted that different cultures need to grow 'their own trees' (as noted by Mamdani in Chapter 5 of this volume), and nurture seeds in their native soil, where the climate allows them to grow. At the same time, the international collaborations and partnerships that are intrinsic to the programme promote the awareness that trees can be grown in many ways and for many different purposes, and that through academic openness, knowledge and skills about how to plant and cultivate entire forests can be created and shared.

This 'organic garden' model builds on what is already there, while also welcoming change by strengthening the ability to build knowledge networks that may develop new and shared theory. The seemingly idealistic presuppositions underpinning the NORHED model will no doubt face challenges as the programme is implemented.

This is not the first book to raise these topics. Nor will it be the last. We hope this book will inspire both critical reflection and new ideas, perhaps even improved practice, and thus form part of an ongoing dialogue.

This book would not have been published without the detailed comments and suggestions provided by our anonymous peer reviewers and the work of freelance copy editor Mary Ralphs. We are thankful for their efforts. We are also grateful for the suggestions and support of our publisher, Francois van Schalkwyk and his team at African Minds.

# Frequently used acronyms and abbreviations

| | |
|---|---|
| (2iE) | International Institute of Water and Environmental Engineering |
| AAU | Association of African Universities |
| ACE | African Centres of Excellence |
| AERC | African Economic Research Consortium |
| AfDB | African Development Bank |
| BRICS | Brazil, Russia, India, China and South Africa |
| CODESRIA | Council for the Development of Economic and Social Research in Africa |
| DAAD | German Academic Exchange Services |
| DANIDA | Danish International Development Agency |
| DDS | Document Delivery Service |
| DFID | Department for International Development |
| EU | European Union |
| IAU | International Association of Universities |
| ILO | International Labour Organization |
| ISESCO | Islamic Educational, Scientific and Cultural Organization |
| IDRC | International Development Research Center |
| IFS | International Foundation for Science |
| IT | information technologies |
| ICT | information and communication technologies |
| Maklib | Makerere University Library |
| MAKIR | Makerere University Institutional Repository |
| MDGs | Millennium Development Goals |
| MISR | Makerere Institute of Social Research |
| NGO | non-governmental organisation |
| NIF | National Islamic Front, Sudan |
| NOMA | Norwegian Medicines Agency |
| NORAD | Norwegian Agency for Development Cooperation |
| NORHED | Norwegian Programme for Capacity Development in Higher Education and Research for Development |

| | |
|---|---|
| NUFU | Norwegian Programme for Development, Research and Education |
| OECD | Organisation for Economic Co-operation and Development |
| PHEA | Partnership for Higher Education in Africa |
| SANORD | Southern Africa–Nordic Centre |
| SAREC | Swedish Agency for Research Cooperation with Developing Countries |
| SDGs | Sustainable Development Goals |
| SIDA | Swedish International Development Cooperation Agency |
| SIU | Norwegian Centre for International Cooperation in Education |
| TRIPS | Trade-Related Aspects of Intellectual Property Rights |
| UK | United Kingdom |
| UNESCO | United Nations Education, Scientific and Cultural Organization |
| US/USA | United States of America |
| USAID | United States Agency for International Development |
| UOBL | University of Bergen Library |

# CHAPTER
# 1

# The role and impact of funding agencies on higher education and research for development

*Göran Hydén*

Financial and political support for higher education and research are generally considered crucial to any country's development. This support has become even more critical in recent decades, with the growing emphasis on creating 'knowledge societies'.[1] With universities deemed so important for progress, their quality and output are constantly measured. However, global ratings and rankings invariably indicate that the best universities are found in higher-income countries, and confirm that, in this arena, like most others, large discrepancies exist between low and high-income countries.[2] Globalisation is changing this situation somewhat, with middle-income countries and 'emerging economies' – such as China, India, Brazil, Malaysia and Turkey – becoming more widely known for offering quality higher education and for funding research. However, many countries, especially those in the lower-income group, are not in a position to spend as much on research and higher education as they might wish. They remain dependent on donor funding to sponsor certain research and tuition programmes and even basic infrastructure and equipment.

In this chapter, I discuss the role and impact of donor funding within the world of higher education and research. The chapter is divided into three sections. In the first section, given the absence of a comprehensive overview and analysis of donor funding for the sector, I attempt to map what donors have done in the past, as well as how they currently work and why. In the second section, I analyse the consequences that seeking external funding for higher education and research has had for low-income countries that do not allocate sufficient domestic resources to fund this sector. In the third section, I suggest various policy priorities for the future. My main argument is that while low-income countries could hardly have done without donor support, its consequences have not always been positive. There is room to consider what might help strengthen local capacities in these countries so that higher education and high-quality research can be pursued in more equitable and sustainable ways.

## Mapping the role of funding agencies

Donor funding for higher education and research is complex and difficult to fully map and understand. Donors use different classifications and categories, which makes it tricky to identify funding flows and where these go.[3] Funding priorities also change fairly often. I attempt to get on top of these reporting issues but I do not pretend to tell the full story (see the Appendix to this chapter for a list of the organisations researched).

Donor support for higher education and research is strongly concentrated in sub-Saharan Africa, although a few countries in Asia such as Bangladesh and Nepal also receive support for higher education from international donors. Donors tend to select countries using three main criteria.

The *first* is donor-driven and countries included are identified as 'principal programme countries' in the donor government's strategy for development co-operation. Following the 2005 Paris Declaration's call to avoid duplication, and organise a kind of 'division of labour' in the donor community, some donors reduced the number of countries they support – the Nordic countries did this, for example.

The *second* criterion relates to colonial legacies, and applies especially to Belgium and France, which both helped to create universities in Africa based on their own models at home. While some universities in the former British colonies have worked hard to 'Africanise' their staff and curricula, this has happened much less in the former Belgian and French colonies, where the higher education sector has continued to be closely related to the systems in the former colonial states.[4]

The *third* criterion is self-selection, and assumes that because institutions in the recipient countries have initiated projects for which they require support, they own the ideas behind them. Where this is the case, donors sometimes support higher education and research even in countries that lie outside their usual range of priorities.

## History of donor funding

Support for higher education and research in many of the world's lower-income countries goes back to the 1950s and 1960s when the US, and later the European countries, began providing considerable support.[5] The US was motivated by its strategy to counter communist influence, initially in Latin America but later also in Africa and Asia. Some European countries followed suit, partly related to compensating for their colonial occupation. The Nordic countries, which had no colonial record to speak of, joined in for more altruistic reasons, especially after African countries gained independence. In all cases, support for higher education was seen as part of nation-building, and can be broadly divided into three phases as outlined below.

### The first wave

This covers the 1960s and 1970s, when support consisted largely of three components. The *first* was funding for 'bricks and mortar'– that is, funds were directed towards the construction of buildings for teaching and research. Laboratories and other equipment needed for the more technical disciplines of the natural and physical sciences were included. Norway's extensive support for the creation of a forestry school at Sokoine University of Agriculture in Tanzania, Germany's funding for the establishment of the College of Engineering and

Technology at the University of Dar es Salaam, and Swiss support for infrastructure development and maintenance at the same institution, are examples of this. The Ford Foundation was also selectively involved in financing the construction of buildings at, for example, Makerere University in Uganda and the University of Ibadan in Nigeria.

The *second* component was technical assistance delivered by academic staff. In the 1960s and 1970s, many of the professors in the new universities in Africa were expatriates from many different countries. The largest contingents were American, British and French, but the Nordic countries also sent academic staff to various African institutions on short-term contracts.

The *third* component was that a large number of young African students were given scholarships to complete their doctoral studies at American and European universities. The Ford and Rockefeller Foundations were major sponsors in the fields of agriculture and the social sciences. Germany focused on more technical fields such as engineering. No particular pattern is apparent in the scholarships offered by the Nordic countries. It should also be noted that many of those still teaching in African and Asian universities, especially in the hard sciences, received their initial doctoral education in what were then communist countries, such as Bulgaria, East Germany and the Soviet Union.

## The reversal

In the 1980s and 1990s, higher education fell out of favour with the donor community. Several African governments adopted the same attitude. Higher education was seen as expensive and as benefitting only a small and privileged group. Evidence of the 'brain drain' did not help. Why should donors support higher education, they argued, when the benefits tended to be so minor for the lower-income countries? The nail in the coffin was a World Bank report, which estimated that in low-income countries the social rate of return (that is, the increase in income) resulting from an additional year of education was on average 13 per cent lower for higher education than for basic education (Psacharopoulos et al. 1986). A subsequent review of 98 countries found that, between 1960 and 1997, the typical social rate of return for primary education was 18.9 per cent, compared to just 10.8 per cent for higher education (Psacharopoulos and Patrinos 2002). Tragically, this 'return-on-investment' philosophy prevailed at the 2000 World Education Forum in Dakar, where the international community agreed that support for primary education would be much more effective in driving broad improvements in social welfare. And, this view was again affirmed in the framing of the Millennium Development Goals (MDGs). As a result, World Bank funding for primary education spiked in the late 1990s (reaching US$ 1.4 billion in 1998) and support for higher education dropped to its lowest level in 2001 (at US$ 120 million).

The World Bank often sets the pace for other donors, but like a large ship, it takes a very long time to turn around. In 1995, when James Wolfensohn took over as its president, the organisation was beginning to rebrand itself as the 'knowledge bank'. Accordingly, their 1998 World Development Report was entitled *Knowledge for Development* (King and McGrath 2004). Two years later, the World Bank published a report with UNESCO, in which it argued that higher education in low-income countries was in a 'perilous' state, and while higher education would not guarantee rapid development, sustained progress would be impossible without it (World Bank 2000). Gradually, the foundations were laid for greater funding of higher education and research.

### The second wave

Today, donor involvement in higher education is widely embraced in what amounts to a second wave of support. The economic benefits to society are taken for granted now that knowledge apparently 'equals power'. In a globalised world, the funding of higher education and research is seen as one way of helping low-income countries to gain greater access to global markets and new technologies. Political support for funding higher education has come from several sources, including the UK's Commission for Africa (via its 2005 report, *Our Common Interest*) and the Danish Africa Commission (via its 2009 report, *Realizing the Potential of Africa's Youth*) (Danish Ministry of Foreign Affairs 2009). Reflecting the priorities of donor countries, most funding is directed towards strengthening the hard sciences and medical faculties. India's Institutes of Technology, which received significant funding during the first wave, are often held up as proof that such investments 'pay off'. If funded at all, the humanities and social sciences (with the possible exception of economics) tend to be seen as lesser priorities.

Ideas about the 'brain drain' have also changed. By building good quality research and education facilities in universities, many countries are working hard to attract academics in the diaspora to return home, thus encouraging 'brain circulation' instead. Institutions in China and India offer the best examples of this. Africa lags behind a bit, but the Network of Ethiopian Scholars encourages Ethiopian scientists in the diaspora and at home to exchange knowledge on local issues. Ghana and Nigeria have similar networks.

## New actors

Support for higher education and research in the South has long been a concern for Western donors, but as wealth accumulates in Asia and the Arab Gulf, new sources of investments in this sector are emerging. These newer actors seem particularly interested in funding the kinds of bricks and mortar developments that are now largely ignored by bilateral Western donors. For instance, the University of Dodoma in Tanzania is being constructed by a Chinese company using a Chinese design. Another example is the Abu Dhabi Fund for Development, which has been in operation since 1971. The full extent of the United Arab Emirates' foreign aid was highlighted in a special report prepared by its Ministry of International Cooperation and Development as follows: 'between 1971 and 2014, government and non-government organisations, charitable and humanitarian institutions in the UAE provided Dh173 billion in foreign aid to 178 countries... Asia received Dh79.4 billion in foreign aid from the UAE during this period, followed by Africa at Dh75.4 billion'. Most of this funding was provided as grants or soft loans, and focused on infrastructure and equipment for various development sectors, including education. In many African countries, basic infrastructure is still badly needed, so this kind of support remains crucial.

China is increasingly offering fellowships for foreign scientists to work at Chinese universities. In January 2009, the Chinese Academy of Sciences announced that it aimed to recruit some 1 500 'top' scientists, professors and doctoral students to work with Chinese researchers. In addition, a special programme, established in the mid-1990s to bring Chinese scholars back home, succeeded in getting 1 300 researchers to return to China by 2009 (Xu 2009). When extending assistance to other countries, China tends to offer short-term and practical courses, as well as 'cultural' education through the Confucius Institutes that have been established on university campuses in several African countries (King 2013).

The Republic of Korea emerged as a donor in the late 1990s, but apart from a few training projects involving South Korean universities and partner institutions in the South, its contribution to higher education and research has so far been minimal. The Korean International Cooperation Agency focuses largely on other aspects of social development.

## What donors do and why

In this section, I begin by outlining the types of support that the OECD countries give to higher education and research, and then examine how donors justify their support for the sector.

### The amounts provided

Given the importance that the international policy community places on statistics and evidence-based policy analysis, I expected it to be reasonably easy to find out what donors spend on higher education and research. This was not the case. What exists is a virtual jungle of figures and claims. Table 1.1 shows how misleading official statistics can be. The figures for the period 2004 to 2008 suggested that the major donors in higher education were not the main development donors,

**Table 1.1 Funding allocated to higher education in low-income countries, 2004–2008 (US$ millions), by donor**

| Donor | 2004 | 2005 | 2006 | 2007 | 2008 |
|---|---|---|---|---|---|
| Germany | 814.12 | 973.33 | 955.74 | 977.15 | 1 094.80 |
| France | 996.24 | 1 140.66 | 1 248.33 | 1 349.45 | 1 072.28 |
| Japan | 294.40 | 497.77 | 471.40 | 425.95 | 488.89 |
| European Community | 13.98 | 125.80 | 162.68 | 209.19 | 185.25 |
| Netherlands | 84.93 | 76.42 | 98.45 | 113.48 | 132.26 |
| Austria | 67.86 | 84.63 | 95.08 | 112.06 | 124.75 |
| Belgium | 80.28 | 51.16 | 92.01 | 113.39 | 105.86 |
| Spain | 38.61 | 59.43 | 53.12 | 43.49 | 99.95 |
| Greece | 17.22 | 26.35 | 17.98 | 56.46 | 72.96 |
| Portugal | 42.67 | 42.14 | 44.09 | 47.02 | 49.02 |
| Norway | 26.91 | 28.72 | 31.21 | 48.38 | 46.04 |
| United States | 39.74 | 17.63 | 23.30 | 13.28 | 42.93 |
| United Kingdom | 0.46 | 0.17 | 1.55 | 54.62 | 40.60 |
| Australia | 21.98 | 7.00 | 28.68 | 40.97 | 26.75 |
| Italy | 5.63 | 1.14 | 8.39 | 5.62 | 17.84 |
| Korea | — | — | 21.47 | 37.21 | 15.59 |
| Switzerland | 3.95 | 10.34 | 11.74 | 11.04 | 12.08 |
| Finland | — | — | 5.47 | 5.05 | 7.00 |
| Canada | 64.90 | 4.83 | 7.48 | 7.43 | 6.68 |
| Sweden | 3.95 | 20.19 | 3.59 | 4.55 | 6.29 |
| Denmark | 0.90 | 1.31 | 2.88 | 1.31 | 2.51 |

*Source:* https://data.oecd.org

such as the UK, the Netherlands or the Nordic countries, but rather Germany, France and Japan.

These statistics, however, do not tally with the figures given by the bilateral agencies themselves. The OECD's statistics for higher education do not include support for research-based education or development research, which has been the mainstay of the mainstream donors. For instance, if we examine the homepage of the Swedish International Development Cooperation Agency (SIDA) using this broader definition, then funding allocated from SIDA's research secretariat to higher education institutions amounted to approximately US$ 100 million in 2009. Moreover, the mainstream donors, unlike those that appear at the top of the OECD list, often provide bilateral support in the form of 'basket funding'. This means that contributions that subsequently flowed into higher education and research were not specifically identified as such. Another factor that skewed the statistics is that various other international and regional inter-governmental and philanthropic organisations that also supported higher education and research are not reflected.

Among the development banks, the World Bank remains by far the dominant one. Since the relatively low allocations of US$120 million that were made towards higher education and research in 2001 and 2004, the World Bank has boosted its funding to this sector considerably. In 2008, the total allocation was US$500 million. By 2015, US$600 million, or 20 per cent of its support for education in sub-Saharan Africa, went into higher education. Most of this went to 19 centres of excellence established at universities across the continent.

In terms of private and philanthropic funders, the Partnership for Higher Education in Africa, which was made up of seven foundations, was the largest single donor, allocating US$300 million between 2000 and 2010. However, this partnership came to an end in 2010, and ongoing funding now continues via some of the individual foundations instead.[6] Other important funders include the Gates Foundation, the UK's Wellcome Trust and Canada's International Development Research Center (IDRC).

## Rationales for funding

Two parameters shape the rationales that donors use to justify supporting higher education. The first is whether they choose to focus their programmes on individuals or institutions. The second is whether their policy perspective justifies educational and cultural or developmental support. To be sure, some donors adopt multiple approaches but their main efforts are nonetheless usually identifiable (see Figure 1.1).

Thus several donors opt for an educational/cultural perspective and focus on individuals. Portugal, with its extensive scholarship programme aimed at strengthening the Lusophone sphere of interest, takes this approach.[7] The Norwegian Programme for Development, Research and Education (NUFU) and NORAD's Programme for Master Studies (NOMA) also focused primarily on training individual scholars in the South (COWI 2009); the International Foundation for Science (IFS) also falls into this category.

France and Belgium are prime examples of countries that provide institutional support from an educational/cultural vantage point. They have been at the forefront of strengthening universities in the Francophone world, not least in Africa. Much of this also applies to Italy and Greece, although their support is not limited to former colonial territories.

**Figure 1.1** A matrix of rationales for donor support

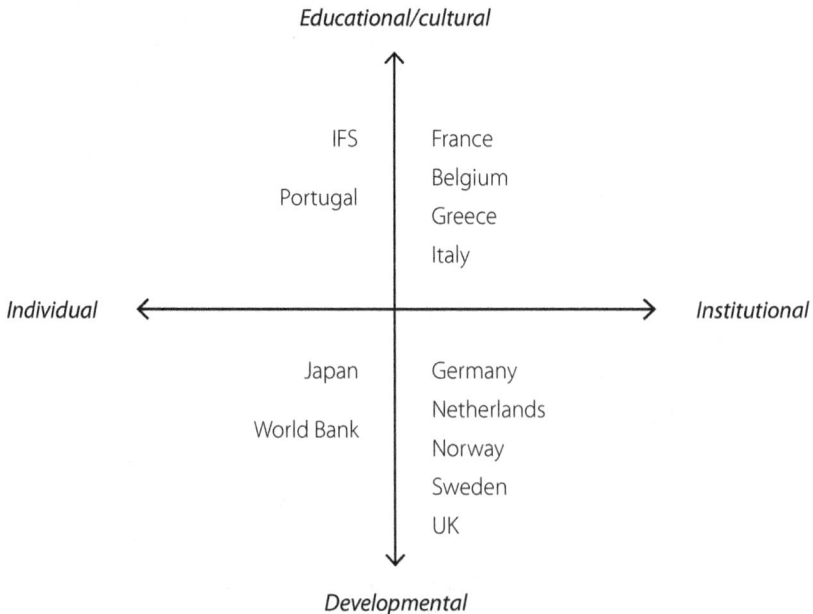

*Educational/cultural*

IFS   France
Belgium
Portugal   Greece
Italy

*Individual* ⟵                          ⟶ *Institutional*

Japan   Germany
Netherlands
World Bank   Norway
Sweden
UK

*Developmental*

The World Bank takes multiple approaches, but among these are a series of scholarships aimed at strengthening capacity to analyse development issues. Japan has a similar programme, which it runs partly through the World Bank. Many of the other southern European donors also tend to justify funding higher education and research in terms of development, but focus more on building institutional capacity. These organisations also lean towards supporting research and research-based education. With the exception of the UK, these countries have no history of close institutional links with the South and tend to be moved by the global development agenda – that is, as this shifts, so too does donor funding. Their support has been less focused on scholarship programmes, and has instead prioritised institutional development and partnerships or networking arrangements between universities in the North and the South as well as, more recently, between institutions in the South.[8] Norway is interesting because it is the only Nordic country that has run ongoing scholarship programmes for students from the South for several decades. The provision of these scholarships explains why Norway features so far above Denmark, Finland or Sweden in the OECD's statistics.

## Types of support

As noted, activities that donors fund can broadly be divided between support for individuals or institutions, and it can also be categorised in terms of whether the support is focused on a single entity or on many. This makes it possible to identify four types of donor support: scholarships, institutional development, networks and partnerships as shown in Figure 1.2. The distinction I make between networks and partnerships is that the former involve individuals, while the latter are built between institutions. In the next few sections, I outline some of the most significant initiatives in each category.

## Scholarships

Scholarships are less dominant than they were before 2000, but, as noted, they still constitute a major part of the support offered,

**Figure 1.2.** Types of donor support

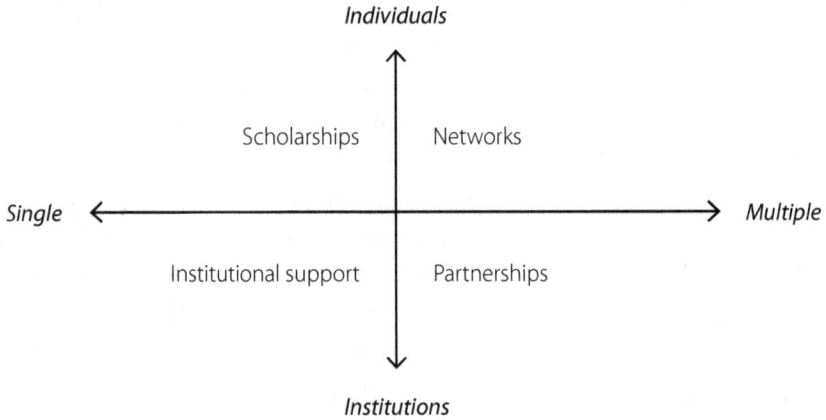

*Individuals*

|  |  |
|---|---|
| Scholarships | Networks |

*Single* ⟵————————————————⟶ *Multiple*

|  |  |
|---|---|
| Institutional support | Partnerships |

*Institutions*

especially by non-OECD donors such as China and India. Several southern European countries also allocate most of their support to
scholarships. *France*, for example, spends approximately half of its aid
on scholarships – mostly in support of postgraduate study in France
and less for study in low-income countries (Lewis 2009).

As shown in Table 1.1, *Germany* is one of the world's biggest supporters of higher education. Much of its funding is managed by the
German Academic Exchange Service (DAAD) and involves the provision
of scholarships for study in Germany. Like the Fulbright Program in the
United States, DAAD does not run academic programmes but offers
scholarships, based on merit, for German students to study internationally, and for students from other countries to study at German
universities. With a budget of over US$500 million, DAAD is the largest
organisation of its kind in the world. It supports approximately 50 000
grantees every year, 11 000 of whom are on long-term scholarships.

Apart from the Fulbright Program, the *United States* supports a
number of scholarship programmes. For example, the United States
Agency for International Development (USAID) has run a graduate fellowship programme since 1963. According to an evaluation conducted
after 40 years of operations, USAID had invested US$182 million on
sponsoring no less than 3 200 graduate students from Africa alone to
study at over 200 American universities. The same evaluation found

that, on completing their studies, 85 to 90 per cent of all beneficiaries had returned to their home countries (Lewis 2009).

Since 2006, the European Commission has supported higher education through partnerships between universities within the *European Union* and the rest of the world. These partnerships involve scholarships that allow students from outside the EU to study at European universities. Between 2006 and 2009, approximately US$400 million was spent on 65 partnerships. According to its website, some 12 000 students and staff benefited from these grants (see EACEA 2016).

*British* support for scholarships is also considerable, and is funded partly by DFID and partly by other government institutions. The Commonwealth Scholarship Commission manages most of the funding, offering over 900 awards a year, not all of which go to Commonwealth countries. The scholarships vary in type. The bulk are for students enrolled for PhDs and masters degrees, but quite a few are targeted at academic staff at universities in lower-income countries. In addition, the Commission makes available what it calls 'split-site' scholarships – these are for students doing postgraduate studies in countries outside the UK, and enables them to benefit from a year of study at a UK university.

The *Netherlands* Ministry of Foreign Affairs has been a generous supporter of scholarships through the Netherlands Organization for International Cooperation in Higher Education and Research (EP-NUFFIC). Its main scholarship programme is the Netherlands Fellowship Programme, which offers funding for PhD and masters degrees, as well as for short courses. The programme is demand-driven in the sense that organisations in the South apply and compete for the fellowships. Specific criteria are applied in the selection process so that half of the fellowships are awarded to female candidates and half of the budget is spent on candidates from sub-Saharan Africa.

Although *Norway's* flagship programme (NUFU) had a broader mandate, its scholarship component was significant. For example, between 2007 and 2012, 194 PhD and 294 masters-level graduates were funded. More than a third of these students were female, and many graduated at universities outside of Norway (SIU 2013).[9]

To this list should be added the support provided by the *World Bank,* which operates two separate programmes. The first is the Robert S McNamara Fellowship Program, which supports young researchers working in low-income countries to spend five to ten months in a university, research or development institution in another World Bank member country. The second programme is the Joint Japan/World Bank Scholarship Program, which is funded by the Government of Japan, and focuses exclusively on supporting graduate studies in subjects related to development. To qualify, students must demonstrate that they have been admitted to a development-related masters programme in a pre-approved university. By 2015, the programme had awarded over 5 000 scholarships selected from more than 65 000 applicants, and disbursed over US$200 million in funding from the Japanese government (World Bank 2015).

Of special interest, too, is the IFS, which is based in Uppsala, *Sweden,* and provides research grants to younger scholars, giving priority to women, following up with short capacity-building courses and grants for obtaining necessary equipment. Its geographic focus is on lower-income countries with weak research infrastructures, the majority of which are in Africa. In 2011, the IFS awarded 219 research grants to students whose work demonstrated high scientific quality, relevance and purpose. To strengthen its presence and role in Africa, the IFS established a 'hub' in Kampala, Uganda. IFS is supported by a consortium of bilateral donors, including Sweden, Norway, the UK, the US, Switzerland and France, as well as private foundations, including the US-based MacArthur Foundation and Switzerland's Syngenta Foundation.

### Institutional support

The development of key institutions has been a major focus for Western donors. In the higher education and research sector, donors have aimed to contribute to the creation of professional environments in which academic pursuits can flourish. In the 1970s, donors gave priority to building national research councils but these were abandoned some ten years later after an evaluation concluded that the funds had been used primarily to build new bureaucracies that had done little to serve the academic community (SAREC 1985).

Subsequent efforts to support institutional development focused on individual institutions, notably those with known track records. Thus, the Nordic donors, especially Norway and Sweden, have given both project-specific and longer-term support to Makerere University in Uganda, the University of Dar es Salaam in Tanzania, and Eduardo Mondlane University in Mozambique. Project support has typically been research-based but also aimed at building departments or faculties. Other donors have paid special attention to upgrading university libraries and some, such as the Bill and Melinda Gates Foundation, have contributed to building and improving the infrastructure needed for the effective use of information technology.[10]

Support for specific university *departments* is often given via institutional collaboration with a corresponding department, usually at a university in the North but there is a readiness to make this a South–South venture too. Departmental support tends to be driven by individual scholars, so it also tends to be research-based and to benefit mainly those who are directly involved in specific research projects. Other benefits generally relate to increased prestige for departments within their institutions or internationally. As in the North, being able to generate research funding is one measure of success, both for individual researchers and their departments.

Funding directed towards whole faculties (or colleges as they are sometimes called) or entire universities usually focuses on cross-cutting issues such as increasing the recruitment of female academics and senior managers, curricular reform, and management training, notably in the field of finance. This kind of support tends to form part of 'core funding' or be provided in the form of funds that can be used to hire consultants. An interesting aspect of Sweden's core support to several universities is the establishment of faculty-wide funds to support small research projects initiated by local scholars.

Institutional governance and management have generally not been of major concern to bilateral donors but have, in some cases, been linked to broader support programmes. For example, Uganda's Makerere University and Mozambique's Eduardo Mondlane University both received money from Norway and Sweden to strengthen university governance. In addition, the Association for the Development of Education in Africa (ADEA), which traces its origins back to 1988, has run a high-profile partnership between the World Bank and the Association of African Universities. ADEA's Working Group on Higher Education has taken the lead in monitoring governance and management issues as well as recommending reforms in this field. Their partnership with the World Bank has helped to direct the attention of university managers in Africa to the experiences of universities in other countries that have gone through similar kinds of expansion processes.

Many donors have attempted to support the growth of centres of excellence. In 2015, the World Bank took the lead in this, and helped fund 19 such centres in West and Central Africa, focused on agriculture, health, medicine or science and technology (World Bank 2014). Joint donor support has been important in creating a number of other such centres.

The International Institute of Water and Environmental Engineering (2iE) is a case in point. Established in 2006, 2iE was set up when two technical colleges that trained engineers and technicians in Burkina Faso merged. Located in Ouagadougou, the country's capital, 2iE's premise is that African development requires students trained at high-quality institutions in Africa. Although it initially catered for French-speaking students only, the institute now has programmes in English. Its degrees are accredited in Europe, and it works with a number of universities and polytechnics, primarily in France and Switzerland. The result is that students worldwide aspire to study there, and its degrees are acknowledged as being on a par with those conferred by European universities. 2iE has extended its network to prestigious institutions in Japan and the US. Created via a public–private partnership, 2iE operates as a foundation and is governed by a board made up of three representatives from each of its four partner categories: African governments, academic institutions, funders and business. Various committees are responsible for matters such as student affairs, academic issues, programme strategy and financial management, and these oversee the day-to-day management of the institution. Its major research themes include climate change and its impact on resources, biodiversity, agriculture, energy, and water issues in Africa. Its courses cover a range of subjects, from mining management to entrepreneurship. The institute has 13 financial sponsors, which include the World Bank, USAID, IDRC, SDC, Japan's International Cooperation Agency (JICA), the UNDP, the EU, the African Development Bank and the French Ministry of Foreign Affairs.

## Scholarly networks

Networks are made up of individual researchers who wish to augment their own activities by interacting with others. In recent years, networking has become common all over the world. Africa, despite its poorer infrastructure, is no exception. Most academic networks focus on a particular sector (such as agriculture), a theme (such as gender), or problem (such as environmental deterioration). I will touch on just a few examples.

The Alliance for a Green Revolution in Africa, based in Accra, is not exclusively a network but serves as such for international and African researchers in the field of agriculture. It is funded by private foundations and bilateral donors.

The Council for the Development of Economic and Social Research in Africa (CODESRIA), based in Dakar, is a social science network, bringing together researchers from all over the continent through a variety of activities. CODESRIA has pursued a broad social science research agenda, but like its sister organisation, the Organization for Social Science Research in Eastern and Southern Africa, based in Addis Ababa, it has also given special attention to issues such as gender. Both organisations are funded by private foundations and bilateral donors.

Gender networks are common both nationally and regionally in Africa. Much the same applies to the environmental sector, in which research networks are often at the forefront of highlighting critical issues, collecting and comparing data, and helping to steer policy discourse. The African Centre for Technology Studies in Nairobi has played a leading role in this area.

## Partnerships

I see partnerships as networks that operate between institutions. USAID's Higher Education for Development was among the first partnership programmes; it sponsored collaboration between universities in the US and lower-income countries between 1987 and 2015. By then, the number of such partnerships exceeded 300 in about 60 different countries. Examples include exchanges and internships between US and Mexican universities, co-operation between schools of public health in East Africa and in the US, and collaboration between Ohio State University and Punjab Agricultural University in India on research into new crops and food products (Lewis 2009).

The European Union's Seventh Framework Programme provides opportunities for a range of individuals and organisations outside the EU to benefit from funding through partnering with European researchers. Such co-operation used to be confined to science and technology but now extends to all EU-funded research. It can involve individuals, public organisations and private companies that have an interest in working with EU institutions, and extends opportunities to individuals and institutions in a hundred different countries outside the EU.

The UK supports partnerships between higher education institutions through its Development Partnership in Higher Education (DELPHE) programme. Since its inception in 2006, it has been managed jointly by the British Council and the Association of Commonwealth Universities. By 2009, it had supported partnerships and multi-institutional projects involving 245 higher education institutions worldwide. Projects range from agriculture, the environment and health to information technology, and also include staff and student training, course redesign and communication workshops (Lewis 2009).

Germany's Higher Education Excellence for Development Cooperation (Ex/CEED) programme is run by the German Academic Exchange Service for the Federal Ministry for Economic Cooperation and Development. Ex/CEED supports institutions that aim to contribute innovatively to the realisation of the Millennium Development Goals and other development programmes. Its aim is to strengthen higher education institutions in the areas of education, research and consultancy. Partnerships it funds include collaborations between German and Southern universities in fields such as sustainable water management, food security, natural resources and public health.

Sweden has been at the forefront of fostering projects that put partners in the North and South on an equal footing. The Swedish model recognises that partnerships that are initiated and dominated by research institutions in the North often have a negligible effect on capacity building in the South. SIDA's policy has been to provide core funding to research-based universities in the South that enables them to work with partners in Sweden or elsewhere, including in the South, and to improve conditions for research – this includes stocking libraries, equipping laboratories, and helping to train academic staff. By providing funding for these core activities, SIDA's expectation is that Southern universities will be able to formulate their own strategies and steer external support into areas that they decide are important, rather than be steered by donors or universities in the North. This principle is one reason that support for development research in Sweden is a relatively small component of SIDA's overall research budget. Support for Swedish researchers is seen as important for maintaining an interest in and capacity for development work among Swedish citizens, but SIDA tries to strike a balance so that the real objective, of building research capacity in the South, is not hijacked along the way (Olsson 2009).

*Canada's* support for research and innovation is managed by the IDRC which, since 1970, has helped researchers and innovators in many countries find ways of overcoming poverty, improving health, promoting democracy and protecting the environment. In carrying out its work, IDRC supports partnerships between Canadian and international organisations on the one hand, and organisations in the South on the other, with the aim of expanding the resource base for research on critical issues. The IDRC is one of very few donors that explicitly emphasise the importance of disseminating research information through scholarly and other networks.

As mentioned, the Partnership for Higher Education in Africa, sponsored by seven private US-based foundations, was a major supporter of higher education between 2000 and 2010. Working in seven countries with 22 universities, this loose network sponsored initiatives identified by the participating institutions in the fields of information and communication technologies; higher education research; regional networks for research and postgraduate training; and a university leaders' forum for exploring the frontiers of knowledge.

The Wellcome Trust launched its African Institutions Initiative with a US$50 million commitment to strengthen Africa's biomedical universities and research institutions through partnerships. More than 50 institutions from 18 African countries are partnered in seven international and pan-African consortiums. Each consortium is led by an African institution and includes research and higher education partners from Australia, Europe and the US. They operate independently and set their own agendas. Activities include: leadership training and professional development; PhD and post-doctoral fellowships; improved infrastructure; competitive grant schemes; and the provision of up-to-date equipment.

The African Economic Research Consortium (AERC) is considered one of the most successful partnerships that donors have helped build. Established in 1988 as a public, not-for-profit organisation, its objective is to strengthen the capacity for independent and rigorous research on issues relating to the management of African economies. Member institutions throughout the region use the network to connect individual researchers. The consortium offers research grants as well as a collaborative training programme for masters and PhD students. Especially innovative is its Joint Facility for Electives, which allows students from a university that does not offer a particular course to take the course with another member institution. AERC publications receive considerable attention within and outside Africa. Researchers supported by the consortium have contributed much to African governance, especially in the field of trade policy, and its collaborative research project on poverty has been instrumental in helping governments develop strategies on the issue. It regularly organises policy-oriented seminars to which government, civil society and private sector representatives are invited. The consortium is governed by a board who are drawn from member institutions, and its professional work is guided by an independent advisory committee made up of

African and international scholars. Its secretariat is based in Nairobi, Kenya. Among those who have served as an executive director is the governor of the Bank of Tanzania, Benno Ndulu. The AERC is supported by nine member funders, and several non-member funders.[11]

A more recent addition to the world of research partnerships in Africa is the Partnership for African Governance and Social Research (PASGR), which was established in 2011 and is also headquartered in Nairobi. It brings together a dozen or so universities from East, Southern and West Africa to conduct joint educational programmes at masters and PhD level. It also organises short courses on research methodologies for academics as well as for representatives of government or civil society organisations that conduct research.

The African Centre for Technology Studies in Nairobi is another example of a network that works closely with the World Agro-Forestry Center on environmental policy.

This list would be incomplete without a reference to the Southern Africa–Nordic Centre (SANORD), which operates out of the University of the Western Cape in South Africa. SANORD grew out of an earlier Norwegian exchange programme with South African universities, and now offers a low-cost arrangement for networking between universities in southern Africa and the Nordic countries. Its 42 member institutions include universities in southern Africa and in the Nordic countries and the Nordic Africa Institute.

There is little doubt that researchers in the South recognise the importance and value of networks and partnerships in the higher education sector. It is also clear that such mechanisms are often most effective when they are initiated by local scholars and operate at various scales and in multiple forums. As one research director has argued, the next important step will be to establish an Africa-wide accreditation scheme (see Muchie 2010).

## The consequences of donor funding

It should be clear from the previous section that donor funding has been a crucial component of the higher education and research sector in low-income countries. Without it, the number of trained scholars in and from Africa would be lower, the width and depth of academic research would be reduced, and researchers would have even less access to libraries and research laboratories. Donor funding has also contributed to enabling African universities to retain cosmopolitan perspectives through exchanges, partnerships and networks. African academics are often the first to acknowledge the role that donors have played in enabling them to pursue their careers in meaningful and positive ways.

What would regional research councils such as CODESRIA have achieved without external funding? What research opportunities would scientists at national universities have had without donor support for libraries and laboratories? How would the quality of teaching have been without the extensive training programmes that donors have funded?

I fully acknowledge that donors' achievements have benefited many individuals in low-income countries. Nevertheless, this story also has a dark side. With the benefit of hindsight, it is clear that not all the consequences of donor funding have been straightforwardly positive. Of course, the donors are not solely responsible for this; they have generally worked in partnership with governments in recipient countries. However, in the higher education sector, at least, many such partnerships have produced results at the cost of national and institutional development in the South.

To be specific, three factors have shaped these partnerships: adherence to a neoliberal economic ideology; commitment to global development goals; and the bureaucratisation of aid relationships. I will now examine each of these factors in more detail to show that although donors might have tried to work as prime drivers of positive change, they also undermined many well-intentioned and carefully prepared schemes for building capacity and professionalism that would have enabled domestic institutions to take responsibility for their own development.

## Adherence to neoliberal economics

The neoliberal economic order that spread across the world in the 1980s arose in response to the incapacity of states to generate national wealth on a sustainable basis. In Africa, for example, national economies seemed to begin well after independence in the 1960s, but by the end of the 1970s, their state-run economies were proving more of a liability than an asset. Producers were punished and consumers favoured in ways that led governing elites to live way beyond what they could afford. Neoliberal economics were meant to rectify this. That is, as these countries transited to neoliberalism, it was envisaged that fewer and fewer resources would be allocated to government institutions, including universities, and that consumers would pay realistic or cost-reflective amounts for services received. The 1980s was an especially difficult decade for African universities. Their incomes fell drastically, and so did the supply of books and equipment necessary to sustain quality education.

Salaries have since bounced back to some extent, and most universities now have career systems in place that reward their employees in ways that compare favourably with those for other public servants. Even so, research institutions face serious challenges, many of which arose as a consequence of neoliberalism. Mahmood Mamdani's chapter in this volume provides a case study of this situation at Makerere University in Uganda, and Mamdani points out that academic remuneration levels, for example, are in no way internationally comparable.

Neoliberalism increased competition between universities, and encouraged the growth of a private higher education sector that lured staff away from the public universities. A report commissioned by UNESCO and the World Bank in 2000 described how the need for donor support in higher education stemmed from what the report called the 'new realities' of 'expansion', 'differentiation' and the 'knowledge revolution' (World Bank 2000).

*Expansion* was explained as resulting from the tremendous increase in student numbers. For example, the University of Buenos Aires and the National University of Mexico grew into 'mega-universities' – both catering for more than 200 000 students. A similar phenomenon occurred across the world. One of the downsides of this rapid expansion has been a real reduction in the quality of the education provided by many institutions.

The huge expansion in student enrolment has been particularly overwhelming for African institutions because academic staffing and capacity has not been increased. Even when universities establish new posts, these are not filled. A capacity deficit has been created, with academic and administrative vacancy rates running at between 25 and 50 per cent (World Bank 2008: 53). This staff shortage can be attributed to many factors, including poor service conditions (Mihyo 2007), a shortage of postgraduate opportunities (Mouton 2008) and low graduation rates (Tettey 2010). It has also led to professors and lecturers teaching in more than one institution.

*Differentiation* refers to the creation of new institutions, many of which are private, to meet the growing demand for higher education. For example, in 1945, Indonesia had just 1 000 university students; yet by 2012, the country had 119 public universities. In addition, 65 accredited private universities and an unknown number of other private institutions were reportedly offering tertiary education in that country. To give another example, Ethiopia had 2 universities in 2000 and 31 universities in 2015. Meanwhile, Tanzania had a total of 26 universities in 2012, 10 of which were public and 16 private. The problem with this is that educational resources, including staff, become very thinly spread. This is particularly true in African countries where the number of well-qualified academics remains small.

The *knowledge revolution* has seen an exponential and continuing increase in access to knowledge in developed countries, but this has yet to have as wide an impact in lower-income countries. Although information technology has made ever-increasing amounts of information accessible, effective and powerful participation in the knowledge economy requires skills that are in short supply worldwide. This is especially true of lower-income countries and even more so in their rural areas. For example, according to a study conducted in 2011, 94 per cent of Rwandans have never used a computer and only 4 per cent feel confident to use one. While 12 per cent of Rwanda's urban population is computer literate, this is true of only 2 per cent of the rural population (NISR 2012).

Donor-to-government cost-sharing has become the most common way of dealing with these realities, and has been strongly recommended by certain economists as necessary for the future (see World Bank 2010). The challenge is to ensure that this does not compromise equity. The University Leaders' Forum (2008) described some examples of scholarships given to poor students from disadvantaged areas of Mozambique, and a loan scheme in Kenya that satisfactorily addresses concerns of both efficiency and equity. Nigeria's Tertiary Education Trust Fund, which receives 2 per cent of national tax revenue, is another good example.

Neoliberalism has done little to enhance academic freedom in Africa. Sure, some progress has been made since the days of one-party states, and the direct control that governments used to exercise over universities is less apparent in some countries. However, many governments continue to use not so subtle means to ensure that public universities pose no political challenge to their rule, making academic freedom precarious in most African countries.

## Commitments to global development

Neoliberalism alone has not only changed the parameters of higher education and research in low-income countries. The donor community's insistence on formulating universal development goals, the MDGs for example, had a similar impact. While it may be difficult to question the moral correctness of working towards education for all, it becomes controversial when this is combined (as it was in the MDGs) with a narrow time frame within which results must be achieved.

African countries, for example, were forced to implement schemes that measured tangible outcomes only – such as the number of schools built or number of girls enrolled in schooling – but which required no consideration of the consequences involved in this overly simplified approach to progress. These forced attempts to get results have been disastrous in countries where governments have no resources to support basic bricks and mortar investment or to meet development goals that have been set above their heads. Many countries cannot afford the ongoing costs of teachers' salaries and textbooks, much less the costs of modernising learning environments with the help of computers. As a result, the quality of education has declined at both primary and secondary levels, and this has affected higher education as well. In other words, the expansion of education provision at the lower levels has contributed to rapidly growing numbers of poorly prepared university students. In effect, higher education institutions now need to allocate more educational resources per student while watching their budgets being cut and student numbers rising.

In addition to the loss of quality, the rapid expansion of the education system has occurred in a context in which very little consideration has been given to what skills the labour market needs and can absorb (Ng'ethe et al. 2008). Graduates, not only of primary and secondary schools but also of tertiary institutions, are often forced to accept employment below their formal educational attainment or end up trying to make a living in the informal sector.

The 'youth crisis' in many countries is very much a result of governments' blind adherence to a set of global goals that have no productive relationship to their own local economic and social realities. Observers have rightly criticised donors' excessive focus on programmes such as the MDGs because they risk undermining the long-term investments required for building scientific capacity (see Dickson 2010). Philippine researcher, Lemuel Cacho (2009), has pointed out that when donors fund science on the basis of market or political considerations, the incentives and opportunities for basic research and local scientific discourse tend to decrease.

Furthermore, the uncritical approach adopted by donors and state institutions to rapid expansion and differentiation means that tertiary institutions are making little effort to build a co-ordinated and efficient education system that enables students to move easily between institutions. This is particularly true of the English-speaking African countries,[12] where competition tends to blur the boundaries between universities and other post-secondary training institutions. To earn enough income, some universities have fallen into 'vocational drift', seizing market opportunities to offer vocational training, while polytechnics and the like are engaging in 'academic drift', and constantly seeking university status (Ng'ethe et al. 2008). Increasingly, the universities and polytechnics are starting to imitate each other rather than innovating in their own fields, and a lacuna is developing between the bottom and the top of the educational pyramid, so that the teaching of many basic technical and vocational skills is being completely neglected.

The rapid expansion of student numbers and the proliferation of private and public institutions has highlighted the need for innovation and reform in the higher education sector. Reform has proven difficult, however, because governments have had their hands full just trying to cope with the educational demands they have helped to generate. In several African countries, for instance, reforms have stalled because, for both political and social reasons, governments have opted to spend more money on student allowances than on investments in new equipment and infrastructure. This means that few of Africa's universities are financially sustainable, and the financial gaps that need to be filled to restore the functionality of the higher education system have grown (see AAU 2004).

## The bureaucratisation of aid relationships

The third factor that has shaped the higher education and research sector is the bureaucratisation of aid relationships. This began in the 2000s, with the processes that led up to the 2005 Paris Declaration, and the statements subsequently adopted in Accra in 2008 and Busan in 2011. Effectively, OECD donors agreed to abandon the political conditions that they had imposed in previous decades as long as recipient governments agreed to take greater responsibility for ensuring that donor funds were spent effectively. At a first glance, this might be seen as having tilted the balance of power in favour of aid recipients. After all, donors were agreeing to channel their funds through recipient governments. However, the reality is that donors continue to determine policy direction and priorities, both globally and at a national level with states they support. Recipient governments control little more than policy implementation, and are now expected to comply with onerous and bureaucratic reporting requirements that demand the creation of multiple and complex monitoring systems.

The OECD's Development Assistance Committee has played a leading role in harmonising donor approaches and methodologies so that the institutional architecture that determines aid relationships has become even more heavily loaded in favour of the donors. The underlying assumption seems to be that the more coherent the policy, the higher the chances of success. Donors, therefore, prioritise recipients that develop policy documents that reflect *the donors'* development goals. Recipient country priorities, and the context in which policies are to be implemented, are of secondary concern (even if, in the writing of proposals and reports, they appear much more important than they turn out to be in practice). As a result, every evaluation is carried out in terms of the goals set by donors, as if *aid effectiveness* is the answer to development in low-income countries.

So-called policy dialogues were established to allow development partners to monitor progress in specific sectors, but these have become increasingly contentious because they tend to be dominated by donors' demands for evidence of results. Government officials in recipient countries are often placed in the awkward position of having to respond to these demands, despite being fully aware that consultants and donors determined the terms and timeframes for measuring the outcomes of specific policy initiatives. The standardisation of donor thinking and practice since the mid-2000s has moved decisions about financing even further away from the political and administrative realities in recipient countries, and the ongoing refinements to methodologies for designing and evaluating donor inputs has done nothing to reduce this distance.

The 'general budget support' that has been an integral part of partnerships between donors and recipient governments since the late 2000s is also problematic. In these cases, donor funds are given in respect of a specific policy or programme but funds are paid into a general fund in the treasury of the recipient country. This offers recipient governments an opportunity to direct the money towards other projects before reporting back to the donor. Such practices are almost inevitable in countries where the revenue base is narrow and tax income falls short of official targets. Expenditure-tracking mechanisms have done little to address this, leading increasingly frustrated donors to intensify the already impatient tone that tends to characterise their voices in partner dialogues.

In addition, the bureaucratisation of aid relationships has narrowed perspectives on the role of higher education and research in society. The higher education sector doesn't fit as neatly into poverty reduction strategies as primary or even secondary education do. As a result, donors not only see higher education and research as less significant, they also tend to overlook the special role that universities and research institutions play in the world. Most notably, the higher education sector's claim to autonomy and freedom from political interference has been ignored. In negotiations with recipient governments, donors treat the sector just like any other.

In the past, the funding of research and higher education tended to be treated as a separate entity and was often made available regardless of other policy priorities in particular countries. With increased bureaucratisation, those attempting to elicit support for this sector have had to try to make it fit into categories that are not compatible with the institutional objectives of academic institutions. In Africa, for instance, governments tend to be authoritarian, but academic freedom is seldom highly valued in donor policy documents. In such contexts, bureaucratised donor relations can give governments a licence to curb academic freedom. To sum up, the current aid architecture has done more harm than good, and this is especially so in relation to higher education and research.

## Policy options for the future

Institutions of higher education and research do not lend themselves to quick fixes. They exist to generate outcomes that become visible only after many years. Measuring results solely in terms of numbers of graduates, or numbers of patents and publications, misses the point about the role that these institutions play in a country's development. Nor do higher education institutions lend themselves to performance assessment within the timeframes that typically apply to donor pro-grammes. Unfortunately, donors have shown little readiness to accept or adapt to the characteristics of this sector.

The story of higher education and research in low-income countries highlighted in this chapter indicates that, despite the dire need for donor funding, this support has also given rise to some negative results. First, because higher education and research was perceived as sitting at the top of the education pyramid, the potential consequences for this sector were never adequately considered when the doors to primary and secondary education were opened to all. Second, higher education and research has fallen victim to the pressure on lower-income countries to comply with neoliberal economic policies and global programmes such as the MDGs. In other words, recipient governments have lost their ability to control the sector in ways that work to the benefit of their countries; quality has been sacrificed for the sake of numbers, and tertiary research and training programmes are too often forced to comply with bureaucratic reporting and monitoring systems that tend to undermine their primary purpose.

Drawing on these lessons and looking to the future, perhaps the primary justification for ongoing or new donor support should be to compensate for the retrogressive consequences of previous activities. Higher education and research in low-income countries needs continued support but on terms that are different from the standard approaches adopted by the OECD donor cartel in the past. In conclusion, I suggest five changes that donors could make to their own policies that have the potential to strengthen higher education and research in both the North and the South.

The first is that compliance with global development goals cannot and should not be the most important criterion for donors when they consider supporting particular countries. The MDGs proved to be a trap – statisticians at the UN and policy-makers in the donor community focused on numbers that often bore little relationship to reality and simply overlooked the stories behind how and why goals were or weren't achieved. Low-income countries should not be subjected to similar treatment in relation to the Sustainable Development Goals (SDGs) that were adopted in September 2015 to guide the global community over the next 15 years. Results are important but they must never again be allowed to be as crucial in determining the existence or the nature of partnerships between donor and recipient governments as they have been since the 2000s. Instead, much more emphasis must be given to local ownership of projects and programmes by recipient countries. It is important to note that even though local ownership was a key tenet of the rhetoric surrounding the 2005 Paris Declaration, in practice, this has been completely sidelined by the focus on policy development, and the entrenching of complex systems for measuring and reporting results. In essence, this first policy change relates to the very nature of the partnership between donors and recipients: *give recipients more say over which priorities should prevail and do not relegate their governments to mere implementers of policies and agendas set by donors in global forums.*

The second suggestion is that timelines for implementation of development programmes in low-income countries must be realistic and not determined solely by narrow political and bureaucratic criteria as was the case in the 2000s. In other words, partnerships must be developed on terms that *both* sides have a reasonable chance of fulfilling. Too often in the past, donor timetables placed undue pressures on recipient governments to be accountable to external actors and forced them to leave unattended many complex social and political issues that take time to address. Whether the aim is to tackle corruption or strengthen higher education and research, strong institutions tend to be built in back-and-forth processes that involve gains and losses over time. Many donors are aware of this, but find it difficult to allow for the time that such processes need, especially if things do not go well from the start or if their own priorities change. Thus, the second policy change is to *ensure that donor commitments are sustained for long enough to enable local actors to learn from their experiences, including from mistakes and missteps that they might make along the way.*

The third change is that support for higher education and research should be removed from the standard aid machinery and approached as an activity with particular needs. Sweden used to have a separate agency for supporting research and higher education – the Swedish Agency for Research Cooperation with Developing Countries (SAREC)

– but this was eventually incorporated into SIDA, and has since disappeared as an entity and lost influence. Allowing national research councils to take on this responsibility might be a step in the right direction, and would strengthen the input of academic peers. However, projects aimed at supporting the development of higher education and research tend to be far more complex than standard peer-review processes can handle. *The idea of special units with responsibility for allocating funds for projects linked to the higher education and research sectors in low-income countries is valid, and donors that fund this sector would do well to adopt it.*

The fourth change needed is for everyone in the sector to accept that so many more universities are competing for scarce resources. For years, many low-income countries had just one national university and the destination of donor funds was a given. Even after new universities were established, some of the 'founding' institutions continued to be the sole recipients of donor funds because they had well-established graduate programmes, and were providing staff for the newer organisations. Now, however, the new institutions are competing with the older ones, arguing that their researchers are just as good. It makes sense, therefore, for donors to consider supporting a national research fund that is accessible, on a competitive basis, to any individual or institution. Admittedly, the establishing of national research councils in the 1970s was not a positive step, but the political climate was more oppressive then, and few senior academics were able to stand up to the bureaucrats. The situation is different now; politics is more competitive and the universities have a core of more experienced researchers who are in a position to ensure satisfactory levels of professionalism. *Supporting research councils, in which members of the academic community can play a leading role without political or bureaucratic interference, could also constitute an important step towards improved institutional governance.* Developing institutions that enjoy a high degree of autonomy from partisan or personalised politics is the most critical governance challenge facing most countries.

The fifth policy shift to consider is that academic institutions fare best when they allow cosmopolitanism to flourish. By cosmopolitanism I mean the product of exchanges, networks and partnerships across national boundaries. African universities have already benefited greatly from support given to such exchanges and it is important that these continue to receive funding. The Nordic governments have played a particularly important role in supporting institutional ties between the North and South, as well as ties between universities in the South. The Danish government also funds a major programme that allows Danish universities to develop closer ties with universities in low-income countries with a view to enhancing both teaching and research capacity on both sides of the equator (Danida Fellowship Centre 2015). *The policy challenge here is to ensure that individuals and institutions in the South have an equal say in these arrangements.* Experience to date suggests that the ostensibly better-qualified individuals in the donor countries take control, not only of planning but also implementing such projects. One way of countering this would be for national research councils in low-income countries (rather than organisations in the donor countries) to allocate money for such collaborative ventures. For example, a funding mechanism in these research councils could consider applications for collaborative ventures with academic institutions in the North alongside one that focuses only on funding for local research projects.

## Appendix

**List of organisations researched**

| Intergovernmental organisations | Private donor organisations |
| --- | --- |
| African Development Bank | Carnegie Corporation of New York |
| African Union | Ford Foundation |
| Consultative Group of International | Gates Foundation |
| Agricultural Research Centers | International Foundation for Science |
| European Union (Erasmus Mundus) | Kresge Foundation |
| OECD/DAC | MacArthur Foundation |
| UNESCO | Mellon Foundation |
| United Nations Institute for Training and | Partnership for Higher Education in Africa |
| Research | Rockefeller Foundation |
| World Bank: Global Development Network | Syngenta Foundation |
| Task Force on Higher Education | Wellcome Trust |

**List of organisations researched**

| Government-funded donor organisations | | Other organisations |
|---|---|---|
| Belgium | University Commission for Development | • Abuja University of Science and Technology |
| Canada | Canadian International Development Agency (CIDA), now merged into Dept of Foreign Affairs<br>International Development Research Center (IDRC) | • Academic Ranking of World Universities<br>• African Centre for Technology Studies<br>• African Economic Research Consortium |
| Denmark | Ministry of Foreign Affairs | • Alliance for a Green Revolution in Africa |
| Finland | Finnish Universities Partnership for International Development (UniPID) | • Association for the Development of Education in Africa |
| France | French Universities Agency (AUF) | • Association of African Universities |
| Germany | German Academic Exchange Service (DAAD) | • Council for the Development of Economic and Social Research in Africa |
| Netherlands | Nuffic | • International Association of Universities |
| Norway | NORAD/NORHED<br>Norwegian Centre for International Cooperation in Higher Education | • International Institute of Water and Environmental Engineering (2iE) |
| Portugal | Camoes Institute | • Network of Ethiopian Scholars |
| Republic of Korea | Korea International Cooperation Agency (KOICA) | • Nigerian Education Trust Fund |
| Sweden | Swedish International Development Cooperation Agency (SIDA) | • Organization for Social Science Research in Eastern and Southern Africa |
| Switzerland | Swiss Development Cooperation | • Southern African–Nordic Centre |
| United Arab Emirates | UAE Interact | • Science and Development Network |
| United Kingdom | Department for International Development (DFID)<br>Commission for Africa<br>Association of Commonwealth Universities | • University World News |
| United States | USAID<br>Higher Education for Development (HED) | |

## Notes

1   Much of this chapter was first published online by the Danish Development
    Research Network in 2010. It is republished here because it helped to spark
    much debate, particularly among the Nordic donors, about the role of fund-
    ing, and many of the points made remain relevant. Some aspects have been
    updated, and some new conclusions and policy recommendations put for-
    ward. Note also that while the Millennium Development Goals (MDGs) are
    mentioned, the Sustainable Development Goals (SDGs) did not exist in
    2009 when the initial research was done.

2   A map reflecting data for the 2015 Academic Ranking of World Universities
    graphically illustrates the uneven distribution of quality higher education
    and research (see http://www.shanghairanking.com). The developed coun-
    tries (OECD members) dominate its list of the world's 500 best universities.
    The colour white denotes countries with no university in the top 500, most
    of East and Central Europe, Central Asia, Southeast Asia, much of Latin
    America and almost the whole of Africa are shown in white. Only five
    African universities, four in South Africa and one in Egypt, make the list.
    None of these are in the top 200, although South Africa's University of
    Cape Town comes close.

3   For example, a distinction is often made between education and research;
    these appear as separate budget categories and are treated differently when
    donors report on their support for academic institutions. Another example
    is that some countries include only academic institutions in their definition
    of higher education while others use the broader notion of tertiary educa-
    tion to include all post-secondary study.

4   Thus, for example, the Belgian University Commission and the French
    Universities Agency, acting on behalf of their respective foreign ministries,
    have been actively involved providing scholarships and broader institution-
    al support to African universities in the Francophone countries. The latter
    institutions follow the French system, which makes it relatively easy for
    French universities and scholars to work with them. The result, however, is
    that, like the French system, the African institutions tend to be fairly con-
    servative and less open to outside influence.

5   The terminology used by donors to describe what they support is often
    vague. Capacity building is the broadest term used but it is often unclear

whether this refers merely to individuals or also covers institutions and/or the policy environment in which higher education and research takes place. Given the inclination of some to apply this term very broadly, it makes sense to think of capacity building as covering all three levels: individuals, institutions, and the policy environment (DFID 2010). In addition, some donors refer to post-secondary, others to tertiary education. Judging from the way the terms are used, tertiary seems to refer more to universities and colleges that award academic degrees, while post-secondary seems to include professional and technical education for which diplomas and certificates can be awarded. Higher education institution is another term that is unspecific. In this chapter, I use it to refer to degree-awarding institutions. The term research-based education is sometimes used to highlight a contrast with regular course-based study.

6    The members of the partnership were the Ford Foundation, the Rockefeller Foundation, the Carnegie Endowment, the MacArthur Foundation, the Mellon Foundation, the Kresge Foundation and the Hewlett Foundation.

7    Countries such as Portugal and Spain, that follow their own priorities, tend to be seen as 'laggards' when it comes to aligning their aid with the principles of the 2005 Paris Declaration and the MDGs (Meyer 2010; OECD/DAC 2010).

8    However, the Commonwealth Secretariat organises most of the scholarships offered by UK universities, and these are not included as part of the UK's bilateral support for higher education.

9    The NUFU Programme began in 1991 and was concluded in 2012, while the NOMA Programme ended in 2014. After several years of co-existence, the two programmes were replaced by the Norwegian Programme for Capacity Building in Higher Education and Research for Development (NORHED), which was launched by NORAD in 2012 and aims to combine the best of both programmes.

10    See the Gates Foundation Global Libraries strategy overview.

11    As of early 2016, the AERC's member donors were DFID, Danida, the Kenyan government, NORAD, SIDA, USAID, the World Bank, the MacArthur Foundation, and the Bill and Melinda Gates Foundation. Other funders include the African Development Bank (AfDB), the African Capacity Building Foundation, German Academic Exchange Services (DAAD) and

the United Nations University, World Institute for Development Economics Research.

12    As noted, the French-speaking countries have long operated within the framework they inherited from France (Mourin 2009).

# References

AAU (Association of African Universities) (2004) *Higher Education in Sub-Saharan Africa with Specific Reference to Universities*. Accra

Cacho, Lemuel (2009) Applied research is ousting curiosity-driven science. *SciDev. Net*, 11 March. Available online

Commission for Africa (2005) *Our Common Interest: Report of the Commission for Africa*, March 2005. Available online

COWI AS (2009) *Evaluation of the Norwegian Programme for Development Research and Education (NUFU) and of NORAD's Programme for Master Studies (NOMA)*. Evaluation Report 7. Oslo: Norad. Available online

Danida Fellowship Centre (2015) Building Stronger Universities, Phase II (BSU II). Available online

Danish Ministry of Foreign Affairs (2009) *Realizing the Potential of Africa's Youth*. Copenhagen

DFID (Department for International Development, UK) (2010) *Capacity Building in Research*, a DFID Practice Paper, June. Available online

Dickson, David (2010) MDGs: A blessing and a curse. *SciDev.Net*, 1 October. Available online

EACEA (European Commission Education, Audiovisual and Culture Executive Agency) (2016) Erasmus Mundus Statistics. Available online

*ICEF Monitor* (2012) New 2035 enrolment forecasts place East Asia and the Pacific in the lead. 3 September. Available online

IDRC (2009) *Innovating for Development: Strategic Framework 2010–2015*. Ottawa. Available online

King, Kenneth (2013) *China's Soft Power and Aid in Africa*. Bloomington, IN: Indiana University Press

King, Kenneth and Simon McGrath (2004) *Knowledge for Development*. London: Zed

Lewis, Sian (2009) Funding for higher education: Facts and figures. *SciDev.Net*, 11 March. Available online

Meyer, Stefan (2010) *Spain in Africa: The Reluctant Newcomer*, FRIDE Policy Brief No 24, Madrid. Available online

Mihyo, Paschal (2007) *Staff Retention in African Universities and Links with Diaspora Study*. Report for the Association for the Development of Education in Africa. Washington DC

Mourin, Sophie (2009) *Lénseignement superieur et la recherché en Afrique subsaharienne: Survol des organizations qui fournissent un appui technique et financier*. Ottawa: IDRC

Mouton, Johann (2008) *Regional Report on Sub-Saharan Africa: National Research Systems*. Paris: UNESCO

Muchie, Mammo (2010) African networks needed to improve higher education. *SciDev.Net*, 17 March

Nge'the, Njuguna, George Subotzky and George Afeti (2008) *Higher Education Differentiation and Articulation in Tertiary Education Systems: A Study of Twelve African Countries*. Report for the Association for the Development of Higher Education in Developing Countries. Washington DC and Accra: World Bank and AAU

NISR (National Institute of Statistics of Rwanda) (2012) EICV3 Thematic Report: Utilities and Amenities, Water and Sanitation, Energy, Housing, Transport and ICT. Kigali: Republic of Rwanda

OECD/DAC (2010) *DAC Peer Review of Portugal*. Paris

Olsson, Berit (2009) Donors must fund the essential conditions for research. *SciDev.Net*, 11 March

Psacharopoulos, Geoge, Jee-Peng Tan and Emmanuel Jimenez (1986) *Financing Education in Developing Countries: An Exploration of Policy Options*. Washington DC: World Bank

Psacharopoulos, George and Harry A Patrinos (2002) *Returns on Investment in Education: A Further Update*. World Bank Policy Working Paper No. 2881. Washington DC

SAREC (Swedish Agency for Research Cooperation) (1985) Tio år med SAREC: En utvärdering av SAREC`s verksamhet med särskild tonvikt på de bilateral insatserna. Uppsala

SIU (Norwegian Centre for International Cooperation in Education) (2013) *NUFU Final Report: 2007–2012*. Oslo

Tettey, Wisdom J (2010) *Deficits in Academic Staff at African Universities*. New York: PHEA

University Leaders' Forum (2008) *Developing and Retaining the Next Generation of Academics*. Accra: PHEA and the University of Ghana

University World News (2010) Higher education financing promises broken. 19 September. Available online

World Bank (2000) *Higher Education in Developing Countries: Peril and Promise*. Report of the Task Force on Higher Education and Society. Washington, DC. Available online

World Bank (2008) *Accelerating Catch-Up: Tertiary Education for Growth in Sub-Saharan Africa*. Washington DC

World Bank (2010) *Financing Higher Education in Africa*. Washington DC: World Bank. Available online

World Bank (2014) World Bank to finance 19 centers of excellence to help transform science, technology, and higher education in Africa. Press release, 15 April. Available online

World Bank (2015) Overview of JJ/WBGS Program. Available online

Xu, Zhiguo (2009) China on the lookout for foreign scientists. *SciDev.Net*, 20 January. Available online

CHAPTER

2

# 'The first philosophers were astronomers': Curiosity and innovation in higher education policy

*John Higgins*

Construction of the first phase of a massive new astronomy project is due to begin in southern Africa and Australia in 2018, at a preliminary cost of approximately US$730 million (Kahn 2015). The intention is to build the world's largest radio telescope, one that enables astronomers to monitor and survey the sky in unprecedented detail. This means, for instance, that astronomers should be able to 'see' how the first stars and galaxies were formed after the Big Bang, gain a better understanding of 'dark energy', and help in the search for extraterrestrial intelligence.[1] In addition to facilitating this fundamental astronomical research, the project – which is one of the largest collective scientific endeavours in history – also promises to yield significant innovations and improve capacity in engineering and ICT. Scientists and engineers will have to rise to the challenges presented by the phenomenal amount of data capture, transmission and processing involved, which is expected to exceed all the data traffic on the entire existing internet.

The project – the Square Kilometre Array (SKA) – involves the building and co-ordination of hundreds of thousands of high- and mid-frequency observation dishes in southern Africa, mostly concentrated in South Africa's semi-arid desert region, the Karoo. At the same time, and operating in conjunction with these dishes, up to a million low-frequency antennae will be set up in Australia. As an international project, the SKA's costs will be shared by some twenty different countries, although the precise amounts to be paid by each country are still to be decided.

The decision to divide the physical location of the instrument between the two main competitors for the bid – Australia and South Africa – came on 25 May 2012, and in September of that year, South Africa's Human Sciences Research Council hosted a celebratory conference on the 'Re-emergence of Astronomy in Africa: A Transdisciplinary Interface of Knowledge Systems'. At the conference, South Africa's Minister of Science and Technology, Naledi Pandor, who fought hard for South Africa's bid to participate in the project, gave the opening address (see Pandor 2012). I begin this chapter by interrogating some of the remarks she made when framing that conference.

A striking feature of Pandor's presentation was her marshalling of powerful arguments in favour of the SKA. This was clearly a response to questions posed by organisations such as the National Science Foundation (NSF) in the USA, as well as the scepticism displayed by some of her fellow parliamentarians. At the centre of her arguments was the question: is it really desirable to devote such a significant portion of national research financing to astronomy? As the NSF put it – with the condescension characteristic of so many Northern donors: 'You are actually wasting money and Africans have no business in the astronomy sciences. Cure your people first. Feed your people first' (see Pandor 2012). As if challenges around hunger, healthcare, poverty and unemployment are not common currency for both 'North' and 'South'.

In addressing this and similar questions, Pandor chose to emphasise the economic and the ideological dimensions of the SKA project. She pointed to the potential for capturing foreign direct investment, and for boosting job creation and skills training, not only in the astronomical sciences but also in IT and a wide variety of engineering disciplines. Above all, she emphasised the desire to 'enhance Africa's scientific capacity' and its consequent standing in the world (Pandor 2012).

The success of the SKA project is likely to bring economic as well as wide-ranging political and ideological benefits to South Africa and other participating countries. In Pandor's bold vision, the SKA project could help to enable a significant (and much needed) strengthening of South Africa's scientific and technological capacities, while improving its general standing in the global knowledge economy.

This is all well and good. In this chapter, though, I focus on a dimension of the SKA project that was (at least in my recollection and in my notes from the event) strikingly absent from Pandor's apologia. This dimension was an intrinsic interest in astronomy itself, and the potential harvest of understanding and interest that the project promises to yield to both specialists and the wider public. I examine this absence and the likely reasons for it, as a way of pointing to some of what I believe to be the ultimately damaging limitations of current higher education policy, both in South Africa, but also across the world. I hope that focusing on this absent dimension will enable us to get a better grip on the necessary and dynamic relations between curiosity and innovation that are too often marginalised by the templates that currently dominate higher education policy.

## The appeal of the Hubble

Let us begin by thinking back to an immediate precursor to the SKA project, the Hubble Space Telescope, which was launched on 24 April 1990, and is still in operation. In 2010, Charles Bolden, NASA scientist and pilot for one of the early missions sent out to do some repairs and improve the Hubble's performance, wrote:

> We grossly underestimated the importance and appeal of [the Hubble] ... I wish I better understood how and why it captivates people around the world in a way no other scientific instrument has before. Hubble takes us on a journey beyond what we know. It is a time machine that has managed to capture the minds and imaginations of people around the world. (Bolden 2010: 8)

Bolden seems to have focused narrowly on the Hubble as a 'scientific instrument'. He seems to have been surprised at the intensity of public interest in astronomy and the power that it holds to 'captivate people around the world', to 'capture [their] minds and imaginations'.

And, indeed, who can not love astronomy? Is there anyone who has never looked up into the night skies with awe and wonder? Can anyone see the images made available by the Hubble, of the Sombrero Galaxy, or the birth of a star, or a black hole, without experiencing powerful feelings of wonder and curiosity? These are precisely the feelings that Bolden wanted to understand better, and the first step in my argument is to suggest that the work of the German philosopher, Ludwig Feuerbach, may help us grasp what eluded Bolden, and what Pandor neglected in her opening address.

This is, I suggest, the simple and powerful appeal of astronomy, with its grounding in the fundamental, and perhaps defining, human trait of curiosity. For this reason, I drew part of the title of this chapter from Feuerbach's line that 'the first philosophers were astronomers', which comes from his influential study, the *Essence of Christianity*, published in 1841, and then, on account of its success, was reissued with a new preface in 1843. In my view, Feuerbach put his finger on the problem identified by Bolden – the question of why the Hubble 'captivates people around the world in a way no scientific instrument has done before'. For Feuerbach,[2] the interest in astronomy runs deep, and embodies the curiosity and ability to contemplate or self-consciously reflect on the world that is widely held to be a constitutive trait of the human animal. 'Man alone,' as Feuerbach wrote (in the sexist idiom of his time),

> has purely intellectual, disinterested joys and passions; the eye of man alone keeps theoretic festivals ... theory begins with the contemplation of the heavens. The first philosophers were astronomers. It is the heavens that admonish man of his destination, and remind him that he is destined not merely to action, but also to contemplation. ([1843] 1989: 5)

With his emphatic repetition of the word 'contemplation', Feuerbach signalled the binary opposition between (positive) contemplation and (negative) action that came, in his socially situated argument, to carry much of his political criticism of the egotistical commercial society that surrounded him, as well as the theoretical emphasis he wished to place on the priority of contemplation over action.

Feuerbach was an iconoclastic figure who challenged the received ideas of his time. To his younger followers, his work was particularly important as it seemed to successfully demolish the theological underpinnings and consequent legitimacy of the authoritarian Christian state of Frederick William IV's Prussia.[3] Feuerbach went so far as to question the Christian belief in the immortality of the soul, and argued that the essence of religious belief was nothing other than the essence of humanity, projected onto the idea and attributes of a Christian deity. In brief, and as he put it, 'Man' – and this is the 'mystery of religion' – 'objectifies his being and then again makes himself an object to the objectivised image of himself thus converted into a subject' (Feuerbach [1843] 1989: 29–30). In the early 1840s, as Engels famously put it, 'Enthusiasm was general; we all became at once Feuerbachians' (Engels [1888] 1977: 592). Marx similarly insisted that it 'is only with Feuerbach that positive, humanistic and naturalistic criticism begins' ([1844] 1992: 281).

Despite Feuerbach's considerable influence in his own time, it is probably true to say that his name is all but unknown today outside the confined conversation of a small circle of professional scholars. For those who do know of him, it is mainly as the object and addressee of one of the shortest yet most influential texts in the Western philosophical and political canon, Marx's Ad Feuerbach, or as it has become known, his Theses on Feuerbach.

## Marx's Theses on Feuerbach

Many have noted the importance of the Theses on Feuerbach for orthodox Marxism.[4] Engels, when publishing some hastily scribbled notes as an addendum to his Ludwig Feuerbach and the End of Classical German Philosophy, canonised them as 'invaluable … the first document in which is deposited the brilliant germ of the new world outlook' (Engels

[1888] 1977: 585). Most other accounts have followed suit, up to and including Althusser's admittedly more complex and conflicted analysis of the relationship between Marx and Feuerbach.[5]

Let me instead isolate and examine just one dimension of Marx's argument in the *Theses:* the binary opposition between contemplation and action that Feuerbach proposed, and that Marx sought to resist and reverse. I hope to show that both this binary opposition and Marx's reversal of it are more complex than they might seem, and also to demonstrate why these arguments are important for considerations of the SKA project and the reigning canons of higher education policy.

In Thesis XI, the final and perhaps most cited of the *Theses on Feuerbach,* Marx famously wrote, 'Philosophers have only interpreted the world, in various ways; the point is to change it' ([1845] 1992: 423). With this closing aphorism, Marx summed up many of his frustrations with Feuerbach, and many of his concerns about his own formative grounding in philosophy.[6]

With regard to Feuerbach, it is important to recognise that Marx's frustrations existed on at least two distinct (albeit related) levels of theory and practice. On a practical level, Marx was disillusioned by Feuerbach's refusal to engage more actively in the ongoing political struggle. On 13 March 1843, Marx complained that Feuerbach 'refers too much to nature and too little to politics' (Marx and Engels 1975: 400). In October of the same year, Feuerbach even declined Marx's suggestion that he write an article criticising Fredrick William IV's appointment of (the once radical but by then conservative) FW Schelling to Hegel's former Chair of Philosophy at the University of Berlin, with the mandate to 'stamp out the dragon-seed of Hegelianism' (Wheen 2000: 54).

Feuerbach did, indeed, interpret the world differently from the ways in which his own mentor, Hegel, had done. In theoretical terms, he sought (as did Marx in following him, and in seeking to extend and correct his theory) to replace Hegel's mystical idealism with realist materialism. This materialism was to be firmly grounded in a sensuous apprehension of the external world, and constituted a renewed scientific empiricism, alert to what Feuerbach regarded as exciting developments in the natural sciences.[7]

For Marx, though, as he put it in the first of the *Theses*, Feuerbach shared the 'defect of all hitherto existing materialism', in that 'the thing, reality, sensuousness, is conceived only in the form of the *object or of contemplation*, but not as *sensuous human activity*, practice, not subjectively' (Marx [1845] 1992: 421, emphasis in original). For Marx, Feuerbach remained trapped in the passive empiricism that Hegel's active idealism had – for all its faults – superseded. In this empiricism, the subject is unable to act, and becomes merely a passive receiver of experience. From this perspective, contemplation is simply *Anschauung* (the mirroring of an external world), and the human subject's capacity for agency, labour and the transformation of the external world – precisely the elements of Hegel's thought that Marx praised and wished to retain – go unrecognised.[8] For Marx, Feuerbach's emphatic emphasis on contemplation over action missed this key dimension in Hegel's thought – the dimension of 'sensuous human activity, practice'. From this perspective, Feuerbach was guilty of regressing to an unmediated form of pure empiricism, in which there was no possibility of articulating the necessary link between theory and practice.

Indeed, Feuerbach's *Essence of Christianity* set up a binary opposition between contemplation and action, in which the sphere of contemplation was overemphasised, and the dimension of action was unduly denigrated. For Marx, Feuerbach was mistaken in seeing the theoretical or 'contemplative' attitude as 'the only genuine human attitude', and in setting against this an idea of practice negatively 'conceived and fixed only in its dirty-Judaical manifestation' (Marx [1845] 1992: 421–422).

In using the phrase 'dirty-Judaical', Marx was referring to the ways in which the negative pole of Feuerbach's binary opposition was charged with a racial bias that ran deep in his thinking, and, indeed, constitutes a significant dimension not only of his history of philosophy, but of German and European philosophy as a whole.[9]

Feuerbach's history of philosophy, which drew on but diverged from Hegel's influential narrative, identified Jewish thought as the main culprit in the wellspring of obsessive egotism that characterises modern commercial society. In the racialising manner of his day, Feuerbach attributed this to the Jewish people, remarking that 'Utilism is the essential theory of Judaism', ([1843] 1989: 113). He went on to argue that

> the Jews have maintained their peculiarity to this day. Their principle, their God, is the most practical principle in the world, – namely, egoism; and moreover egoism in the form of religion. Egoism is the God who will not let his servants come to shame. Egoism is essentially monotheistic, for it has only one, only self, as its end. Egoism strengthens cohesion, concentrates man on himself, gives him a consistent principle of life; but it makes him theoretically narrow, because indifferent to all which does not relate to the wellbeing of self. Hence science, like art, arises only out of polytheism, for polytheism is the frank, open, unenvying sense of all that is beautiful and good without distinction, the sense of the world, of the universe. The Greeks looked abroad into the wide world that they might extend their sphere of vision; the Jews to this day pray with their faces turned towards Jerusalem. ([1843] 1989: 114–115)

For Feuerbach, 'Practical perception is a dirty perception stained with egotism' ([1843] 1989: 196, translation amended), while action is negatively identified with a 'purely practical view' that 'subordinates Nature only to the ends of egoism'. This egoism 'contains and expresses nothing but the command to make nature – not an object of thought, of contemplation, but – an object of utilisation' ([1843] 1989: 117). In this, Feuerbach covertly criticised the emerging commercialism of his day, but in terms that were highly charged with the anti-Semitic thinking of his time.[10]

Against this 'purely practical view', Feuerbach put forward a 'theoretic view of Nature', and its embodiment of the precepts of the Greek philosopher Anaxagoras, that humans are 'born to behold the world' and that the 'standpoint of theory is the standpoint of harmony with the world' (Feuerbach [1843] 1989: 113).[11]

For Marx, of course, theory never was, and could never be, 'a standpoint of harmony with the world'. Rather it was a means of analysing a world that might present itself as harmonious, but only so as to conceal its cracks and rifts, and its destabilising inequalities.[12] Little wonder that in establishing his theoretical and political distance from Feuerbach, Marx reversed the polarity of Feuerbach's binary opposition, shifting the emphasis decisively towards practice, and insisting on the 'significance of "revolutionary", of "practical-critical" activity' (Marx [1845] 1992 Thesis I: 422). Accordingly, Marx asserted that 'Man must prove the truth, i.e. the reality and power, the this-sidedness of his thinking in practice' (Thesis II: 422), and argued that 'All social life is essentially practical. All mysteries which lead theory to mysticism find their rational solution in human practice and in the comprehension of this practice' (Thesis VIII: 423). Marx's theoretical and political critique of Feuerbach came together in his famous statement, already cited: 'Philosophers have only interpreted the world, in various ways; the point is to *change* it.'

With a slight change of phrasing, much the same sentiment could be said to animate contemporary higher education policy and its attitude towards academic study. Policy-makers might argue that academics have only interpreted the world; the point is to change it, or, more specifically, the point of higher education is to innovate and contribute to the growth of the economy; that is what change is.[13]

As Roger King (among others) observed:

> Everywhere we find the view (not necessarily well-evidenced) that universities help to provide economic well-being and comparative national advantage through providing the research and the education personnel necessary to enable countries to compete effectively in the global economy. (King 2010: 37)

Similarly, Scandanavian scholars Olsen and Maassen have emphasised that academic teaching and research have been reduced to 'key instruments for economic growth and mastering international competition'. Consequently, as they have observed, the 'possible role of universities in developing democratic citizens, a humanistic culture, social cohesion and solidarity, and a vivid public sphere' has been almost entirely obliterated (Olsen and Maassen 2007: 7, 9).[14]

The emphasis on applied research, to the exclusion of anything else, is evident everywhere. Note, for example, the World Bank initiative on promoting excellence in the applied sciences in Africa and the recommendations of the 2012 ministerial review of the science, technology and innovation landscape in South Africa, which openly privileges 'applied sciences and experimental development' over other forms of learning and research (MRCNSC 2012). In my view, this emphasis on practice over theory, or applied science over curiosity-driven research, repeats the dynamics of Marx's reversal of Feuerbach's binary between theory and practice, contemplation over action. It is therefore worth returning to Marx's discussion as a way of understanding some of the limitations of the dominant forms of contemporary higher education policy.

Given the reappearance of this opposition between theory and practice, with practice now positively charged, it is worth attending to some of the conceptual difficulties involved in the reversal or inversion. A useful starting point is one of Althusser's remarks concerning Marx's not infrequent recourse to reversal or inversion to characterise his process of critical thinking. With characteristic textual insight, Althusser pointed to the simple fact that the figure or image of inversion or reversal can be 'no more than an image and has neither the meaning nor the rigour of a concept' (Althusser and Balibar 1977: 153). This cautionary note (made *à propos* Marx's general relation to Hegel) is particularly important when it comes to thinking through the formulations of a central canonical text such as the *Theses on Feuerbach* where, as argued above, Marx attempted to invert Feuerbach's binary opposition of theory and practice.

As I have argued elsewhere (see Higgins 2009), canonical citation has a tendency to reduce the complex textuality at work in thinking and writing to the transparency of a pure and authoritative statement. Acting in this way, it embodies the policing functions of canonicity and is generally intended to close an argument rather than open it up for further analysis. Thus the process of potential understanding is brought to a halt in a way that is both entirely arbitrary and yet culturally (and politically) sanctioned.

The reduction of real textual complexity to the transparency of pure and authoritative statement is particularly apparent in many casual readings (or rather citations) of the *Theses on Feuerbach*. In particular, it is evident in the fact that Thesis XI and its recapitulation of the theory/practice opposition has come to stand as a rallying cry or *mot d'ordre* for many orthodox Marxists.[15]

Nonetheless, going against the grain of an orthodox interpretation, which takes the primacy of practice over theory for granted (as in Stalin's blunt statement that 'theory must serve practice'),[16] a number of commentators have pointed to the real complexity of thought and argument in the hastily scribbled and incompletely articulated *Theses*. This is particularly the case for Thesis XI and its implicit articulation of the theory–practice opposition.

Antonio Gramsci (1978: 334) for instance, argued (against Croce and others) that it was far from Marx's intention to maintain such a binary opposition, and to simply set a commitment to 'practical action' against a commitment to philosophical thinking and analysis. Similarly, in one of the most thorough analyses of the *Theses* that we have, Ernst Bloch insisted that Marx's endorsement of practice must not be confused with an American-style pragmatism, which claims that 'truth is nothing more than the commercial usefulness of ideas' (an apt enough description of the brute core of contemporary higher education policy) (Bloch 1986: 275). Real practice, insisted Bloch, 'cannot take a single stride without having consulted theory economically and philosophically' (277), and he pointed (quite rightly) to the example of Marx's *Capital* which, even on the most cursory reading, embodies something very different from an unthinking commitment to action as an alternative to theory and patient analysis. *Capital* – and indeed Marx's work as a whole – surely shows the need for the most 'painstaking examination' and 'philosophizing contextual exploration of the most difficult reality' (Bloch 1986: 278).

Holding theory and practice as alternatives in a binary opposition, no matter which way round, betrays the complexity of the relations between the two that Marx's work sought constantly to demonstrate.[17]

What is too easily lost in the binary opposition – whichever way you play it – is the necessary interplay between theory and practice. This was the conclusion of all but the most sloganeering of Marxist thinkers.

But is it the conclusion of higher education policy-makers today? Certainly, Minister Pandor's failure to name anything other than the practical benefits and spin-offs of the SKA project in her keynote speech highlighted the pressures on state officials and policy-makers to acknowledge application and not investigation, practice and not theory, conclusion rather than curiosity. The 'most difficult reality' for all those who wish to pay more than lip-service to enabling innovation is that innovation so often emerges from the unintended consequences of research and enquiry. It is therefore crucial to ensure that a portion of academic enquiry is devoted to pure and non-instrumental research.

After all, we would do well to remember that – viewed from a Feuerbachian perspective – the emergence of the natural sciences can be read as an unintended consequence of the deep human curiosity about the stars. Over time, this bifurcated into the two distinct modes of thinking and analysis that we now call astronomy and astrology. Who would have thought that from that pure, driving curiosity about the heavens, the extraordinary international SKA project would emerge? I submit that part of our enthusiasm for this project should be to celebrate human curiosity, and to recognise all that is implicit in Feuerbach's observation that 'the first philosophers were astronomers'.

Ultimately, active curiosity constitutes the middle ground between too simple a binary opposition between contemplation and action, and must be recognised as *central* rather than marginal to higher education policy and practice.

## Notes

1    For a full account of, and update on, the project, see the SKA website.

2    As for others, in a tradition extending from Aristotle: for an extremely useful general survey of the tradition, see Fisher (1998), while for a discussion

of astronomy in relation to curiosity, see Adam Smith's 'Essay on Astronomy' (1980).

3    For a useful placing of Feuerbach's politics in the context of their time, see Breckman (2001).

4    For detailed analysis and useful commentary, see Labica (1987).

5    Much of Althusser's work was concerned to repeat, in a more contemporary idiom, the classic orthodox Marxist claims for Marxism as a science, with the breakthrough coming via Marx's decisive break with Feuerbach in and around the Theses. However, Althusser was also consistently and repeatedly drawn to some elements of Feuerbach's thinking. See, in particular, how his interest in Feuerbach's projection theory of religious belief – central to the Essence of Christianity – anticipates the later theory of ideology in 'On Feurbach' in his *The Humanist Controversy and Other Essays* (2003).

6    Marx's remarks were addressed as much to himself as to his former philosophical mentor. In particular, the relationships between philosophy and action are central to Marx's thinking at this time, and prompted in part by his collaborator Moses Hess's 'The Philosophy of the Act' (Hess ([1843] 1964)).

7    For details of Feuerbach's interest in and training in the natural sciences of the nineteenth century, see Wartofsky (1977).

8    As Marx put it, 'Hegel conceives the self-creation of man as a process, objectification as loss of object, as alienation and as supersession of this alienation ... he therefore grasps the nature of labour and conceives objective man – true, because real man – as the result of his own labour' (Marx [1844] 1992: 386, emphasis in original).

9    For a useful account of this in German Idealism, see Mack (2003).

10   Marx – although far from free of casual anti-Semitism, despite his own Jewish blood – pointed out that it is not Judaism that is the problem, but rather the commercial system in which it is embedded and performed. As he argued in his reply to Bruno Bauer's tract, On the Jewish Question, 'Emancipation from haggling and from money ... would be the same as the self-emancipation of our age' (Marx [1843] 1992: 236, emphasis in original).

11   In his *History of Philosophy* ([1892] 1995: 319), Hegel famously praised Anaxagoras as 'a sober man amongst drunkards', as the one who opened

thinking to truly philosophical speculation and credited him with the crucial recognition that philosophy had to deal with the analysis of totality.

12   This point is well made by Emmanuel Renault, who rightly noted how 'philosophy will fight against the world by exposing the irreconcilable contradictions, of which negative dialectic is the theory' (Renault 1995: 39, my translation).

13   For a fuller discussion of this element in higher education policy, see my book, *Academic Freedom in a Democratic South Africa*, particularly Chapter 5, 'Making the case for the humanities' (Higgins 2013).

14   For a detailed account of the democratising features of humanist education, see Nussbaum (2010), and for an excellent general critique of current trends in higher education, see Collini (2012).

15   Labica's wise conclusion is worth noting here, and particularly his emphasis on how 'the different theses are much more complex than they at first appear', and that on many occasions their different interpretations mark the line between orthodoxy and heterodoxy in the Marxist tradition (Labica 1987: 125, my translation).

16   Quoted in Gramsci (1978: 334).

17   For two useful recent guides to the complexity of Marx's thinking in *Capital*, see Harvey (2010) and Jameson (2013).

## References

Althusser, Louis (2003) *The Humanist Controversy and Other Essays* (translated by GM Goshgarian). London and New York: Verso

Althusser, Louis and Étienne Balibar (1977) *Reading Capital* (translated by Ben Brewster). London: New Left Books

Bloch, Ernst (1986) *The Principle of Hope: Volume One* (translated by N Plaice, S Plaice and P Knight). Cambridge, MA: MIT Press

Bolden, Charles F (2010) Foreword. In: Edward Weiler *Hubble: A Journey through Space and Time*. New York: Abrams

Breckman, Warren (2001) *Marx, the Young Hegelians, and Radical Social Theory*. Cambridge: Cambridge University Press

Collini, Stefan (2012) *What are Universities For?* Harmondsworth: Penguin

Engels, Friedrich ([1888] 1977) Feuerbach and the end of classical German philosophy. In: Karl Marx and Friedrich Engels *Selected Works in One Volume*.
London: Lawrence and Wishart

Feuerbach, Ludwig ([1843] 1989) *Essence of Christianity* (translated by George
Eliot). New York: Prometheus

Fisher, Philip (1998) *Wonder, the Rainbow and the Aesthetics of Rare Experience*.
Cambridge, MA: Harvard University Press

Gramsci, Antonio (1978) *Selections from the Prison Notebooks* (translated by
Quentin Hoare and Geoffrey Nowell Smith). London: Lawrence and Wishart

Harvey, David (2010) *A Companion to Marx's Capital*. London and New York:
Verso

Hegel, GWF ([1892] 1995) *Lectures on the History of Philosophy, Volume One*
(translated by ES Haldane). New York: Bison

Hess, Moses ([1843] 1964) The philosophy of the act'. In: Albert Fried and Ronald
Sanders (eds) Socialist Thought: A Documentary History. Cicago: Aldine
Available online

Higgins, John (2009) On representation: Citizenship and critique in Said and
Marx. In: Heather Jacklin and Peter Vale (eds) *Re-Imagining the Social in South
Africa: Critique, Theory and Post-Apartheid Society*. Durban: UKZN Press

Higgins, John (2013) *Academic Freedom in a Democratic South Africa*. Johannesburg: Wits University Press

Jameson, Fredric (2013) *Representing Capital: A Reading of Volume One*. London
and New York: Verso

Kahn, Tamar (2015, 23 July) Department awaits Africa budget allocations for
SKA. *Business Day*

King, Roger (2010) Governing knowledge globally: Policy internationalism and
higher education in the age of globalization. In: John Brennan, Lore Arthur,
Brenda Little, Allan Cochrane, Ruth Williams, William Locke et al. *Higher
Education and Society: A Research Report*. CHERI: London

Labica, Georges (1987) *Les Thèses sur Feuerbach*. Paris: Presses Universitaires de
France

Mack, Michael (2003) *German Idealism and the Jew: The Inner Anti-Semitism of
Philosophy and the German Jewish Responses*. Chicago, IL: Chicago University
Press

Marx, Karl ([1843] 1992) On the Jewish question. In: Karl Marx *Early Writings* (translated by Rodney Livingstone and Gregor Benton). Harmondsworth: Penguin

Marx, Karl ([1844] 1992) Economic and philosophical manuscripts. In: Karl Marx *Early Writings* (translated by Rodney Livingstone and Gregor Benton). Harmondsworth: Penguin

Marx, Karl ([1845] 1992) *Theses on Feuerbach.* In: Karl Marx *Early Writings* (translated by Rodney Livingstone and Gregor Benton). Harmondsworth: Penguin

Marx, Karl and Friedrich Engels (1975) *Collected Works Vol. 1: Marx: 1835–1843.* London: Lawrence and Wishart

MRCNSC (Ministerial Review Committee on the National System of Innovation) (2012) *Department of Science and Technology Ministerial Review Committee on the Science, Technology and Innovation Landscape in South Africa: Final Report,* March. Available online.

Nussbaum, Martha (2010) *Not for Profit: Why Democracy Needs the Humanities.* Princeton NJ: Princeton University Press

Olsen, Johan P and Peter Maassen (2007) European debates on the knowledge institution: The modernization of the university at the European level. In: Peter Maassen and Johan P Olsen (eds) *University Dynamics and European Intregration.* Dordrecht: Springer

Pandor, Naledi (2012) Introduction. In: Re-emergence of Astronomy in Africa: Transcript of Proceedings from the Transdisciplinary Interface of Knowledge Systems Conference, 10–11 September, Cradle of Humankind, Moropeng, South Africa

Renault, Emmanuel (1995) *Marx et l'idée de critique.* Paris: Presses Universitaires de France

Smith, Adam (1980) The history of astronomy. In: Adam Smith *Essays on Philosophical Subjects.* Oxford: Oxford University Press

Wartofsky, Marx W (1977) *Feuerbach.* Cambridge: Cambridge University Press

Wheen, Francis (2000) *Karl Marx: A Life.* London: W Norton and Company

# CHAPTER
# 3

## Research training, international collaboration, and the agencies of Ugandan scientists in Uganda

*Eren Zink*

In this chapter, I compare three models of PhD training available to Ugandans today. The three models are: full-time programmes abroad, full-time programmes in a Ugandan institution, and the so-called sandwich model,[1] which combines study abroad with study in Uganda. I pay particular attention to how these models strengthen or curtail the agency of Ugandans who subsequently pursue scientific careers in Uganda.[2] My findings have relevance for other countries where the means for carrying out scientific research (including funding, equipment, and advanced training opportunities) originates primarily from international sources.

In many ways, completing a PhD degree is a rite of passage towards becoming an independent researcher who can design research projects and compete for research funding. And while completing a doctorate in the Ugandan context is no exception, it does differ from studying in wealthier countries in the sense that universities are dependent on foreign governments and organisations to fund and support PhD training. After decades of structural adjustment and other neoliberal policies that have shrunk state funding for research and tertiary education in favour of fee-based financing mechanisms, Ugandan university budgets are stretched exceedingly thin. This, combined with a drastic expansion in the size of the student body, which far outpaces increases in faculty numbers, means that universities have very little core funding to invest in infrastructure, equipment, curriculum development or postgraduate supervision (Kabeba Muriisa 2010; Mamdani 2007; Obong 2004).[3] As a result, PhD opportunities for Ugandans, and for many in other sub-Saharan African countries, arise only to the extent that funding can be mobilised from foreign universities and/or development organisations (see Bradley 2008; Moyi Okwaro and Geissler 2015). This reliance on foreign funding fundamentally undermines the credibility and status of higher education institutions as research universities (Halvorsen 2010).

For many scientists in lower-income countries, beginning their PhD training is an opportunity to permanently move abroad, to a country where salaries, infrastructure and incentives are more conducive to carrying out research (Gaillard and Gaillard 1997). My focus, however, is on the experiences of Ugandan scientists who study locally or return home after obtaining their PhDs abroad. By foregrounding Ugandan scientists' experiences of, and reflections on, their PhD training, this study offers a vantage point from which to better understand the manner in which local and foreign actors participate in the co-production and reproduction of Uganda's research environments.

In the spirit of Ferguson's (2006) entreaty that scholars pay more attention to the ways in which African actors contest their marginalisation in a globalising world, I show how Ugandan scientists turn their experiences of transnational mobility and cultural immersion in higher-income countries into assets in the context of their later work in Uganda. Drawing on actor-network theory (Latour 2005) and the application of science studies to low-income-country contexts (Donovan 2014; Rottenburg 2009a; Zink 2013), I show that the actants, and the relationships between them that matter in the assemblage of Ugandan science, include scientific equipment, supervisors and empirical material, as well as cultural and gendered engagements with kin, colleagues, places and histories. Based on a comparative analysis of three models of PhD training I reflect on the different degrees to which each model facilitates Ugandan scientists' efforts to assemble and maintain actor-networks that align with their own goals, and with the continued decolonisation of knowledge production in Uganda.

## Participants in the study

The interviews and participant observations that inform this chapter were carried out with 45 Ugandan scientists between 2013 and 2015. The group included men and women, all of whom were well-connected internationally, and their ages ranged between 25 and 70 years. Trained in fields related to health, agriculture, and natural-resource management, they were all enrolled in or had completed their PhDs. Most were married, and many had had children prior to beginning their PhDs. Most had published at least one journal article in an international peer-reviewed journal by 2013, and were engaged in research, development and/or consultancy projects with foreign partners.

In addition, I conducted a survey among a partially overlapping population of Ugandan scientists during 2014. The survey included 40 multi-part questions on their experiences of higher education and research collaboration; 57 completed questionnaires were received. The study presented here also forms part of a larger study pursuing similar lines of inquiry in Zimbabwe and Ghana.

## Overview of research training models in Uganda

For the purposes of this chapter, I divided the PhD training programmes that are available to Ugandan scientists into three groups based on patterns of mobility and supervision. The first is full-time PhD programmes in Uganda supervised by at least one senior faculty member at a domestic institution. The second is full-time foreign PhD programmes carried out at an institution outside Uganda, and supervised by at least one faculty member at that institution. Students who enrol for full-time foreign PhDs tend to spend nearly all their time, with the possible exception of visits for vacations and fieldwork or data–collection, outside Uganda. The third is sandwich programmes that are characterised by co-supervision by faculty members at a Ugandan and a foreign institution, with the PhD candidate regularly travelling between the two institutions. 'Sandwich students' usually collect data in Uganda and complete courses abroad, while doing analysis and writing in both countries. Such students can receive their degree from either the foreign or the Ugandan university, or both.

My analysis of these three different groups highlights the differences in student mobility patterns, time spent researching and writing, as well as the location of the supervisor or supervisors. In the pages that follow, I show that social, economic and political relationships with foreign actors and institutions are integral aspects of the actor-networks that produce PhD degrees across all three models.

Sandwich programmes and full-time foreign PhDs are generally financed via international development-aid programmes – as part of capacity-building initiatives, or as sub-components of ongoing research collaborations between institutions and researchers. Full-time domestic training opportunities, even if not always explicitly incorporated into a foreign-funded research-capacity-building programme, are also often the result of ongoing international research and/or training collaborations. The lack of domestic investment in equipment, supplies and supervision means that opportunities for students who enrol for PhDs at universities in Uganda are often sustained on the crumbs of foreign development programmes.

In 2012, approximately a thousand Ugandans with PhDs were living in Uganda. A survey carried out by the Ugandan National Council for Science and Technology, tracing the careers of more than half of these individuals, found that 47 per cent had received their degrees from foreign universities located mainly in the United Kingdom and the United States (UNCST 2012). The remaining 53 per cent had received their degrees from Ugandan institutions, primarily from the famous Makerere University (formerly the University of East Africa) in Kampala (Sicherman 2005; UNCST 2012).

That more than half of the Ugandans who have a PhD graduated from a Ugandan institution should not be taken to imply a degree of independence from foreign funding and partners. A large portion of the Ugandan degrees came about as a result of international collaborations, whereby students are trained in two institutions, one in Uganda and one foreign, with supervision by at least one Ugandan and one foreign supervisor. Sweden is a strong advocate of the sandwich model, and at least 20 per cent of Ugandans who received their PhDs from a Ugandan institution had participated in a Swedish–Ugandan sandwich programme, sponsored by Swedish development funding (Sembatya and Ngobi 2014). Although the data are scarce and incomplete, my own survey and the two other surveys cited all indicate that in 2013, 70 to 80 per cent of the PhDs held by individuals at Ugandan higher education and research institutions were awarded at a foreign university in Europe or North America, or through sandwich programmes involving partner institutions in Europe. It is important to note that only about 20 per cent of all PhD holders in Uganda are women (UNCST 2012). This reflects the social and cultural barriers to access and success in higher education for women in Uganda.

## Full-time training abroad

In terms of acquiring in-depth and cutting-edge scientific knowledge from internationally respected scientists, as well as the skills to use advanced scientific equipment, many of my informants saw full-time study abroad as the optimal path for PhD studies. For example, Dr Mbazira[4] leads a scientific institution that works at the interface of research and its application, but not long ago he was training towards a PhD in the medical sciences in the US. Sitting in his neat air-conditioned office in a newly constructed building away from the hectic streets of Kampala, he told me that for Ugandan scientists pursuing a full-time PhD abroad, and in the US in particular, the 'advantages are enormous'. He went on to explain:

> One, you get state-of-the-art knowledge. Two, it is excellent for networking. You interface with the global experts in almost all of the fields. And this is regardless of which university you are studying at because there are all of these conferences and meetings, and they give you an opportunity

to interact with specialists ... That is something that you
cannot put any price value to because you never know what
some interaction or network that you made at one time in
life ... you never know when it is going to materialise, and
things keep coming up. (interview, 17 October 2014)

Study programmes such as the one pursued by Dr Mbazira offer students an opportunity to acquire a deeper knowledge than might be
possible in Ugandan programmes. This is partly related to the easy
availability of journals, books, reliable internet connections and access
to scientific equipment. In addition, supervisors and fellow PhD students have time, and are willing to make themselves available, for
meetings and discussions.

Beyond this privileged access to the human and material actants
that facilitate the completion of a PhD, the special advantage of full-
time training abroad is that it is relatively easy to create contiguous
stretches of time to concentrate on one's own work. A three- or four-
year foreign PhD programme removes young Ugandan scientists from
their social and economic obligations to most of their family, friends,
colleagues and institutions in Uganda. This drastic and often emotion-
ally painful curtailment of their sociality creates a vacuum that can be
filled with lab time, reading, writing and networking with other scientists. Few PhD programmes leave any space for the extra jobs or
consultancies that have become the norm for academics in Uganda, and
work permits are rarely included in student visas anyway.

A few lucky candidates may be able to bring along and support a
spouse and perhaps a young child on their modest stipends. But those
with larger families and/or spouses who have careers of their own must
generally leave even these closest relations at home. This means that,
apart from intermittent Skype connections, the time that would otherwise be spent eating, playing with children and attending weekend
events with the family no longer competes with research time.
Furthermore, invitations to funerals and weddings that often oblige
Ugandan-based researchers to leave their stations for a few days or a
week at a time, to attend to their commitments to their extended

families, no longer hinder the completion of an experiment, attendance at a seminar, or the finishing of a draft text.

Despite these advantages, and partly because of their immediate social and economic costs, 75 per cent of participants in this study indicated that they would prefer a sandwich programme or an entirely domestic programme to full-time study abroad. This is explained by the fact that the fulfilment of Ugandan scientists' aspirations (and those of scientists from other sub-Saharan countries) is not exclusively dependent on access to the most expensive and advanced scientific equipment or the ability to produce new knowledge for audiences at the wealthiest of universities. Too often, such paths lead away from Uganda, via the brain drain, and spending years abroad can make reintegration into professional and family networks exceedingly difficult (Gaillard et al. 2015).

For scientists who intend to live and work in Uganda, full-time training abroad can work at cross-purposes to their goals to live in and contribute to improving the quality of life in their homeland, to support their families, and someday build a home to which they can retire. For most scientists that I met, and for women in particular, the prospect of spending several years in a foreign country, far from their immediate and extended families, was an unwelcome idea. Women who had studied abroad full-time generally did so when they were young and before they had children. Dr Kisembo, for example, explained that 'problems related to families would be the main problem' for students who enrol in full-time training programmes. She hoped donors would note that

> these programmes where someone has to go away from home for over six months, for the ladies especially, they are not good ... You can go, and [when you] come back the marriage can't work anymore. (interview, 1 May 2014)

Men who studied abroad full-time, and missed out on seeing their children for years, generally described their separation as a personal hardship, but prevailing gender norms mean that such separations are less risky for the stability of their marriages. While a man might expect support from his wife for deciding to spend several years abroad study-ing for a PhD, it is rare for a Ugandan woman to be able to justify to her husband that she should do the same. In general, gendered cultural norms with respect to duties towards children and spouse were the primary factors that women scientists identified as limiting their advancement in academic careers.

Beyond risking family and social relations, full-time study abroad can also significantly undermine individuals' chances of obtaining work in Uganda after completing their degrees. The learned and embodied knowledges obtained abroad sometimes replace other forms of knowl-edge that are essential for success in Uganda. With experience of training for a masters degree at an elite university in Europe, and later for a PhD in another African country, Dr Nalwanga reflected on the dangers that full-time studies can pose to the relevance of Ugandan scientists in their own country:

> I've seen colleagues that do high-tech science in molecular biology. They get a very advanced degree and they have han-dled all these machines … But then they come back to a lab where they don't even have a PCR machine, which is a routine thing. So how are they going to manage? … You don't want to train abroad and then come back and you seem to be redun-dant … yet you are not. (interview, 28 April 2014)

The redundancy that Dr Nalwanga describes occurs as a result of train-ing programmes that encourage scientists to engage in research related to the scientific priorities of their supervisors in the host countries. Redundancy can also result from the tendency to become overly reliant on scientific equipment that is standard in foreign countries, but which might not be available in Uganda due to prohibitive costs and/or the lack of infrastructure.

To cope with laboratories characterised by a scarcity of technicians and spare parts, as well as an intermittent supply of electricity and an overabundance of dust and humidity, Ugandan scientists require the kind of knowledge and creativity seldom cultivated in wealthy research environments. On returning to Uganda, the networks and knowledge that one imagined might open doors to international research funding and opportunities are often undermined by the impossibility of assembling the tools and human resources perceived to be necessary to facilitate local research. Hence, while the facts produced by scientists may travel across continents in the form of 'immutable mobiles' (Latour 1990), the actor-networks that Ugandan scientists enrol in (and are enrolled by) to produce PhD degrees are not nearly as adept at making the same kinds of transcontinental transfers.

From the perspective of training leaders in scientific research in Uganda, full-time study abroad can be disastrous. As Dr Mugisa, a Kampala-based scientist explained, his institution has had serious problems with PhD programmes that enrol their researchers in full-time studies abroad:

> We tend to lose a lot of our people to that environment. Even though in academics now we are saying that ... with globali-sation we can't have brain drain ... and that wherever you are you can contribute to the global knowledge. But, looking at it from a selfish point of view, this institution goes over there to train and build its capacity, and it keeps losing its best sci-entists to other environments. (interview, 5 May 2014)

Dr Mugisa's critical stance towards full-time study abroad is based on its power to weaken social ties and alter scientific subjectivities. He is not alone in this view. Another recently retired professor explained that those who do eventually return are often so disoriented that many are lost to science, while others require months or years before they can begin to be productive. Another influential senior academic was vehe-ment that Ugandan institutions should 'scrap these people' who had trained abroad full-time and had no pre-existing position in Uganda to return to.

In the course of my research, I met several scientists who had resigned from positions at Ugandan research institutions to take up scholarships to study abroad full-time, and had then experienced great difficulties in returning to their careers in Uganda. This was partly due to a mismatch between their new expertise and the local science infrastructure, but it was also linked to bureaucratic obstacles that prevent the absorption of qualified scientists who do not have existing employment contracts. Scientists who were offered a temporary leave of absence from their positions to undertake full-time study abroad were more easily, but seldom unproblematically, reabsorbed if they chose to return.

In general, the scientists I interviewed appreciated the quality of training they could gain by studying abroad, but they found the erosion of their scientific, social and economic ties in Uganda too costly to merit the sacrifice. And while full-time study abroad has the potential to equip scientists with the skills, networks, resources and ambitions to produce forms of scientific knowledge that are internationally appreciated and publishable, it does not necessarily equip them with the skills, networks, resources and ambitions that help them thrive in contemporary Uganda. Hence, despite the rapid advances in internet and related technologies that ease communication across great distances, long-term physical absence for training abroad significantly challenges Ugandan scientists' abilities to sustain their place in the actor-networks that matter most to them in Uganda.

## Full-time training at home

If full-time research training abroad is generally perceived to be contrary to the interests of scientists in Uganda, and to the interests of Uganda's scientific community more broadly, then full-time training at home might be expected to offer a solution. Post-colonial critiques of international science and development highlight the value of indigenous knowledge systems and the importance of resisting the domination of the modernist ideologies that originate in the metropoles (Kelly 1979; Tikly 2004). Other voices call for 'South–South' collaborations, whereby partners from several Southern countries pool resources to address problems of shared importance (Hassan 2001). In both instances, those who advocate the de-linking of scientific training from Northern actor-networks are concerned that African scientists forfeit too much of their own agency when they enrol (and are enrolled) in higher education institutions in the North. However, for the researchers and professors that I met in Uganda, the advantages of full-time training at home relate less to the avoidance of what Eric Wolf (1966) might call patron–client ties with a global reach than they do to strengthening and maintaining their own local social, kinship and economic relations.

Dr Mugisa, who studied abroad for his PhD and whose current professional position affords him insight into the experiences of a range of Ugandan PhD candidates registered at multiple institutions, describes the main advantage of staying home as follows:

> The basic advantage is that you are at home, which is familiar ground for you. You don't deal with issues of being away from home and missing your family. And at work everyone knows you and you are familiar with the facilities. You can multi-task and do any number of things. Many people will pursue their social careers as well and get good jobs at the same time that they are students. (interview, 5 May 2014)

Mugisa's references to family, 'social careers' and employment speaks to the entanglement of personal, entrepreneurial and scientific aspects of Ugandan scientists' lives. The attainment of a PhD is not only, or even primarily, a rite of passage in becoming an independent producer of new knowledge. Instead, it is a component of the broader project of producing material wealth and reproducing nuclear and extended family networks. Scientists who are firmly emplaced in the Ugandan context, and thus able to negotiate, reproduce and expand the actor-networks that underpin their work, often also have certain advantages in accessing the empirical materials that are central to the success of knowledge production. As Dr Ochieng explains, his local emplacement facilitates the collection of samples for his agricultural research:

> The advantage is that you are in your local environment. You can move around easily to all parts of the country, and collect strains of the virus from all over. I have contacts all over. I

can contact district officers and then go to the farms, and it
is not a problem. (interview, 7 May 2014)

According to Dr Ochieng, the institutional gatekeepers, who guard the
material basis of much agricultural and medical research in Uganda, are
more likely to grant access to local PhD students, who are also employed
by public institutions and whose local social networks are still intact.
Conversely, researchers, from Uganda or elsewhere, who are explicitly
attached to foreign research or training programmes, will have more
difficulties in this regard.

However, while long-term integration into the local context does
seem to simplify some matters for those who embark on a local PhD
programme, the scientists I consulted generally agree that full-time
domestic programmes are a poor alternative to the sandwich programmes described in more detail below. These scientists cited low
salaries, sporadic supervision and limited opportunities for personal
engagement with scientific communities outside of Uganda to explain
their views.

Salaries and supervision are related. Salaries earned by academics at
public universities in Uganda are considered by the scientists themselves to be insufficient to support their livelihoods. Even full-time
employees spend a considerable amount of time on activities that generate additional income so that they can achieve what they see as an
acceptable standard of living.[5] One consequence of this is that local
supervision of PhDs is done on a more or less voluntary basis – in the
words of Dr Mugisa, it is as if 'someone is just doing you a favour'.

This means that PhD supervision is not only provided in a begrudg-
ing and inconsistent way, but also creates a kind of indebtedness to the
supervisor. Students are expected to service this informal 'debt'
through the co-authorship of publications and the rendering of unpaid
assistance in the form of teaching and research. This further slows
down the students' progress towards completing their degrees. As such,
the relationship between supervisor and PhD student can be

understood as belonging to a substantive cultural economy character-ised by transactions linked to scientific recognition, knowledge and labour (see Halperin 1994).

With a handful of exceptions, most PhD candidates in Uganda enrol at the country's oldest and most prestigious higher education institu-tion, Makerere University. At Makerere and elsewhere, local PhD programmes depend directly or indirectly on foreign funding. Funds might be earmarked for PhD training or cobbled together by senior scientists from one or more different projects from which they can allocate small amounts of funding towards supporting a PhD student's fieldwork and analysis. Either way, research priorities are strongly influenced by the interests of the foreign partners, but in such cases, the PhD student seldom benefits from direct engagement with those partners. Thus, completing a PhD exclusively in Uganda narrows the range of people, as well as the material and symbolic resources, that can be incorporated into the actor-networks that produce the degree, with-out significantly reducing the students' or the universities' dependence upon foreign resources.

Institutional hindrances to accessing primary empirical data sources may be less formidable for local PhD students, but laboratory equip-ment and consumables that can assist their analysis, together with access to such basics as electricity and transport can be difficult. And while it is rare for anyone to complain about the quality of supervision available in Uganda, it is widely acknowledged that the small number of trained and experienced scientists in Uganda limits the breadth of dis-ciplinary expertise that PhD students can draw upon. The result is that local PhDs are perceived by Ugandan scientists as taking far too long to complete and as constrained by inadequate tools. While still dependent upon foreign resources, local degrees also offer too little exposure to foreign collaborators and research environments. The skills developed from such exposure, perhaps more so than specific personal relation-ships, were perceived by respondents in this study as essential for success in subsequent efforts to mobilise international funding for further research.

## The sandwich-training model

On an icy winter afternoon in 2014, David Ebine and I sat in a busy European café talking about his PhD training. At the time, he was nearing the end of a sandwich programme and he compared the opportunities he had to study at home with programmes spent partly or wholly abroad:

> I also wanted to study abroad. The reason being that doing a PhD in Kampala can take you, if you are not careful [laughing], ten years. I think it is a systems issue, mixed with one's own personal commitments. So, most people who would like to do PhDs prefer doing them abroad because usually the turnaround time is short. It is almost half of the time it would take [in Uganda]. (interview, 14 February 2014)

Here, Ebine reiterated a common criticism of local PhD programmes and identified a key advantage of sandwich programmes and full-time study abroad: PhDs are finished far more quickly abroad than they are in Uganda.

For Dr Mpagi, an agricultural scientist who is active in several international and regional professional networks, the sandwich model has the added advantage that 'in the end you become relevant' (interview, 28 April 2014). For him, this relevance is a direct outcome of the multi-site nature of the training and of the PhD student's mobility.

Time spent abroad offers brief but significant respites from a wide range of social and economic commitments and obligations – from extra teaching at a private university, to managing a small business, to attending family events. As a result, PhD students tend to be far more focused and effective in the months they spend abroad. At the same time, the brevity of these interludes means that ties to place, family, and colleagues are not significantly eroded, nor are the capacities for creativity and patience that are essential for successful work in Ugandan institutional contexts. Meanwhile, continued dependence upon supervisors and, often, data collection in Uganda, counter the temptation to design and carry out research that might be highly valued in foreign institutions but not so much in Uganda.

As such, the sandwich model offers training in a liminal space that is neither mainly Ugandan nor mainly foreign. This liminality can be an asset to anyone seeking to broker disparate actor-networks while maintaining some creative space in which to achieve their own goals. Successful Ugandan scientists who continue to work in their homeland after completing their PhDs have learned to navigate and manipulate opportunities in a liminal zone that amalgamates local and foreign influences in ways that exceed the traditional bounds of what might be called a field of science (Bourdieu 2004).

To borrow from Sheila Jasanoff (2004), the Ugandan research environment is co-produced through the actions of individuals, organisations and material actants with diverse geographical origins. Sandwich-training models tend to be preferred by Ugandan scientists because these models are well suited to the environment. Sandwich models offer high quality training while preserving scientists' social and material ties to their home country. The model thus also favours the cultivation of a scientific subjectivity that seeks to engage with research questions that are closely tied to issues of concern in Uganda, while permitting the mobilisation of a variety of resources from both near and far.

## Mobility, training and understanding one's future partners

Another advantage of scientific mobility, and one that is often missed in studies on science research in low-income countries, is the value of exposure to new social and cultural environments (for an exception, see Ynalvez and Shrum 2009). Temporary mobility offers scientists an insight into the fractured geographies and uneven advantages of different research environments, while at the same time offering them opportunities to cultivate understandings of other cultures and academic traditions. In other words, immersion in foreign research, education and cultural contexts, equips Ugandan scientists to better understand and negotiate with foreign collaborators later in their careers.

Acquiring some life experience in countries such as the US, the UK, the Netherlands, Sweden or Japan can improve Ugandan scientists' abilities to participate in internationally-sponsored projects, and to further their own individual and institutional interests within the context of such projects. These skills can be deployed in managing the kinds of known-unknowns that sustain partnerships with foreign actors despite the 'inherent political-economic contradictions' that lurk just below the surface of many collaborative research projects (Geissler 2013:13). A personal experience of mobility and immersion in another culture can also be an advantage to scientists who return to Uganda and seek to build collaborative research architectures that include the boundary objects (Star and Griesemer 1989) and slippery spaces that are necessary for facilitating the flow of resources across actor-networks and towards partly, or wholly, contradictory ends (Zink 2013).

As such, sandwich programmes can be an asset in the decolonisation, if not endogenisation (see Crossman 2004), of Ugandan science even as it continues to engage with global networks. Instead of reproducing and embodying power inequalities in new Ugandan PhDs, the sandwich model, through its periodic mobilities, offers researchers experiences and tools to engage and negotiate more successfully with foreign actors and their science agendas in Uganda. Unlike PhD programmes abroad, which can create significant hiatuses in Ugandan scientists' networks in Uganda, sandwich programmes seldom undermine the potential for graduates to become powerful actors in Uganda. The sandwich model also differs from local PhD programmes that, while firmly embedded in local social and scientific networks, obliquely disempower students through their indirect dependence upon foreign funds and research interests.

Reflecting on his PhD training in Europe, Dr Oloya noted that one of the greatest rewards of his experience was the sense of empowerment that allowed him to see himself as an equal to his European colleagues. It was while studying overseas that he first realised 'Hey! I'm not stupid after all,' and allowed him to see himself as an expert when offering guidance to foreign colleagues from other countries and foreign institutions. As he explains:

> When you talk about genetic sequencing and DNA technol-
> ogy, you say, 'Ah, that is core science, that it is very tough. We
> can't do it, it is for the Europeans, and it is for the Americans.'
> But through training abroad you realise 'OK, I can also do it'.
> And then the Europeans, the fellow students, they say,
> '[Oloya], I'm finding a problem here and here, how do you do
> solve it?' Then you go through this and you solve the prob-
> lem. You say 'OK, I can also help somebody.' It gives you
> confidence. (interview, 13 May 2014)

For Oloya and others, this confidence was cultivated further by foreign supervisors who invited Ugandan PhD students into their home, per-sonally served them a cup of coffee or tea, and asked them how they would tackle a research issue or encouraged them to pursue their own ideas. Several respondents compared this with their experiences of supervision in Uganda, which tend to reproduce existing hierarchies and favour obedience above independence. Of course, not all Ugandan students enjoy such warm relations with their foreign supervisors. However, to the extent that collegial relations and friendships do develop across geographic and political-economic spaces, supervisor–student relationships are demystified, and hierarchies begin to erode (albeit even partially), thus enabling Ugandan scientists to engage and negotiate more effectively with international collaborators.

Later, when PhDs have been completed and graduates are continu-ing with their careers, experiences abroad also help Ugandan researchers to understand and accommodate what might otherwise seem to be irrational behaviour on the part of their foreign collaborators. Dr Nalwanga, for example, described her foreign colleagues' loss of confi-dence on encountering what to them were shocking research conditions in a Ugandan hospital's maternity ward:

> They said: 'you mean a woman can deliver on the floor? ...
> How do we go and talk to such a woman to participate in a

research project? ... How will we conduct research in a centre which delivers a hundred [babies] per day, when in our centre [in Europe] we have a hundred per month? How will we be able to take the samples? How are we going to counsel [the women]?' ... They said all those kinds of things. But to me these things are normal. I've done research [in such contexts]. (interview, 28 April 2014)

Having trained in their country through a sandwich PhD programme, Dr Nalwanga knows the environments that European researchers are more familiar with. She has experienced the clean hallways, ample beds and basic comforts of European hospitals, just as she has experienced conditions in regional public hospitals in Uganda. Her experience has enabled her to assist and advise her foreign colleagues, and to facilitate the continuation of their scientific work. She explained that foreign partners often

don't know much about the local setting, and it is up to us to really tell them the true picture. [And] it matters! Otherwise some of them, at one point, feel like they are exploiting patients. They are like, 'how do we come then and take all these samples for DNA analysis ... when a women can't even feed herself?' (interview, 28 April 2014)

For Dr Nalwanga, the conditions in which her research is conducted is one of the reasons why her research matters. Like many of her colleagues, she was once a doctor working at a hospital with few medical resources, and treating a seemingly never-ending queue of individual patients with frighteningly advanced medical conditions. What was, for her, the depressing prospect of spending her career reacting to individual cases without being able to effect systemic change in terms of preventative healthcare was one of the factors that motivated her to pursue a career in clinical research. Through her research, which is carried out in collaboration with foreign partners and using foreign funds, Dr Nalwanga is hopeful that she might be able to help mitigate future suffering rather than merely reacting to avoidable and preventable medical emergencies. Dr Nalwanga believes that her experience abroad makes her a more effective support to her foreign partners, whose funds and equipment are essential to the success of her research.

While Dr Nalwanga's example is dramatic, others are more amusing. Dr Tumushabe recalled a flushed and frustrated Scandinavian researcher in a northern Ugandan town who stood in the street demanding a receipt from a *boda boda* [motorcycle taxi] driver:

> If you only studied here in Uganda, then you would be won-
> dering 'is he crazy, looking for a receipt from a *boda boda*?'
> [*laughing*]. Yet, the *boda* driver is taking your money. Maybe
> he has worked with you the whole day and you are going to
> pay him 30 000 shillings. That is a lot of money. Money you
> cannot receive later [without a receipt]. So, [training abroad
> and] learning among those environments helps you to know
> how to respond to and understand a different culture in the
> future. Scandinavian people are strict [*chopping the side of one
> hand against the palm of his other*]. If you have been with them,
> you won't wonder why they are irritated, why they are not
> renewing your project [when you can't show receipts for
> some project costs]. (interview, 1 May 2014)

The *boda boda* story is comical, but it also highlights two serious issues. First, foreign collaborators' concerns and actions sometimes make little sense in a Ugandan context. Second, understanding those actions and their implications can be important for the sustainability of future research and collaboration opportunities.

Understanding partners' and funders' perceptions of the legitimate costs involved in a research project and of how those costs should be accounted for, is fundamental to building trust in international collaborations. Only after spending months in Scandinavia, getting to know Scandinavian researchers, their research environments, and their version of audit culture (Power 1994), does a sweaty argument with a *boda boda* driver make any sense. In the long run, being able and/or willing to try to make sense of the underlying assumptions inherent in such encounters is a skill that helps make transnational collaborations sustainable in contexts where very research might otherwise seem impossible.

## Conclusions

The research-training programmes described here are elements within a larger transnational economy of scientific knowledge production whereby labour, equipment, data and access to empirical material are exchanged between local and foreign actors and institutions. While some foreign institutional and individual partners might engage with Southern researchers for altruistic reasons, significant material and symbolic rewards are available to foreign actors who engage with the Southern science community. Many Northern scientific careers, commercial innovations, and medical breakthroughs rely on access to the plants, animals, viruses and social and physical processes that are only, or most easily, accessible in the South. Meanwhile, in the securitised North, where low-income countries are viewed as potentially destabilising sources of disease, refugees and environmental pollution, access to and expertise about these countries is a priority for wealthy governments seeking to neutralise or curtail such threats.

Despite occasional periods of political tumult and violence, Uganda has long been an attractive research site for scientists from Europe and North America. It has offered (and continues to offer) a welcoming political, social and physical climate in tropical Africa with access to plants, animals, bacteria, viruses and human bodies that are the essential raw material for much Northern research (Elliott et al. 2015; Tilley 2011). By offering foreigners access to such material, Ugandans can garner rewards such as funding, equipment, access to training opportunities abroad, and foreign expertise. These resources have the potential to contribute to the renewal and development of research capacity, enabling Ugandans to carry out scientific research and to speak with increasing authority in both local and international fora. Meanwhile, the rising number of highly trained researchers in Uganda, combined with the growing influence of local institutional review boards and the Uganda National Council for Science and Technology, permit local researchers to demand more meaningful and beneficial collaborations in exchange for allowing foreign researchers and institutions access to Ugandan sites.

Both historical and contemporary evidence shows that scientists in lower-income countries are able to wield influence and agency in (and sometimes against) foreign actors from the North (Lowe 2004; Osseo-Asare 2014; Pollock 2014; Prince and Marsland 2014; Rottenburg 2009b; Tilley 2011; Zink 2013). However, the balance of power between research collaborators still obviously favours actors in the wealthier countries (Crane 2013; Droney 2014; Olukoshi and Zeleza 2004; Tousignant 2013). Both my own informants, and the publications of a diverse group of scholars (see, for example, Elliott et al. 2015; Juma and Yee-Cheong 2005; Osseo-Asare 2014), seem to agree that it is important and necessary for African scientists to foreground their own priorities for science research in Africa. In my view, opportunities for scientists from low-income countries to participate in sandwich research training programmes are clearly an asset in this struggle.

In comparing the three different models of PhD training that are available to Ugandan scientists, Dr Mugisa succinctly encapsulated the perspective of most of the scientists I encountered in my investigation:

> I think if you compare the three modes: the one at home, which now tends to create capacity but over a long period of time, and also does not create capacity with a richness of experiences. Then you have the sandwich programme, which shortens the length of stay on the programme but then with a very high probability of people coming back to their sta-tions. Then the other one where you have probably even a shorter stay on the programme, but chances of fleeing the station, people not coming back. I think the one that we really would prefer is the sandwich programme up until the capacity at home is grown – the capacity to supervise, the infrastructure, and the resources. (interview, 5 May 2014)

Dr Mugisa points to the richness of experience and the likelihood of return as key factors informing his preference. His emphasis on the importance of scholars returning to their 'stations' might surprise observers who see the 'brain drain', and the constant flow of people from resource-poor to richer research environments, as a natural phenomenon. However, his view resonates with my observations of, and conversations with, scientists in Uganda, who frequently pointed out the beauty of their country and the value they place on being at home.

I found a consensus in Uganda that the sandwich model of training offers Ugandan scientists opportunities to strengthen their positions in Uganda's scientific community and in society more generally. These programmes also provide opportunities for Ugandan scientists to improve their positions in relation to international partners and counterparts. Given that Uganda's research environments are, and will in all likelihood continue to be, co-productions between actors and actants from both inside and outside Uganda (as well as inside and outside of science) (Latour 1987), the power of Ugandan scientists to act as strong agents is strengthened, not weakened, by their exposure to multiple scientific and cultural contexts.

These insights should also serve as a caution to institutions that would like to accelerate the shift towards local PhD training models, based on the growing number of qualified and experienced scientists in low-income countries. In my view, PhD training opportunities in the South should continue to expand to the extent that they can derive resources from international collaborations that are primarily *scientific* in nature (as opposed to those focused on capacity building), and to the extent that national governments direct funds to their own PhD training programmes. A shift to a full-time local model by international actants supporting science capacity building has the potential to erode the agency of scientists if it takes place before the following conditions are met in lower-income countries:

- National institutions must be well-equipped with the tools necessary for research.
- Reliable conduits must be established through which scientists

can access the reagents and other consumable resources that research depends on.

• Significant national funding is directed toward locally defined research priorities.

• Academic salaries are sufficient to enable individuals to focus on research and not need to seek other sources of income that consume their time and their energy.

These conditions are not yet met in Uganda or in most sub-Saharan African countries. As such, the sandwich model, through its co-produced, multi-local and liminal learning and research environment is better suited to the goals of institutions that aim to strengthen the agency of scientists who are working in lower-income countries.

Lastly, it is important to acknowledge that the costs and values associated with the three models differ widely. The costs of full-time training programmes abroad are high while their value for science in Uganda is relatively low, given that so few of their recipients return home. Meanwhile, if we apply the narrow models of financial accounting that have become normative in understanding value in contemporary audit culture, the sandwich model may seem prohibitively expensive when compared to local PhD programmes. Sandwich PhDs entail high salary costs for foreign supervisors, as well as airfares and living stipends for students in high-income countries. However, the actor-network theory approach used here highlights the value of various kinds of relationships, knowledges, skills and hands-on experience with modern scientific equipment, that are commonly externalised in conventional calculations of the return on investment from the different training models. My findings indicate that these elements of PhD training are precisely the ones that become key assets for Ugandan scientists as they attempt to further decolonise science in their country. Consequently, until local research environments are further improved, a substantive economic calculation of value clearly favours sustained investment in sandwich models of PhD training.

## Notes

1   I use the term 'sandwich model' rather loosely to cover PhD programmes where degrees are awarded by a foreign institution, a domestic institution, or jointly by more than one institution. The important aspect is that the PhD is supervised by senior scientists who are based locally and internationally, and that the PhD candidate is mobile, spending significant amounts of time abroad and at home during the course of their PhD programme.

2   I have limited my observations to the science sector as my research focused on academics working in the health sciences, agricultural sciences, and in natural resource management.

3   See also Chapters 4, 5 and 6 in this volume.

4   Pseudonyms are used for all of the interviewees quoted in this chapter; their anonymity was guaranteed as a condition of their participation in the research.

5   This includes paying for their children to attend the more expensive primary and secondary schools that have more chance of preparing pupils for university study.

## References

Bourdieu, Pierre (2004) *Science of Science and Reflexivity*. Chicago: University of Chicago Press

Bradley, Megan (2008) On the agenda: North–South research partnerships and agenda-setting processes. *Development in Practice* 18(6): 673–685

Crane, Johanna Tayloe (2013) *Scrambling for Africa: AIDS, Expertise, and the Rise of American Global Health Science*. Ithaca: Cornell University Press

Crossman, Peter (2004) Perceptions of 'Africanisation' or 'endogenisation' at African universities: Issues and recommendations. In: Paul Tiyambe Zeleza and Adebayo Olukoshi (eds) *African Universities in the Twenty-First Century: Knowledge and Society*. Dakar: CODESRIA

Donovan, Kevin P (2014) 'Development' as if we have never been modern: Fragments of a Latourian development studies. *Development and Change* 45(5): 869–894

Droney, Damien (2014) Ironies of laboratory work during Ghana's second age of optimism. *Cultural Anthropology* 29(2): 363–384

Elliott, Alison, Barbara Nerima, Bernard Bagaya, et al. (2015) Capacity for science in sub-Saharan Africa. *The Lancet* 385(9986): 2435–2437

Ferguson, James (2006) *Global Shadows: Africa in the Neoliberal World Order.* Durham, NC: Duke University Press

Gaillard J and AM Gaillard (1997) Introduction: The international mobility of brains: Exodus or circulation? *Science, Technology and Society* 2(2): 195–228

Gaillard, Jacques, Ann-Marie Gaillard and VV Krishna (2015) Return from migration and circulation of highly educated people: The never-ending brain drain. *Science, Technology and Society* 20(3): 269–278

Geissler, PW (2013) Public secrets in public health: Knowing not to know while making scientific knowledge. *American Ethnologist* 40(1): 13–34

Halperin, Rhoda H (1994) *Cultural Economies Past and Present.* Austin: University of Texas Press

Halvorsen, Tor (2010) Introduction. In: Kassahun Berhanu, Tor Halvorsen and Mary Mwiandi (eds) *Reshaping Research Universities in the Nile Basin Countries.* Kampala: Fountain

Hassan, Mohamed HA (2001) Can science save Africa? *Science* 292(5522): 1609–1609

Jasanoff, Sheila (2004) The idiom of co-production. In: Sheila Jasanoff (ed.) *States of Knowledge: The Co-Production of Science and Social Order.* London: Routledge

Juma, Calestous and Lee Yee-Cheong (2005) *Innovation: Applying Knowledge in Development.* Earthscan: London

Kabeba Muriisa, Roberts (2010) It is not all about money: Financial governance and research in public universities in Uganda. In: Kassahun Berhanu, Tor Halvorsen and Mary Mwiandi (eds) *Research Universities in the Nile Basin Countries.* Kampala: Fountain

Kelly, Gail P (1979) The relation between colonial and metropolitan schools: A structural analysis. *Comparative Education* 15(2): 209–215

Latour, Bruno (1987) *Science in Action.* Cambridge: Harvard University Press

Latour, Bruno (1990) Visualisation and cognition: Drawing things together. In: Michael Lynch and Steve Woolgar (eds) *Representation in Scientific Practice.* Cambridge, MA: MIT Press

Latour, Bruno (2005) *Reassembling the Social: An Introduction to Actor-Network Theory*. Oxford and New York: Oxford University Press

Lowe, Celia (2004) Making the monkey: How the Togean Macaque went from 'new form' to 'endemic species' in Indonesians' conservation biology. *Cultural Anthropology* 19(4): 491–516

Mamdani, Mahmood (2007) *Scholars in the Marketplace: The Dilemmas of Neoliberal Reform at Makerere University, 1989–2005*. Dakar: CODESRIA

Moyi Okwaro, Ferdinand and PW Geissler (2015) In/dependent collaborations: Perceptions and experiences of African scientists in transnational HIV research: Transnational collaborations and HIV research. *Medical Anthropology Quarterly*: 29(4): 492–511. DOI: 10.1111/maq.12206

Obong, Quintas Oula (2004) Academic dilemmas under neoliberal education reforms: A review of Makerere University, Uganda. In: Paul Tiyambe Zeleza and Adebayo O Olukoshi (eds) *African Universities in the Twenty-First Century*. Dakar: Codesria

Olukoshi, Adebayo O and Paul Tiyambe Zeleza (2004) The African university in the twenty-first century: Future challenges and a research agenda. In: Paul Tiyambe Zeleza and Adebayo O Olukoshi (eds) *African Universities in the Twenty-First Century*. Dakar: Codesria

Osseo-Asare, Abena Dove Agyepoma (2014) *Bitter Roots: The Search for Healing Plants in Africa*. Chicago: University of Chicago Press

Pollock, Anne (2014) Places of pharmaceutical knowledge-making: Global health, postcolonial science, and hope in South African drug discovery. *Social Studies of Science* 44(6): 848–873

Power, Michael (1994) *The Audit Explosion*. London: Demos

Prince, Ruth Jane and Rebecca Marsland (eds) (2014) *Making and Unmaking Public Health in Africa: Ethnographic and Historical Perspectives*. Cambridge Centre of African Studies Series. Athens: Ohio University Press

Rottenburg, Richard (2009a) *Far-Fetched Facts: A Parable of Development Aid*. Cambridge, MA: MIT Press

Rottenburg, Richard (2009b) Social and public experiments and new figurations of science and politics in postcolonial Africa. *Postcolonial Studies* 12(4): 423–440

Sembatya, Vincent A and Robert K Ngobi (2014) *Mapping the Careers and Mobility of Makerere University Doctoral Graduates*. Kampala: Makerere University, Directorate of Quality Assurance

Sicherman, Carol (2005) *Becoming an African University: Makerere 1922–2000*. Kampala: Fountain

Star, Susan Leigh and James R Griesemer (1989) Institutional ecology, translations and boundary objects: Amateurs and professionals in Berkeley's Museum of Vertebrate Zoology, 1907–1939. *Social Studies of Science* 19(3): 387–420

Tikly, Leon (2004) Education and the new imperialism. *Comparative Education* 40(2): 173–198

Tilley, Helen (2011) *Africa as a Living Laboratory: Empire, Development, and the Problem of Scientific Knowledge, 1870–1950*. Chicago: University of Chicago Press

Tousignant, N (2013) Broken tempos: Of means and memory in a Senegalese university laboratory. *Social Studies of Science* 43(5): 729–753

UNCST (Uganda National Council for Science and Technology) (2012) *The Careers and Productivity of Doctorate Holders (CDH) Survey*. Kampala, Uganda

Wolf, Eric R (1966) Kinship, friendship, and patron-client relations. In: Michael Banton (ed.) *The Social Anthropology of Complex Societies*. New York: Praeger

Ynalvez, MA and WM Shrum (2009) International graduate science training and scientific collaboration. *International Sociology* 24(6): 870–901

Zink, Eren (2013) *Hot Science, High Water: Assembling Nature, Society and Environmental Policy in Contemporary Vietnam*. Copenhagen: NIAS Press

# CHAPTER

# 4

## The status of research at three Ugandan universities

*ABK Kasozi*

In this chapter, I review research at three Ugandan universities. My main focus is Makerere University in Kampala but I also make some observations about the Mbarara University of Science and Technology and the Uganda Christian University in Mukono. I argue that although Makerere University has achieved some impressive results in research, the lack of local funding, an unfriendly legal framework, inadequate research-management systems, and an overemphasis on teaching at the expense of research, are undermining its struggling research capacity. This study shows that micro-level co-operation between academic staff and institutions of the North and the South should supplement, and eventually overtake, African universities' existing agreements with large multilateral institutions such as the World Bank, the IMF, UNESCO, the OECD, ISESCO and so on. Such co-operation will enhance the research function of African universities.

### Understanding the background

Most of Africa's universities were established to train a handful of the more obedient local elites as civil servants so that they could be relied on to keep the colonial system's administrative and economic systems running smoothly. Higher education has therefore always been, and still is, elitist.

The role of African universities did not change as the continent achieved political independence. Between 1960 and 1980, African universities remained 'development institutions', designed to produce the workforce that African countries needed for state administration (Yesufu 1973; see also the Accra Declaration). Research was never emphasised, and even teaching staff were able to access only the bare minimum in terms of equipment, books and facilities. From the 1970s to the 2000s, many African states weakened to the point of collapse (Harrison 2004), and years of mismanagement by military and authoritarian regimes seriously undermined Africa's universities. Most universities lost any autonomy they might have hoped to win with the ending of colonialism; nationalisation turned most of them into government institutions and they began to be governed as state departments.

When multilateral organisations such as the World Bank and the IMF imposed their conditionalities on collapsing African states from the 1980s onwards, the accompanying neoliberal policies further undermined African universities. Based on a theory that rates of return on higher education were lower than those from basic education, and that higher education primarily benefited private and not public interests (Psacharopoulous 1980; Psacharopoulos et al. 1986), African countries were encouraged to spend less on higher education. The World Bank considerably reduced its own spending on higher education in Africa (Banya and Elu 2001; Carrol 2005; Kasozi 2009). In 2008, the World Bank noted that its 'official development assistance to postsecondary education averaged just US$110 million a year between 1990 to 1999' and that its 'financing for tertiary education on the continent, which had averaged US$103 million annually from FY90–FY94 declined to US$30.8 million per year from FY95–FY99' (World Bank 2008: 1, 2). African governments were encouraged to view higher education as a luxury and enormous budget cuts to higher education spending drastically weakened universities in a number of African countries. From 1980 to 2002, public expenditure per student fell from US$6 800 to

$1 200, and by the mid 2000s, it had dropped to a per student average of $981 in 33 sub-Saharan African countries (World Bank: 2008: xxvii).

The funding cuts dealt a major blow to research and knowledge production in universities, and by 2008, the continent's academics were contributing less than 3 per cent of articles published in international journals (Paul Zeleza quoted in Cloete et al. 2015: 8). In Uganda, from 1985 to 2005, the Ministry of Education allocated an average of between 9 and 11 per cent of its budget to higher education, and over 60 per cent to basic education.[1] The Ugandan government still sees universities primarily as teaching institutions, and has barely funded research since the mid 1990s. In the 2014/2015 financial year, research at Ugandan universities was allocated just 420 million shillings (about US$210 000) in state funding.[2]

It is clear therefore that the education policies of the World Bank and other multilateral financial institutions have had disastrous consequences for African institutions of higher learning. While advancing their own ideological agendas, these macro-level 'same-size-fits-all' policies have neither emphasised the knowledge production function of universities nor have they facilitated the production of the next generation of academics in Africa.

## The urgency of research and knowledge

So, how can Southern institutions support one another to enhance research and knowledge accumulation while working with their Northern counterparts? Can collaboration between North and South at institutional and faculty levels enhance research capacity in the South and give both Southern and Northern collaborators greater insight into global problems?

In this information age, knowledge plays a key role in development (World Bank 2000, 2002, 2006, 2008). Human societies need knowledge to manage all their activities and resolve problems that arise. Higher education institutions, particularly universities, are major sites of knowledge production. Because of this, universities should be at the centre of any country's innovation system (this includes public and private research centres funded by industry and commerce). But universities do not only produce knowledge, they also pass on knowledge to the next generation, award academic and professional qualifications, recruit social elites and diffuse dominant ideologies into society (Castells 2001; see also Cloete et al. 2015). Unfortunately, African universities have never fully carried out their knowledge-creation functions effectively for a number of reasons, some of which I discuss briefly in the sections that follow.

## Gaps in the creation of home-grown knowledge

Ideally, collaboration between North and South, at the inter-faculty, inter-institutional or bilateral-agency levels should advance home-grown knowledge. Instead, multilateral agencies tend to draw up blueprints of knowledge for emulation and implementation by weaker Southern partners. These blueprints are often loaded with cultural and ideological content generated by the major powers.

The importing of these conceptual models that are allegedly 'universally applicable' is one of the major causes of slow development in Africa (Okolie 2003). African farmers, for example, tend to embrace only those agricultural technologies that are not contrary to their beliefs or ways of life, and which are affordable, safe and sustainable. However, most of what is taught in our agricultural faculties and colleges is based on Western agricultural practices. These assume that mechanised, large-scale commercial farming is the ultimate goal, despite its high costs, and disastrous social and environmental impacts. For this reason, most African academics agree that scholars who have knowledge and experience of African conditions must produce Africa-centred knowledge.

Researchers and teachers in African universities should be trained in the environments they are likely to work in if they are to appreciate the problems they will be called upon to resolve. In this way, they will ask the right questions when confronted with problems for resolution. Due to the lack of funding, homegrown researchers and supportive research environments, most of what is taught in African universities is imported. Virtually all the knowledge quoted in the Science Citation

Index is produced in developed countries. No wonder Africa remains peripheral in terms of knowledge production (Altbach 2002, 2003). Although African-produced academic articles rose from 1 250 in 1996 to 5 200 in 2006, this still comprised only about 2.3 per cent of global output (Musiige and Maassen 2015). Clearly, this is an area where improvement is needed and collaboration is feasible.

## Too little funding for research

How can African scholars co-operate to lobby governments to fund research as a major function of universities? Most African leaders see universities as teaching institutions and therefore do not sufficiently fund knowledge production. Yet, poor funding is a key reason for the lack of research outputs from sub-Saharan Africa. From 2008 to 2012, most developing nations spent the equivalent of 3 to 4 per cent of their country's total GDP on research and development. In the same period, African countries spent the equivalent of less than 1 per cent of their (much smaller) GDPs on 'mainstream science-based' research (Sanyal and Varghese 2006; Teferra and Altbach 2003). Uganda performs even worse than the rest of sub-Saharan Africa when it comes to funding research. In 2007, the country spent the equivalent of 0.41 per cent of its GDP on research and development and relied on external funding for a good percentage of its research expenditure (Cloete et al. 2015: 151).

Looking back to how this came about, Mamdani has reported that, in 1993, 'both the [Makerere] University and the government sus-pended research funding' (2007: 131). Although the government then allocated 300 million shillings (about US$3 million at the time) towards research in its 1994/1995 budget, general state policy was to do away with research funding. In December 1996, the 'government scrapped scholarships for graduate studies' (Mamdani 2007: 131) and linked all further training to public staffing requirements. This meant that gov-ernment funding for all other types of research – including basic research, applied research, strategic research, and the training of a national cadre of highly skilled researchers at universities – was scrapped. According to statistics supplied by the Ministry of Education for the period 2000 to 2007, basic research was not funded.[3] Fortunately reasonable funding from donors helped to fill part of the vacuum.

## Issues of institutional autonomy

How should university autonomy be understood, and how do different types of autonomy influence the way research is done? A major obstacle to expanding and enhancing research at Makerere and other Ugandan universities is the lack of institutional autonomy and academic freedom. In Uganda, universities have passed through various stages, being: institutions for training African colonial functionaries (1948–1963); regional and independent universities (1963–1970); national institutions governed from the Ministry of Education (1970–2001); and semi-autonomous institutions with key management areas still controlled by the state (since 2001). The Universities and Tertiary Institutions Act of 2001 granted Ugandan universities some freedoms, but they remain stifled in many ways. For example, section 6A of the Act (as amended in 2006) states:

> The Minister may issue directives of a policy nature to all institutions of higher education, whether public or private, and the institutions shall give effect to those directives.

Accordingly, although, under section 41, university councils have powers to 'fix scales of fees and boarding charges', the government prevented Makerere University's council from increasing fees in the 2004/2005 academic year and again in 2014. In addition, section 62(3) of the Act forbids public universities from spending any money not approved by the Ugandan parliament, and section 59(5) states that no public university has the right to invest any of its funds without approval of the minister of education. The Treasury can also ask public universities to remit monies collected to the government under section 44(4) of the Public Finance and Accountability Act. All these legal restrictions means that universities in Uganda, particularly public universities, have no power to freely manage their finances, and therefore cannot accumulate funds for academic or research purposes.

## Types of research conducted at Ugandan universities

Research activities in Ugandan universities can be classified into six broad categories. A few staff and students do the critically important basic or *disinterested research* conducted solely with the aim of searching for truth. However, research with immediate practical outcomes for implementation is preferred. The majority of academics and institutions therefore seek out and conduct *applied research* with the aim of resolving specific social or scientific problems.

Makerere and Mbarara universities are involved in a number of research projects that aim to find solutions to various medical, agricultural and social problems. The College of Agriculture at Makerere University has done pioneering work in its efforts to modernise agriculture, prevent animal and plant diseases and conserve the environment. The Mountains of the Moon University, in the town of Fort Portal in Central Western Uganda, conducts a number of research projects in horticulture and ecology.

Meanwhile public and chartered university institutions are permitted to train postgraduate students to carry out *training-based research,* to fulfil the requirements of masters and doctoral degrees. Virtually every academic in Uganda attempts to obtain *consultancies*, which sometimes bring new information to light. Both local and international issues are addressed, and the research is often carried out on behalf of businesses or NGOs. Perhaps the most sought after form of research is *donor-driven*. A number of foreign donor agencies have supported research in Uganda. Most donor-driven research has focused on social and scientific issues. In the process, new knowledge has been produced and academics have been trained. Many of the beneficiaries have been the applied science-based faculties that work in sectors such as agriculture, forestry, health and technology. External donors are, understandably, interested in funding areas that they consider important. Lastly, some academics conduct *publication-driven research* aimed at increasing their publication records with a view to promotion and academic advancement.

## Research and research capacities

Despite all the obstacles they face, Ugandan academics persist in conducting research, disseminating their results, and training postgraduate students. In this section, I focus on the status of research and research capacity at Makerere University and then briefly touch on two other higher education institutions. All three institutions have benefited from collaborating with universities and researchers from the North.

### Makerere University

Research capacity depends on qualified academic staff, adequate facilities, a friendly legal framework that gives institutions the freedom to conduct research, and a good graduate-training system. Makerere University was established as a training institution (Sicherman 2005). Not only has it stuck to this tradition but new universities have followed its example. The massification of tertiary education has made Makerere University's problems more acute by dramatically increasing the need for additional lecturers. As shown in Table 4.1, in the 2012/2013 academic year, Uganda had only 973 PhD graduates, but in the same year over 200 000 students were registered to study at the country's 30 universities (UNCHE forthcoming).

In the 2012/2013 academic year, about 69 per cent of the country's PhD graduates were at, or associated with, Makerere University (see Table 4.2). That is, of the university's 1 585 academic staff, 640 or approximately 40 per cent had terminal degrees. Of the administrative staff, 23 had PhDs and another 12 non-administrative support staff also held this qualification.

The staff attrition rate at Makerere University increased when retirement was made mandatory for employees when they reach 60 years of age. Many seasoned academics were forced to leave and the university was unable to replace them with people of similar calibre. Of late, however, professors aged between 60 and 70 can be hired on contract, but this issue is being debated and had not been finalised when this chapter was written. Competition from smaller universities, as well as from the public and private sectors, is also having an impact on

**Table 4.1: Distribution of academic staff in Uganda by qualification, 2004–2013**

| Qualification | 2004/05 | 2005/06 | 2006/07 | 2010/11 | 2011/12 | 2012/13 |
|---|---|---|---|---|---|---|
| PhD (%) | 549 (10%) | 558 \|(11%) | 746 \|(12%) | 858 (11%) | 914 (11%) | 973 (10%) |
| Masters (%) | 2 221 (42%) | 2 167 (41%) | 2 651 (41%) | 2 967 (38%) | 3 657 (42%) | 3 455 (37%) |
| Bachelor (%) | 1 715 (33%) | 1694 (32%) | 1 949 (30%) | 2 621 (34%) | 2 923 (34%) | 2 585 (27%) |
| PGD (%) | ?? (0%) | 153 (3%) | 224 (3%) | 209 (3%) | 269 (3%) | 264 (3%) |
| Other (%) | 764 (15%) | 686 (13%) | 895 (14%) | 1 214 (16%) | 939 (11%) | 2 187 (24%) |
| Total (%) | 5 249 (100%) | 5 258 (100%) | 6 465 (100%) | 7 785 (100%) | 8 594 (100%) | 9 464 (100%) |

*Source:* UNCHE (forthcoming)

reducing the proportion of senior staff at Makerere. In 2014, for example, the university's academic staff dropped from 1 585 to 1 447.

## Postgraduate training

Despite having attracted the highest number of the country's PhD graduates, Makerere's facilities in terms of book-to-student ratios, internet access, library space, classroom space, laboratory facilities and administrative infrastructure, are not particularly conducive to research. Nevertheless, the training of the next generation of academics at doctoral level is integral to higher-education-based research, and contributes to the vibrancy of the research culture at any university. One area of collaboration that can, and I think it has, benefited both North and South is the training of doctoral students at Northern institutions, as long as Southern students continue to have study periods and assignments in the local environments in which they will be expected to work after they have graduated. Makerere University has benefited from such collaboration, and a number of postgraduates have received financial and intellectual assistance from institutions from abroad. Table 4.3 lists the numbers of doctoral students who graduated

Table 4.2: Qualifications of academic, administrative and support staff at Makerere University, January 2014

| Academic department | Full-time staff | | | | Part-time staff | Grand total |
|---|---|---|---|---|---|---|
| | PhD | Masters | Bachelors | Sub-total | Various degrees | |
| Agricultural and Environmental Sciences | 118 | 4 | 61 | 183 | 14 | 197 |
| Business and Management Sciences | 36 | 10 | 69 | 115 | 12 | 127 |
| Computing and Information Sciences | 25 | 2 | 62 | 89 | 1 | 90 |
| Education and External Studies | 54 | 4 | 55 | 113 | 3 | 116 |
| Engineering Design, Art and Technology | 55 | 5 | 86 | 146 | 6 | 152 |
| Health Sciences | 70 | 11 | 203 | 284 | 19 | 303 |
| Humanities and Social Sciences | 137 | 11 | 120 | 268 | 4 | 272 |
| Natural Sciences | 89 | 4 | 59 | 152 | 9 | 161 |
| Veterinary Medicine | 37 | 4 | 54 | 95 | 2 | 97 |
| School of Law | 16 | 5 | 23 | 44 | 2 | 46 |
| Jinja campus | 3 | 13 | 8 | 24 | 0 | 24 |
| Admin and support staff | 35 | | | | | |
| Total | 675 | 73 | 800 | 1 513 | 72 | 1 585 |

*Data source:* Obtained from Makerere University's administrative staff linked to colleges, department and research units

from Makerere University between 2008 and 2014. Several of these had dual registration at Makerere and an overseas institution. Immersion in a local area helps students learn to ask relevant questions and helps them to frame their conclusions appropriately, while visiting overseas institutions helps students to appreciate global issues and problems and broadens their experience of academic study.

**Table 4.3: Doctorates completed at Makerere University, 2008–2014**

| College/discipline | 2008 | 2009 | 2010 | 2011 | 2012 | 2013 | 2014 |
|---|---|---|---|---|---|---|---|
| Agriculture and Environmental Sciences | 1 | 6 | 3 | 12 | 8 | 7 | 12 |
| Business and Management Sciences | 1 | 0 | 0 | 5 | 3 | 8 | 8 |
| Computing and Information Sciences | 0 | 1 | 2 | 3 | 4 | 4 | 0 |
| Education and External Studies | 1 | 3 | 1 | 5 | 10 | 12 | 6 |
| Engineering, Design, Art, and Technology | 1 | 3 | 4 | 4 | 1 | 6 | 4 |
| Health Sciences | 0 | 5 | 1 | 4 | 9 | 3 | 4 |
| Humanities and Social Sciences | 0 | 4 | 20 | 7 | 4 | 6 | 13 |
| Law | 0 | 0 | 0 | 0 | 0 | 3 | 0 |
| Total | 4 | 22 | 31 | 40 | 39 | 49 | 47 |

*Data source:* Senate Graduation Books

## Research output

From 2005 to 2012, Makerere University made significant strides in terms of disseminating its research results. With increased foreign funding, Makerere's research outputs, in the form of publications and doctoral theses, increased tremendously, accounting for over 70 per cent of Uganda's publication output (Cloete et al. 2015: 116). Table 4.4 gives the picture.

In an assessment of Africa's 'flagship' universities published by Cloete et al. in 2015, Makerere University was ranked second to South Africa's University of Cape Town in terms of research and publication output for the period 2007 to 2011, and first in terms of international co-operation for the period 2006 to 2012. However, in spite of this success, there are four major weaknesses that Makerere and its stake-holders must resolve if the institution is to maintain and improve its knowledge-production function.

Firstly, the institution is dependent on external funding for these activities. Figure 4.1 shows some of the donors that funded research

**Table 4.4: Research-related publications and doctoral theses produced by disciplines at Makerere University, 2010–2012**

| Fields of study | 2010 | 2011 | 2012 |
|---|---|---|---|
| Business and Management | 3 | 4 | 10 |
| Science and Technology | 2 374 | 2 293 | 2 164 |
| Humanities and Social Sciences | 22 | 13 | 21 |
| Education | 22 | 33 | 27 |

*Data source:* Directorate of Quality Assurance, Makerere University

via the university from 2000 to 2012. By 2013, 80 per cent of the US$85 million available for research funding came from foreign donors (Musiige and Maassen, 2015: 122). In my view, there is nothing wrong with foreign funding. Many universities in the North *and* South obtain foreign funding that opens the door to opportunities that any university should be happy to receive. It is, however, unsustainable for any university to rely *primarily* on external funding because these funds are affected by several variables that the universities cannot control. Donors' priorities change, diplomatic relations with donor governments can be unpredictable, and strict conditions or forms of soft manipulation can be imposed on recipients. Makerere University urgently needs to develop a strategy for sustaining its research output and ensuring that it has funding sources that can be depended on if donors decide to close their taps.

Secondly, Makerere is still mainly an undergraduate teaching institution. By late 2014, undergraduate students made up more than 80 per cent of total enrolment, and staff could not handle the teaching load effectively. Further, too few staff are qualified to teach postgraduates. With just 675 (43 per cent) of staff holding PhDs, 57 per cent of the academic staff were qualified to teach undergraduates only. They could supervise neither doctoral students nor carry out serious research. Table 4.5 highlights this problem in more detail.

As shown in Table 4.5, most programmes, especially those in the College of Arts and Humanities, were oversubscribed and understaffed. Only the Colleges of Health Science, Natural Science and Veterinary Science met the National Council for Higher Education's benchmarks

**Figure 4.1:** Research funding given to Makerere University by donors, 2000–2012

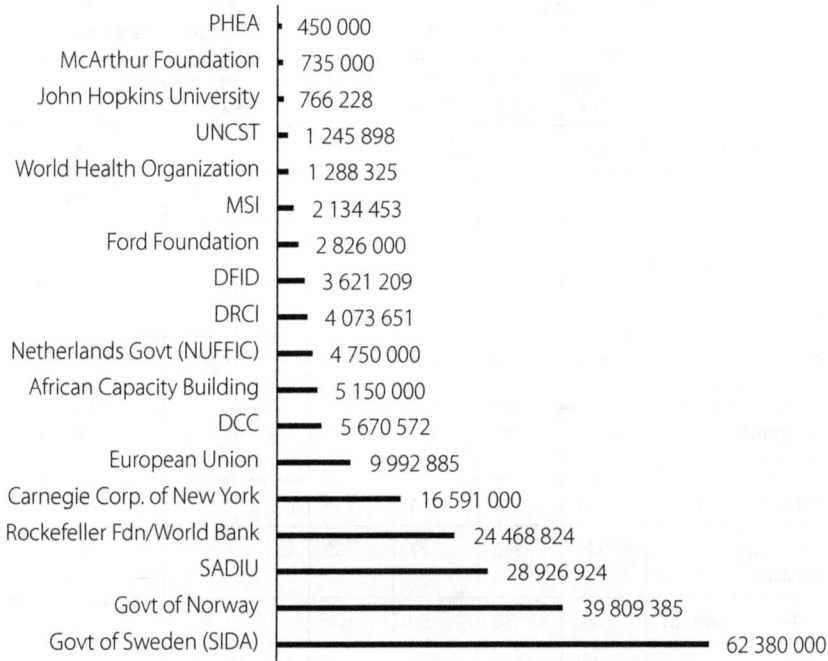

|  |  |
|---|---|
| PHEA | 450 000 |
| McArthur Foundation | 735 000 |
| John Hopkins University | 766 228 |
| UNCST | 1 245 898 |
| World Health Organization | 1 288 325 |
| MSI | 2 134 453 |
| Ford Foundation | 2 826 000 |
| DFID | 3 621 209 |
| DRCI | 4 073 651 |
| Netherlands Govt (NUFFIC) | 4 750 000 |
| African Capacity Building | 5 150 000 |
| DCC | 5 670 572 |
| European Union | 9 992 885 |
| Carnegie Corp. of New York | 16 591 000 |
| Rockefeller Fdn/World Bank | 24 468 824 |
| SADIU | 28 926 924 |
| Govt of Norway | 39 809 385 |
| Govt of Sweden (SIDA) | 62 380 000 |

*Note:* PHEA = Partnerships for Higher Education in Africa; UNCST = Uganda National Council for Science and Technology; MSI = Millenium Science Initiative of the UNCST; DFID = Department for International Development, UK; IDRC = International Development Research Centre; CDC = Centers for Disease Control and Prevention; USAID = US Agency for International Development
*Data source:* Directorate of Quality Assurance, Makerere University

for staff-to-student ratios. It is no coincidence that faculties and colleges that are less crowded publish more research than the overcrowded ones. For example in 2012, the faculties related to science and technology produced more than 90 per cent of Makerere's research output (2 164 compared to 58 for Business, Humanities and Education combined, as shown in Table 4.4). This was also true in 2010 and 2011.

Thirdly, the management of research at Makerere, as in most Ugandan universities, is disorganised. After experiencing much frustration while trying to obtain data from various academic units at the university, my research assistant noted that, 'There is no central office that records and documents research projects and the publications of

**Table 4.5: Undergraduate student/staff statistics at Makerere University, December 2014**

| College | Students | | | Staff | Ratio of students per staff member | Ratio recommended by the UNCHE |
|---|---|---|---|---|---|---|
| | Female | Male | Total | | | |
| Agriculture | 927 | 1 471 | 2 398 | 151 | 16 | 10 |
| Engineering | 835 | 2 458 | 3 293 | 143 | 23 | 10 |
| Education | 3 139 | 3 658 | 6 797 | 118 | 58 | 15 |
| Health Science | 592 | 1 145 | 1 737 | 313 | 6 | 8 |
| Humanities and Social Sciences | 5 389 | 3 437 | 8 826 | 215 | 41 | 24 |
| Business and Management | 2 472 | 3 054 | 5 526 | 128 | 43 | 24 |
| Computing and Information | 1 982 | 2 529 | 4 511 | 94 | 48 | 24 |
| Natural Science | 380 | 904 | 1 284 | 153 | 8 | 10 |
| Veterinary Medicine | 241 | 536 | 777 | 89 | 8 | 8 |
| Fort-Portal campus | 21 | 38 | 59 | n/a | n/a | |
| Jinja campus | 207 | 244 | 451 | n/a | n/a | |
| Law Development Centre | 550 | 855 | 1 405 | 43 | 32 | 24 |
| Business School | 3 807 | 2 403 | 6 210 | n/a | | |
| Total | | | 43 274 | 1 447 | | |

*Note:* Makerere University is divided into a number of colleges on its main campus, and has two up-country campuses, one at Fort Portal to the west and one at Jinja to the east.
*Sources:* UNCHE (forthcoming) and the Directory of Quality Assurance, Makerere University

staff at unit or departmental levels.' (Two exceptions to this are described in the next section of the chapter.)

Lastly, the creation of Makerere University's college system was rushed. The roles of the colleges and the faculties in relation to academic departments are not properly defined. In most universities, departments are hives of research and teaching activities, the recipients of research and innovation funding and the distributors of privileges and sanctions. But these roles were blurred when the colleges were established as a kind of superstructure above the departments and faculties. As a result, deans of faculties and principals of colleges struggle to manage their academic and financial affairs. To sustain even the modest momentum attained in research activities to date, Makerere's researchers and administrators must improve their management of this important university function.

## Research at other universities in Uganda

In Uganda, public and chartered private universities are permitted to offer graduate programmes. As part of a broader research project, I surveyed 15 tertiary institutions (see Appendix 1 for a full list of Uganda's tertiary institutions). Most had similar problems to those experienced at Makerere University. However, due to the lack of staff and facilities, some had begun to 'churn out' improperly trained doctoral candidates. In 2012, for example, the Uganda National Council for Higher Education (UNCHE) used its powers to ask one institution to review more than 40 PhD degrees that it had planned to award in one academic year![4] Nevertheless, I identified two institutions – Mbarara University of Science and Technology and the Uganda Christian University – that I think organised and managed their research functions slightly better than Makerere University, although their outputs were relative to their respective sizes. Although both institutions are much smaller in terms of enrolment and infrastructure, they have laid good foundations for the management of research. Both institutions have created elaborate mechanisms for collaborating with international academics and research institutions, and some of their staff and students benefit from these collaborations. These two university institutions are briefly reviewed below.

### *Mbarara University of Science and Technology (MUST)*

MUST's research efforts are well organised. Its Centralized Institutional Research Innovations and Management Office (CIRIMO) co-ordinates effectively with units (departments) that report directly to faculties or institutes. In addition, the university has a *Grants Management Manual*, a strategic plan for research, and a 'Research Innovations, Management and Uptake Policy'. At the time of writing, MUST's research policy was being reworked and was expected to be approved shortly thereafter. In addition, the medical faculty has its own research administration office and its own strategic plans.

In the 2014/2015 financial year, MUST received 75 million shillings (US$37 500) from the Ugandan government and 260 million shillings (US$130 000) from non-taxable revenue for research – a total of 335 million shillings. This was distributed to the institution's five faculties as follows: Faculty of Medicine, 85.5 million shillings (US$42 750); Faculty of Science, 85.5 million shillings (US$42 750); Institute of Computer Science, 55 million shillings (US$27 500); Institute of Management Science, 55 million shillings (US$27 500); and Institute of Interdisciplinary Training and Research, 50 million shillings (US$2 500).

The university also obtained funding from a number of state agencies and foreign governments including the National Institute of Health, the Center for Global Health, the European Union, the United Nations (through World Vision), the Bill and Melinda Gates Foundation, Grand Challenge Canada, VLIR-UOS (for the Belgian government), Google, the Ugandan Ministry of Health, the Rockefeller Foundation, as well as from the governments of Sweden, the Netherlands, the UK, the US and others.

What is impressive is that the university spent 335 million shillings (US$167 000)(about 4 per cent) of its annual budget of 7 810 million shillings (US$4 million) on research in the 2014/2015 financial year.

MUST does not have its own publishing unit, but certain faculties have plans to start publishing their own journals. Researchers for the Institute for Tropical Forest Conservation, a semi-autonomous postgraduate research institute linked to the university have published work in highly regarded ISI journals such as *Conservation Biology*, *Oryx*, *Forest Ecology and Management* and *The Lancet*, among others.

MUST also collaborates in various ways with a number of institutions nationally and internationally. These include: Massachusetts General Hospital, the University of Calgary, the University of California

San Francisco, Harvard University, Johns Hopkins University, the University of British Colombia, MUST Bogoye, Case Western Reserve University, Indiana University, the University of Minnesota, Ghent University, Oxford University, the University of KwaZulu-Natal, Moi University, Makerere University, Gulu University, Busitema University and Kampala International University (Western Campus).

All five of MUST's faculties prepare students for bachelors, masters and PhD degrees. In addition, research teams of staff and students undertake non-degree-related research through MUST's Epicentre Research Base. Meanwhile, the Consortium for Affordable Medical Technologies (CAMTech) aims to accelerate innovations in medical technology and build entrepreneurial capacity to improve health in low-and middle-income countries.[5]

## Uganda Christian University, Mukono

Alumni of the Uganda Christian University have an excellent reputation among employers in Uganda. That the university has begun to put a modest research infrastructure in place is evident from the following:

- 1 per cent of the university's total budget is allocated to research and publications. In the 2013/2014 financial year, this amounted to about 370 million shillings (US$185 000).
- The institution also receives some research funding from Christian donor organisations, and collaborates with several international Anglican research and training institutions.
- The university's research activities are organised under the umbrella of its School of Research and Postgraduate Studies.
- The university has a fully-fledged research policy, a student research manual, a digital repository, an open-access policy, as well as a university bulletin in which academics and students can publish information about their research.
- At the time of writing, only one staff member's work had been included in international journal listings.

The university's research infrastructure includes the new Ham Mukasa Library, which has good ICT facilities and dedicated staff. The shortage of terminal degree holders in Uganda is, however, hampering the institution's efforts to train its staff and enrol larger cohorts of postgraduate students.

## Conclusions

Although Uganda's higher education sector is both cash-strapped and legally disempowered, research activities are still taking place at several of the country's tertiary institutions. However, most Ugandan universities see themselves mainly as teaching institutions, and do not aim to produce substantial new knowledge. University management teams tend to perceive their institutions primarily as places of teaching, and seem to see research as a lower priority. In my view, co-operation between national, regional and international institutions is needed to advance the basic notion that knowledge production *should be* a major function of *all* universities.

As relative latecomers to the establishment of universities, polytechnics and research centres as centres of knowledge creation, Africa must collaborate with regions and states that have nurtured such institutions for centuries. However, Africa needs homegrown thinkers who are able to use locally focused conceptual models to resolve local problems.

To avoid repeating mistakes made in the past, levels, types and methods of cross-regional co-operation must be carefully defined. Co-operation and relationships should hinge on the assumption that universities are primarily centres of knowledge creation and that good teaching is the *product* of quality research.

While, in the past, international and multilateral bodies allocated most of their resources to co-operation at a macro level, it is high time that more emphasis is placed on the micro levels of individuals, faculties and institutions, via country-specific and bilateral relationships. Unfortunately, even this form of co-operation is likely to remain unequal in terms of financial and intellectual resources. The North tends to have more of both than the South. To remedy this, the South must take responsibility for funding their own research and teaching institutions. The South must nurture their own academics and develop local research capacities in their universities and other research institutions. Donors cannot forever bear the burden of funding research in Africa's universities.

Defined co-operation can help African academics to devise ways of lobbying governments not only to increase funding, but also to free universities from government-imposed red tape. For now, in a number of countries in the South, universities' research efforts are crippled by their lack of funding and an absence of institutional autonomy. Yet, the need to improve the knowledge production function of universities in the South remains (Cloete et al. 2015).

In my view, it is better to train doctoral students in their native environment if they are to participate in resolving local problems. In addition, while the South needs to increase its numbers in this area, it is important to acknowledge that students from the North gain much from study trips to the South and from consulting Southern academics.

The following are key areas that must be addressed:

- Co-operation at the micro level between faculties and institutions, and bilateral relations between countries in the North and South should be encouraged because this is likely to be less loaded with mismatched ideologies.
- The need to transform African universities from being mainly teaching institutions to both instructional and knowledge-producing institutions should be an area for urgent co-operation.
- The dearth of research funding from government and other state institutions in the South should be addressed, and ought to be led by Southerners themselves. Northern academics can help with strategic advice but they cannot go lobbying in our corridors of power.
- North–South co-operation must be acknowledged as being of benefit to both parties. While the South can benefit from the resources of the North, the latter can benefit from experiencing problems of global development, as well as from the insights and resilience that can be derived from different worldviews.

As shown, the universities of Makerere and Mbarara and the Uganda Christian University have begun conducting reasonable amounts of new research in a small set of disciplines; however, their ability to continue to do so is threatened by unstable funding regimes and a lack of autonomy in key areas of financial management. In addition, the mismanagement of research activities, a lack of qualified academic staff and the absence of a well-structured programme for training the next generation of academics, pose serious threats.

## Appendix 1: Accredited universities in Uganda in 2012/2013

| Name | Website | District | Founded in |
|---|---|---|---|
| **Public universities** | | | |
| Makerere University | www.mak.ac.ug | Kampala | 1922 |
| Mbarara University of Science and Technology | www.must.ac.ug | Mbarara | 1989 |
| Gulu University | www.gu.ac.ug | Gulu | 2002 |
| Kyambogo University | www.kyu.ac.ug | Kampala | 2002 |
| Busitema University | http://busitema.ac.ug | Busia | 2007 |
| Muni University | | Arua | 2013 |
| **Private universities** | | | |
| Islamic University in Uganda | www.iuiu.ac.ug | Mbale | 1988 |
| Ndejje University | www.ndejjeuniversity.ac.ug | Luwero | 1992 |
| Uganda Martyrs University | http://www.umu.ac.ug | Mpigi | 1993 |
| Bugema University | www.bugemauniv.ac.ug | Luwero | 1994 |
| Uganda Christian University | www.ucu.ac.ug | Mukono | 1997 |
| Busoga University | www.busogauniversity.ac.ug | Iganga | 1999 |
| Nkumba University | www.nkumbauniversity.ac.ug | Wakiso | 1999 |
| Kampala University | www.ku.ac.ug | Kampala | 2000 |
| Kampala International University | www.kiu.ac.ug | Kampala | 2001 |

| Name | Website | District | Founded in |
|---|---|---|---|
| Aga Khan University | www.aku.edu | Kampala | 2001 |
| Kumi University | | Kumi | 2004 |
| Kabale University | www.kabaleuniversity.ac.ug | Kabale | 2005 |
| Mountains of the Moon University | www.mmu.ac.ug | Kabarole | 2005 |
| African Bible University | http://africanbiblecolleges.org/uganda | Wakiso | 2005 |
| Uganda Pentecostal University | http://upu.ac.ug | Kabarole | 2005 |
| Bishop Stuart University | www.bsu.ac.ug | Mbarara | 2006 |
| St. Lawrence University | www.stlawrenceuniversity.ac.ug | Kampala | 2007 |
| Muteesa I Royal University | http://www.mru.ac.ug | Kampala | 2007 |
| All Saints University, Lango | www.asul.ac.ug | Lira | 2008 |
| International Health Sciences University | www.ihsu.ac.ug | Kampala | 2008 |
| Cavendish University of East Africa | www.cavendish.ac.ug | Kampala | 2008 |
| International University of East Africa | www.iuea.ac.ug | Kampala | 2010 |
| African Rural University | http://arua.ac.ug | Kibaale | 2011 |
| Islamic Call University College | | Kampala | 2011 |
| Livingstone International University | http://livingstone.ac.ug | Mbale | 2011 |
| Victoria University | http://vu.ac.ug | Kampala | 2011 |
| St Augustine International University | www.saiu.ac.ug | Kampala | 2011 |
| Virtual University of Uganda | www.virtualuni.ac.ug | Kampala | 2011 |
| Uganda Technology And Management University | http://utamu.ac.ug | Kampala | 2013 |
| Africa Renewal University | http://africarenewaluniversity.org | Wakiso | 2013 |
| Nsaka University | http://nsakauniversity.ac.ug | Jinja | 2013 |

## Appendix 2: Other degree-awarding institutions in Uganda

| Name | Website/email | District | Founded in |
|------|---------------|----------|------------|
| **Public** | | | |
| Uganda Management Institute | www.umi.ac.ug | Kampala | 1969 |
| **Private** | | | |
| Team Institute of Business Management | www.teamibm.ac.ug | Kampala | 2010 |
| ESLSCA International Business School | http://uganda.eslsca.net | Kampala | 2013 |
| Ernest Cook Ultrasound Research and Education Institute (ECUREI) | ecurei@yahoo.com | Kampala | 2013 |
| International School of Business and Technology (ISBAT) | info@isbat.ac.ug | Kampala | 2013 |

*Note:* This category of institutions was created by the Universities and Other Tertiary Institutions (Amendment) Act of 2006. Since the Act was passed, one public and four private institutions have been licensed. Among these, the Ernest Cook Ultrasound Research and Education Institute, located at Mengo Hospital in Kampala, specialises in medical research, while the other three offer business management programmes. These institutions account for approximately 2 per cent of students enrolled at higher education institutions.
*Source:* UNCHE

## Notes

1   This information was supplied to me by the Statistics Department at Uganda's Ministry of Education and Sports.

2   This figure is from the Uganda National Council for Higher Education in Kampala. Note also that Ugandan shilling–US dollar equivalents provided in this chapter are approximate and reflect the value of the Ugandan shilling in 2014 when the allocations were made.

3   These reports were made available to me by the Statistics Department of the Ministry of Education and Sports.

4   This occurred during my term as executive director of UNCHE. I felt it was part of my duties to review the issuing of terminal degrees.

5   CAMTech was established after a memorandum of understanding was signed in 2012 between MUST and Massachusetts General Hospital.

# References

Altbach, Philip (2002) Centres and peripheries in the academic profession: The special challenges of developing countries. In: Philip Altbach (ed.) *The Decline of the Guru: The Academic Profession in Developing and Middle-Income Countries.* Boston: Centre for International Higher Education, Boston College

Altbach, Philip (2003) African higher education and the world. In: Damtew Teferra and Philip Altbach (eds) *African Higher Education: An International Reference Handbook.* Bloomington and Indianapolis: Indiana University Press

Banya, Kingsley and Juliet Elu (2001) The World Bank and financing of higher education in sub-Saharan Africa. *Higher Education* 42: 1–34

Carrol, Bidemi (2005) Private monies, public universities: Implications for access and university behaviour, a study of Makerere University. PhD thesis, Stanford University

Castells, Manuel (2001) Universities as dynamic systems of contradictory functions. In: Johan Muller, Nico Cloete and Shireen Badat (eds) *Challenges of Globalisation: South African Debates with Manuel Castells.* Cape Town: Maskew Miller Longman

Cloete, Nico, Peter Maassen and Tracy Bailey (2015) *Knowledge Production and Contradictory Functions in African Higher Education.* Cape Town: African Minds

Harrison, Graham (2004) *The World Bank and Africa: The Construction of Governance States.* London and New York: Routledge

Kasozi, ABK (2009) *Financing Uganda's Public Universities: An Obstacle to Serving the Public Good.* Kampala: Fountain

Mamdani, Mahmood (1993) University crisis and reform: A reflection on the African experience. *Review of African Political Economy* 58: 7–19

Mamdani, Mahmood (2007) *Scholars in the Marketplace. The Dilemmas of Neoliberal Reform at Makerere University, 1989–2005.* Kampala: Fountain

Musiige, Gordon and Peter Maassen (2015) Faculty perceptions of the factors that influence research productivity at Makerere University. In: Nico Cloete, Peter Maassen and Tracy Bailey (eds) *Knowledge Production and Contradictory Functions in African Higher Education.* Cape Town: African Minds

Okolie, Andrew C (2003) Producing knowledge for sustainable development in Africa: Implications for higher education. *Higher Education* 46: 235–260

Psacharopoulous, George (1980) Returns on education: An updated international comparison. In: T King (ed.) *Education and Income*. World Bank Staff Working Paper No. 402. Washington, DC: World Bank

Psacharopoulos, George Jee-Peng Tan, and Emmanuel Jimenex (1986) *Financing Education in Developing Countries: An Exploration of Policy Options*. Washington, DC: World Bank

Sanyal, Bicas C and NV Varghese (2006) *Research Capacity of the Higher Education Sector in Developing Countries*. Paris: UNESCO

Sawyerr, Akilagpa (2004) African universities and the challenge of research capacity development. *Journal of Higher Education in Africa* 2(1): 213–242

Sicherman, Carol (2005) *Becoming an African University: Makerere 1922–2000*. Kampala: Fountain

Teferra, Damtew and Philip Altbach (eds) (2003) *African Higher Education: An International Reference Handbook*. Bloomington and Indianapolis: Indiana University Press

UNCHE (Uganda National Council for Higher Education) (forthcoming) *State of Higher Education and Training in Uganda: 2012/2013*. Kampala

World Bank (1999) *World Development Report: Knowledge for Development*. Washington, DC

World Bank (2002) *Constructing Knowledge Societies: New Challenges for Tertiary Education*. Washington, DC

World Bank (2006) *Higher Education and Economic Development in Africa*. Washington, DC

World Bank (2008) *Accelerating Catch-Up: Tertiary Education for Growth in Sub-Saharan Africa*. Washington, DC

World Bank and UNESCO (2000) *Higher Education in Developing Countries: Peril or Promise*. Washington, DC

Yesufu, Tijani Momodu (ed.) (1973) *Creating the African University: Emerging Issues in the 1970s*. London: Oxford University Press

# CHAPTER
# 5

## Undoing the effects of neoliberal reform: The experience of Uganda's Makerere Institute of Social Research

*Mahmood Mamdani*

I did my O levels at Old Kampala Secondary School in 1962, the year of Uganda's independence. In that year, the US government gave an independence gift to the Ugandan government, which included 24 scholarships. I was one of those airlifted to the US where I obtained several degrees over ten years. I returned in 1972.

Those who were given scholarships can be divided into two: those who never returned and those who did. Those who did were soon frustrated by the fact that the conditions under which they were supposed to work were so far removed from those in which they had been trained. Material amenities and infrastructure were minimal, as was a political and research environment conducive to intellectual work. Within a matter of years, sometimes months, many of those who returned began looking for jobs overseas, or moved out of academia into government or business or elsewhere.

I draw one lesson from this experience: the model does not work. It focused on selecting bright young high-school graduates for training oversees and assumed that, on our return, we would function as so many individual change agents or 'modernisers'. Today, academics in African universities must instead train postgraduate students in the institutions in which they will have to work. The next generation of

African scholars, or at least most of them, must be trained at home. This means that issues of institutional reform have to be tackled alongside those of postgraduate study, so that postgraduate education, research and institution-building form part of a single integrated whole.

I would like to put this in the context of the history of higher education in Africa. Rather than claim a single African history, I contrast the older colonies, such as South Africa and Egypt, with countries, such as Uganda, that were colonised after the Berlin Conference of 1884 and 1885. In the older colonies, Britain embarked on a 'civilising' mission (building schools and universities), whereas after the Berlin Conference, the colonial powers tended to regard the products of modern education as likely to subvert colonial rule.

## The history of higher education in Africa

The history of higher education in Africa began over a millennium ago. It is well known that centres of learning existed in different parts of Africa – such as at Al-Azhar in Egypt, at Al-Zaytuna in Tunisia and at Sankoré in Mali – prior to Western domination of the continent. And yet, this is of marginal significance when it comes to understanding contemporary higher education institutions in Africa, which are so rooted in our colonial experience. The fact that knowledge production is everywhere based on a disciplinary mode developed in Western universities during the nineteenth and twentieth centuries is testimony to this.

Britain and other Western powers colonised the African continent in successive phases. The northern and southern parts of the continent were the first to be colonised in the seventeenth and eighteenth centuries. As noted, the British initially thought of colonialism as a 'civilising mission'; the schools and universities they built were hallmarks of this. By the early twentieth century, however, when they were colonising the lands between the Sahara and the Kalahari, the British authorities had become far more concerned with maintaining order and power, while extracting raw materials and exporting their own rural poor, than with 'civilising' or 'developing' the lands they ruled.

Centuries of colonial experience – particularly in India – had taught the British that education can be double-edged. Thus, while teaching people to read and write and reflect might make them more productive, the risk is that their thinking is less easily controlled. In the older colonies, the educated elites were the first to demand independence. When denied this, the same elites began to organise the broader populations. This gave us the nationalist movement. Frederick Lugard, who headed British colonial missions in Uganda (from 1890 to 1892) and in Nigeria (from 1900 to 1906), wrote that Britain must avoid 'the Indian disease' in Africa, by which he meant that 'the natives' must not be educated (Lugard 1965).

It is unsurprising then that, by the 1960s, the whole of East Africa had just one university: Makerere; and the whole of Nigeria had only one university: Ibadan. This means that, unlike in South and North Africa, the universities that now exist in the lands south of the Sahara and north of the Limpopo are products of nationalism, not colonialism. In this region, no African country could claim to be truly independent until it had, alongside its national flag, national anthem and national currency, a national university.

## Nationalism and the university

Everywhere, the development of universities was a key nationalist demand. Nigeria, for example, had one university and a thousand students at independence. By 1991, the country had 41 universities and 131 000 registered students (Bako 1993: 150). The figures for countries in East Africa are similar. And yet, the very nationalists who created the post-colonial universities soon came into conflict with the new institutions. There are two sides to this story. Nationalists are seldom democrats. This is true the world over. George Washington saw opposition as treason, so did Indira Gandhi, Kwame Nkrumah, Gamal Abdel Nasser, and even Julius Nyerere.

The African political world of the late 1960s and early 1970s was about single-party nationalism. In this single-party world, universities were the only institutions that were free to run campaigns and hold elections. Naturally, opposition thinkers gravitated to these universities. At the same time, university students saw themselves – as they still do – as the leaders of tomorrow, born to rule.

Recall the language student leaders used when describing their present and imagining their future: students were organised in 'guilds'; their leaders were called 'presidents'; presidents' assistants were called 'ministers'; and together they called themselves a 'cabinet'. For their part, the governments of the day saw such students as incubators of opposition – as both actual and potential political threats. No longer just hubs for producing knowledge, post-colonial universities turned into so many political nuclei. When governments silenced dissent at such universities, it wasn't innovative research programmes that they saw as a threat, but the participation of students and academics in national politics.

In 1972, Makerere University celebrated its fiftieth anniversary. Idi Amin came to address us. He arrived with a battalion of soldiers. He stood right in front of the Main Hall. Amin was blunt. Pointing to the battalion surrounding the square, he said: 'I brought the soldiers with me so when you lift your heads from your books, you know who has power.' And then he added, mischievously and meaningfully: 'On my way, I stopped in Mulago [the University hospital] to look at your records. I saw that most of you are suffering from gonorrhoea. I will not tolerate you spreading political gonorrhoea in Uganda.'

If African governments saw activist students and staff as potential opponents, many students and academics saw themselves as ministers-in-waiting, some even as presidents-in-waiting. Thus, even when their language and critique was radical, their practice was elitist, and their elitist universities were in constant conflict with ruling parties. As a result, the governments began to run the universities as if they were parastatal organisations, forgetting that they are meant to be public institutions. It is no surprise that successive governments have treated the universities like so many water faucets; taps that can be turned on or off depending on political expediencies. Under such conditions, very little institutional planning worth the name is possible.

Like its sister campuses on the continent, Makerere University was an elitist and a colonial institution. Like the society of which it was part, Makerere was never intellectually independent. Before independence, it formed part of a colonial network that was subordinate to the University of London. After independence, this network soon became dominated by America, and held together by American funding organisations, mainly the Rockefeller Foundation. No matter how elitist it became, however, Makerere University was never seen as fit to run itself. Nor was it ever expected to become a research institution. Few departments had postgraduate programmes, as it was assumed that postgraduate work would be done in Britain or America.

Yet, Makerere is proud of its colonial legacy, thinking of itself as the 'Harvard of Africa'. If Makerere was ever this, it was a colonised Harvard. Harvard is a research university in two senses of that term. First, it is a site of research; second, it produces researchers. Every research university has to grow its own timber (whether it then uses or exports this timber is a secondary question), and the key sites for growing researchers are university PhD programmes. Ask anyone at a research university to identify the heart of its research, its vital and dynamic centre, and they will point to their doctoral programmes. Research universities integrate research and teaching in a single, organic relationship.

Makerere University, at least the part of it that I am most familiar with, the College of Humanities and the Social Sciences, has never been a research institution. The example of the Makerere Institute of Social Research (MISR) illustrates my point. Established in 1948 as the East African Institute of Social Research, and renamed a decade later, MISR became known globally as a research site. But MISR never produced researchers. The assumption was that those undertaking research at MISR, whether non-Ugandans in the colonial period or Ugandans after independence, would be trained elsewhere.

## Post-colonial visions

Two different post-independence visions of the role of higher education can be identified. One was state-driven. An example of this was Tanzania's University of Dar es Salaam, where I taught for six years in the 1970s. The downside of that experience was that the government tended to treat the university as a parastatal, and continually undermined academic freedom. The upside was the university's creation of a historically informed, inter-disciplinary, curriculum.

The second post-independence vision, which emerged later, was market-driven. Makerere University is a prime example of this. I spent nearly two decades at Makerere, from 1980 to 1996. During the 1990s, the university combined the policy of fee-paying students (privatisation) with the introduction of a market-driven curriculum (commercial-isation). The effects were contradictory: income from fees showed that it was possible to broaden higher education's financial base; commercialisation opened the door to a galloping consultancy culture.

Both visions had a common failing: neither developed a postgraduate programme. Over nearly three decades, I do not recall a single discussion on postgraduate education at either Dar es Salaam or Makerere. To reflect on this is to realise that everyone assumed that postgraduate education would happen elsewhere, through staff-development programmes at overseas 'centres of excellence'. This assumption was so deep-seated that it became part of academic common sense.

### Neoliberal reform

MISR is a part of the university's College of Humanities and Social Sciences. The Faculty of Arts in the College has been noted for its enthusiastic and uncritical embrace of neoliberal reforms since 1990. Not surprisingly, most students at the university are enrolled in the College of Humanities and Social Sciences. The neoliberal project has transformed the life of both students and lecturers in the College.

I will borrow a Malthusian metaphor to make my point: the rise in student admissions at the College of Humanities and Social Sciences between 2000 and 2015 has been geometric, but the increase in the teaching staff and the physical facilities has been arithmetic. Lecture halls have burst at the seams, and tutorials have been discontinued.

Lecturers' lives have also changed dramatically. Payment varies depending on the number of hours they teach, with the result that the average teaching load resembles that of a secondary-school teacher. In addition, almost every activity has been monetised. Staff are paid an allowance to invigilate an examination or to mark a script, even to attend meetings (departmental, faculty, college or senate). Although not all meetings elicit a sitting or transport allowance, the general practice is that the higher your designation, the more eligible you are to receive such allowances. In 2012, Ugandan newspapers carried a story of millions that were paid out in allowances to the search committee for the post of vice-chancellor.[1] In the neoliberal university, there is no such thing as good citizenship.

In the late 1980s, with the government seeing the university as a parastatal, the World Bank began to play a role. From the World Bank's viewpoint at that time, university education was not only elitist, but a luxury that countries such as Uganda could ill afford. Two conclusions flowed from this. One, the cost of university education should be paid mainly by the (elite) families of (elite) students, and not by the state. Two, the government should shift its focus from higher to primary education where the costs are much lower and the same amount of money can apparently benefit many more students.[2]

The logic was elegant but populist, and faulty. It has had disastrous consequences for higher education, not just in Uganda but everywhere it has been applied. The World Bank's argument has two main problems. First, primary schools cannot thrive without a thriving university system. Without the universities, who will train the primary school administrators and teachers? Who will design the curricula? Second, it is nonsense to think that higher education benefits only, or even mainly, those who teach, work or study in the tertiary sector. This is like arguing that a hydropower plant benefits only the plant's management and the workers; it ignores the millions whose factories and houses, offices and streets, are lit by the power it generates. The point is that every element of a country's infrastructure, whether it be a power plant, a road or a university, has a social benefit.

In the 1990s, with rapid development in East Asia, the World Bank realised its mistake. It has since changed its mind. It now preaches 'knowledge-led growth', but its converts in Uganda and elsewhere are lagging behind (as converts often do). That the World Bank has changed its mind does not mean it should shirk responsibility for its mistakes. The Bank claims to be a champion of the free market. Well, the first law of the market is that if you make a bad investment, you pay for it. The World Bank has a long history of making bad investments, but it is difficult to recall even one instance where this organisation has paid for its wrongdoings. Its default response has been to withdraw, leaving its clients to pay the bills – the bank has the luxury of not living by the rules it imposes on others.

### Privatisation and commercialisation

The World Bank's approach created three problems. First, it exacerbated the under-financing of Africa's public universities. The expectation was that students and their families would carry the costs of higher education via fee payments. Yet, the reality in most African countries is that cost-based fees would deny most citizens access to higher education, and governments have shied away from the political consequences of this. Moreover, it must be noted that nowhere in the world do universities cover most of their costs via fees. The bulk of their income comes from endowments bequeathed by wealthy donors or the public purse.

The second problem flowed from the first. The neoliberal solution to the financial crisis of Africa's public universities was to expand student enrolment. To enlist the support of the academic staff in this, Makerere University decided to let each unit keep the bulk of the fees paid by students, and allow the academic staff decide how to use this income. This created a division between different faculties, leaving those with high enrolments cash-heavy, and those with low enrolments cash-strapped. The more the university divided into 'wet' and 'dry' faculties, the greater the disparities between the 'top up' allowances given to academic and administrative staff, both between and within units. Gradually, the university began to fragment from within.

The third problem has been the spread of the consultancy culture. Essentially, poorly paid academics morphed their research work into consultancy contracts as a way of making ends meet. For consultants, research is all about finding answers to problems defined by a client – consultants tend to think of research as finding answers, not formulating questions. Consultancy culture has been further institutionalised through short courses in research methods that teach students to gather and process quantitative information, from which they can cull 'answers'.

In response to the conditions created by these three problems, intellectual life in many African universities has been reduced to the bare bones of classroom activity. Extra-curricular seminars and workshops have migrated to hotels. Workshop attendance has to include transport and per diem allowances. All this is part of a larger process that I see as the 'NGO-isation' of the university. Academic papers have turned into corporate-style audio-visual presentations. Academics read less and less. A chorus of buzzwords has replaced lively debates.

Countering these problems calls for the building of a meaningful intellectual culture. To my knowledge, there is no model for this on the African continent today. It is something we must create. The old model looked for answers outside the problem, and it was utopian because it imposed externally formulated answers. A new model must look for answers within the parameters of the problem. For a start, we need to move beyond simply understanding the problems and begin to identify initiatives that seek to address the problems. In what follows, I describe two such initiatives at Makerere University: the first is an external programme introduced by the Swedish International Development Co-operation Agency (SIDA), and the second is an internal initiative developed at MISR.

## The SIDA programme

SIDA is Makerere's largest donor. Since the mid 2000s, it has poured millions of dollars into graduate education at Makerere. In 2008, SIDA commissioned a group of three Swedish researchers to evaluate their assistance to Makerere. They worked with a Ugandan research assistant, Nelson Kakande, and published their findings in 2010 (see Freeman et al. 2010).

The researchers asked the right kinds of questions, including, how do you develop a research agenda, and why does money *alone* not solve the problem? Nevertheless, they were unable to answer any of the questions posed. When compiling their report, the study team began by admitting its own limitations. The main limitation, they said, was lack of time. SIDA brought forward the timing of their visit to Uganda which gave them hardly any time to prepare for their visit. As a result, the team 'was not able to develop questionnaires, perform surveys, or collect data prior [to] the site visit, nor to seek perceptions from Makerere participants about the survey and interview results from Sweden during the Makerere site visit' (2010: 10). Among other things, the study thus suffered from a 'lack of data about activities and outputs of SIDA-funded graduate students and senior researchers/supervisors' (2010: 10). In my view, even if the team had been given more time and more data, no external evaluation was likely to answer these questions; it needed to be guided by an internal reflection.

### *How do you develop a research agenda?*

Developing 'research capacity' is the main objective of SIDA's assistance. As a small country surrounded by powerful neighbours in a rapidly globalising world, Sweden understands that independent research is indispensable to maintaining intellectual independence, and forms the basis of social, economic and political independence. That is, the Swedes understand that if you want to act independently, you have to develop the capacity to think independently.

To this end, the study team made three recommendations: 'indigenous development of research themes', the formation of 'research groups as foundations for continuing teamwork', and 'collaboration within and across disciplines and geographic boundaries' (2010: 38). They noted that the first is the most important. Why this emphasis on 'indigenous' development? Why not import research themes from esteemed foreign universities or ask foreign advisors to provide them? The simple fact is that a decent research agenda can only be formulated on the basis of an understanding of one's own reality. There is no recipe that can be shared. It has to be home grown. The first step towards intellectual independence for a research community is for it to develop its own research questions.

At the same time, no individual should ever develop research questions in splendid isolation. We all need the insights provided by peer-to-peer networks in all aspects of this work, from constituting research teams to holding seminars. These forums function as sites for internal debate and brainstorming. A question the SIDA study team asked but did not answer was: how can Makerere University play 'a stronger role in developing Uganda's research agenda?' (Freeman et al. 2010: 49).

### What money alone cannot do

A conundrum lies at the heart of the report. The team gave a comprehensive account of what has been achieved through increased funding. Pride of place went to the development of an elaborate research infrastructure: 'The enormous enhancement in *research infrastructure* (ICT, library, laboratories, and a Demographic Surveillance Site) has transformed the research environment' they said (2010: 35). And yes, all the necessary artefacts are in place –information and communications technology, a library, laboratories, demographic surveillance facilities, academic networks, publications, external collaboration and support, journals, even research groups.[3] Only the live subject is not quite present. Certainly, the library has expanded, more journals are available, both as hard copies and online, yet the culture of reading is declining. The problem is deeper. Even as we rightly celebrate these advances in material infrastructure, we cannot ignore signs that the failure to address the human factor may result in perverse uses of these very material advances.

The study team identified three major limitations when it comes to the human factor. The *first* was managerial: 'starting "big" in a setting where resources are very limited and systems for managing grants and contracts across the university are very weak, increases risks of funds not being used for purposes intended and for inefficiency'. They warned against the temptation to start big noting that, 'bigger investments may hold promise for significant gain in research capacity, but at relatively high risk' (2010: 38). Needless to say, this is salutary advice.

The *second* problem has to do with thesis advisors: 'Overwhelmingly the most frequent complaint,' reported the study team, is 'delay by overcommitted Ugandan supervisors' (2010: 22). But this was a complaint to which the team had no response except to note: 'External funds have not and cannot resolve the "overload" dilemma for researchers or those operating the research infrastructure' (2010: 8).

Why can money alone not solve the 'overload' problem? Because no matter how much you pay professorial advisors, it will not change the fact that their days, like everyone else's, consist of just 24 hours. The only way to solve the problem is to increase the size of the pool of advisors. Instead, both SIDA and the evaluation team looked for a short-term solution: collaboration with Swedish academics:

> Collaboration with Swedish university colleagues markedly enhanced supervision, publication in the science disciplines, and preparation of a new generation of research mentors for growing numbers of PhD and masters students, including increasing the proportion of women ... (from 25% in 1990 to 46% in 2008). (2010: 7)

The result was also the introduction (or some may say cloning) of Swedish practices at Makerere. The 'adoption of doctoral committees, the option of published papers to meet the thesis requirement, public thesis defences, and exclusion of supervisors from examination committees' (2010: 7) are some examples. Will greater dependence on Swedish supervisors in the short run enhance the supervisory capacity of Makerere's academics in the medium term? Or will it give rise to other, unintended and unanticipated, problems?[4]

Some negative effects are already evident. If a student has both a Ugandan and a Swedish supervisor, how should each be remunerated? Equally or in line with remuneration practices in each country? There is no easy answer to this. To reconcile two unequal standards of remuneration, Swedish and Ugandan, is difficult. SIDA decided to remunerate Swedish supervisors using Swedish standards and Ugandan supervisors using Ugandan standards. This means, however, that a Swedish supervisor is paid 'about US$22 000 per student, which is 'about twice the entire salary of a senior Ugandan supervisor' (Freeman et al. 2010: 23). Naturally, Ugandan supervisors resent this. As noted in the report, 'Supervisors were very concerned about disparities in rewards for supervision between Swedish supervisors and themselves' (2010: 23).

The *third* problem concerned the students themselves:

> Supervisors highlighted differences in today's students, many of whom they say read few books and articles, instead taking content from more generic web sources, 'regurgitating', cutting and pasting to assemble papers, rather than engaging in more rigorous analysis preferable to the 'old timers' – unless guided, and pushed, by supervisors. (2010: 23)

How much of this can be dismissed as a generational divide and how much needs to be seen as evidence of the university's failure to develop a research culture? Supporting evidence comes from students themselves: 'some [PhD students] expressed serious reservations about presenting their work [in PhD seminars], out of concern that colleagues could appropriate their ideas' (2010: 22).[5] What do you do when perceived solutions are turned on their heads? When some students fear their ideas may be stolen in seminars, and others use the internet as an alternative to reading books – indeed, as an easy way of stealing ideas, otherwise called plagiarism? How do you develop a reading culture among students?

The value of the SIDA evaluation is that it underlined the primacy of the human factor. Lack of money is a problem, but it is not the most important problem. More important than how much money we have is *how we use it.* If we fail to recognise this, throwing money at problems is more likely to exacerbate them than solve them.

## Sustainability

The greatest shortcoming of the SIDA evaluation is that it failed to place Swedish assistance to the graduate programme at Makerere in the larger context of Makerere's own development. As a result, it made recommendations that were mainly timidly managerial– confined to areas of oversight and implementation. In my view, implementing these recommendations would simply increase bureaucracy without addressing the heart of the problem.

As explained, the university's lack of research capacity needs to be located historically. The heart of the problem lies in how the university has been conceptualised through the two main phases of its history. In the colonial period, it was assumed that Makerere's teaching and research faculty would be trained elsewhere, preferably in the UK. Then the cash-strapped post-colonial university became an entry point for the World Bank, which put the institution through the grinder of market-oriented reform, the main consequence of which was to destroy the quality of teaching and undermine existing research capacity. Some parts of the university, such as the arts faculty, participated in this initiative enthusiastically, and were wrecked; the science faculty, which resisted the reform, emerged with the least damage. I have written about this elsewhere (see Mamdani 2007).

If history is important in understanding the onset of the problem, it is perhaps even more important to an understanding of why the problem keeps recurring.

## The MISR initiative

When I arrived at MISR in June of 2010, we had seven researchers, including myself. I began by meeting each one for an hour and asking what research they had done since joining the institute. The answers were a revelation: everyone seemed to do everything, or rather anything: at one point primary education, the next primary health, then roads, then HIV/AIDS, whatever was in demand! This was when I learnt to recognise the first side-effect of consultancy: consultants have no expertise. They can lay claim only to a way of doing things, of gathering data and writing reports. They are Jacks or Janes – or Musokes or Mirmebes – of all trades, and masters of none.

Even though consultancies were MISR's main focus, some research was happening. However, it was all externally driven – the result of demands made by European donor agencies that the European universities they support to conduct research on Africa must also 'partner with' African universities. Rather than giving rise to institutional partnerships and collaboration, this has led to individual local researchers being incorporated into externally driven research projects. Too often, this resembles an outreach programme far more than a partnership between equals.

I suggested to my colleagues that we prioritise upgrading the library. The size of our collection had actually decreased over the previous decade. MISR's ten-year strategic plan called for purchasing about a hundred books over the ten-year period. This pointed to the second side-effect of the consultancy culture: consultants don't read, not because they can't or are not interested – but because reading has become a luxury, an after-work activity. Most consultancies require one to read nothing more than field data and notes.

My colleagues and I discussed these consultancy-related issues in meeting after meeting, and came up with a two-fold response. Our short-term response was to begin a programme of seminars, two a month. This required every staff member to present a research proposal that surveyed the literature in their field, identified key debates and located their query within those debates. In addition, we agreed to meet as a study group, also twice a month. As part of this process, we prepared a list of key texts published in the social sciences and humanities over the previous forty years to read and discuss. For the long term, we decided to create a multi-disciplinary, coursework-based, PhD programme to train a new generation of researchers. In January 2011, we held a two-day workshop with scholars from the University of the Western Cape in South Africa and Addis Ababa University in Ethiopia to brainstorm the outlines of this programme. In the next section, I sum up the ideas generated at that workshop.

## Reflections on postgraduate education in the humanities and social sciences

The central question facing higher education in Africa today is what it means to teach the humanities and social sciences in the current historical context, and specifically in post-colonial Africa. What does it mean to teach humanities and social sciences in locations where the dominant intellectual paradigms are products, not of Africa's own experience, but of a particular Western experience that theorises specific aspects of Western history and is concerned, in large part, with extolling the virtues or expounding on the shortcomings of the Enlightenment? How can we teach this paradigm, knowing that, as it has spread to other parts of the world, it has done so mainly by submerging its own particular origins and specific local concerns in terms of (ostensibly universal) scientific objectivity and neutrality?

I have no problem with reading Enlightenment texts; in fact, I see this as vital. The problem is, if the Enlightenment is said to be an exclusively European phenomenon, then the story of the Enlightenment excludes Africa and most of the rest of the world. How can it then serve as the foundation of university education in Africa? The assumption is that there is a single model, and that this can be derived only from the dominant Western experience. Accepting this is to reduce research to no more than a demonstration that societies around the world either conform to or deviate from the one model. The tendency is to dehistoricise and decontextualise all discordant experiences, both Western and non-Western. The effect is to devalue original research and intellectual production in Africa. Thus the global market tends to relegate Africa to providing the raw material ('data') to outside academics who process it and then re-export their theories back to Africa. Research proposals increasingly turn into descriptive accounts of data collection and of the methods used to collate this data; collaboration is reduced to assistance. The result is a general impoverishment of both theory and debate.

The expansion and entrenchment of intellectual paradigms that stress quantification above all else has led to a peculiar intellectual dispensation in Africa today. The dominant trend is for research to be primarily positivist and quantitative, carried out to answer questions formulated outside the continent, not only in terms of location but also in terms of historical perspective. This trend is directly reinforced via the 'consultancy' model, and indirectly through the ways in which research funds are channelled and through other forms of intellectual disciplining.

From this point of view, the proliferation of short methodology courses that aim to teach students and academics the quantitative methods necessary to gather and process empirical data are ushering in a new generation of native informers. In addition, the collection of data to answer pre-packaged questions can never be a substantive form of research as it displaces the fundamental practice of formulating the research questions that are to be addressed. When this happens, however, researchers turn into managers who supervise data collection.

This challenge to autonomous scholarship is not unprecedented. Indeed, autonomous scholarship was similarly denigrated in the early post-colonial states, when universities were conceived of as providing the 'manpower' [sic] necessary for national development, and original knowledge production was seen as a luxury. Even when scholars saw themselves as critical of the state, such as during the 1970s at the University of Dar es Salaam, intellectual work ended up being too closely wedded to a political programme. Thus, although that university nurtured a generation of pubic intellectuals, they failed to reproduce themselves. This same fate awaits future African academics if research is not put back into teaching, and if African PhD programmes are not seen as crucial to the training of the next generation of scholars.

Our initiatives at MISR were born from these reflections. We began with the conviction that the key to research is the formulation of a research problem. We reached consensus that the definition of a research problem should stem from both a critical engagement with society at large and a solid grasp of the disciplinary literature (world-wide), so as to identify the key debates and locate specific queries within those debates. Faced with a context in which the dominant model promotes consultants, not independent researchers, we decided to create a PhD programme based on significant preparatory course-work, thus instilling in students the capacity to both rethink old questions and formulate new ones.

Our PhD programme has been offered since 2012, and seeks to combine a commitment to local and regional knowledge production, rooting itself in relevant linguistic and disciplinary terms, and reflect-ing critically on the globalisation of modern forms of knowledge and modern instruments of power. Rather than opposing the local and the global, we seek to understand the global from the vantage point of the local. This means, we aim to understand alternative forms of aesthetic, intellectual, ethical, and political traditions, both contemporary and historical. Our objective is not just to learn *about* these forms, but also to learn *from* them. Over time, we seek to nurture a scholarly commu-nity that is equipped to rethink – both intellectually and institutionally – the very nature of the university and the function it should serve locally and globally.

### The curriculum

Coursework covered in the first two years is organised around a set of core courses taken by all students. These are then supplemented by electives grouped in four thematic clusters:
- Genealogies of the political: covering discursive and institutional histories of political practices and thought.
- Disciplinary and popular histories: ranging from academic and professional modes of history writing to popular forms of retelling the past in vernacular languages.

- Political economy: understanding global, regional and local power relations.
- Literary and aesthetic studies: consisting of fiction, the visual and performing arts, and cinema studies.

From a curricular perspective, the objective is for an individual student's course of study to be driven by investigation and not by orthodoxy. This approach gives primacy to the reading of key texts in related disciplines. In practical terms, students spend the first two years coming to grips with the literature and building a bibliography. In the third year they write a critical essay on this bibliography. In the fourth year, they embark on their own research year, and finally write this up in the fifth.

## Interdisciplinarity

In the nineteenth century, European universities developed three different domains of knowledge production – the natural sciences, the humanities, and the social sciences – based on the notion of 'three cultures'. Each of these domains was then subdivided into 'disciplines'. From 1850 to the Second World War, this pattern became institutionalised in three key ways, namely:
- Within universities, as chairs, departments, curricula and academic degrees for students;
- Between and beyond universities, as national and international discipline-based associations of scholars and journals;
- In the libraries of the world, as the basis for classification of scholarly works.

The intellectual consensus that sustained this project began to break down after the 1960s, partly because of the growing overlap between disciplines and partly because of a shared problematique. For example, the line dividing the humanities from the social sciences became blurred with the increasing 'historicisation' and hence 'contextualisation' of knowledge in the humanities and the social sciences.

The development was best captured in the report of the Gulbenkian Commission chaired by Immanuel Wallerstein (see Wallerstein 1996). As interdisciplinarity began to make inroads into disciplinary speciali-sations, the division between the humanities and the social sciences paled in the face of the growing chasm between quantitative and quali-tative perspectives in the study of social, political and cultural life. However, because it is so difficult to shift strongly entrenched habits in organisations, these intellectual developments were not matched by comparable organisational changes. Thus, although the number of interdisciplinary and regional institutes has multiplied, collaboration has rarely bridged the divide between the humanities and the social sciences. The challenge of postgraduate studies in the African univer-sity is how to produce truly interdisciplinary knowledge without giving up the ground gained within the different disciplines.

We have learned a number of lessons over the past few years. The most important is that we need to deepen our understanding of what it means to 'grow our own timber'. We could have started a PhD pro-gramme at MISR and borrowed the curriculum from Columbia or Harvard. We could then have become a satellite of those great institu-tions, but without the creativity that distinguishes them. In our very first semester, we confronted the question: what should we teach, at this time and in this place? What should be the content of our curriculum?

Our search for answers to that question has been protracted. Following a brainstorming session with colleagues from Ethiopia and South Africa, we held five workshops in 2011 under the umbrella title, 'Contemporary Debates' (see Mamdani 2013). Our idea was to invite scholars from around the world and from diverse intellectual traditions, whose works were defining the terms of the debate in the fields of gender in the public sphere, political economy, political studies, cultural and literary studies, and historical studies.

In 2012, we shifted our focus to hosting lecture series by key schol-ars. Professor Wang Hui of Tsinghua University in Beijing gave lectures on his four-volume intellectual history of the Chinese-language, *The Rise of Modern Chinese Thought*. Professor Partha Chatterjee from the Centre for Studies in Social Sciences in Calcutta gave a series of lectures on political theory and the Indian school of historiography known as subaltern studies. Through such encounters we began to put together a new curriculum that is global in content but crafted from local, regional and continental perspectives.

The question of perspective is important because research is not about finding answers to preset questions. It is about formulating new questions in response to both the evergreen flow of life and ongoing scholarly debates. The questions we ask depend on who we are, where we are, and the dilemmas we confront. Our first batch of students began to formulate their research questions in 2014 and answering them in the course of 2015. Our first batch of PhDs graduated in 2016.


## The kernel of reform

I have two very practical suggestions for Makerere University. The first is to substantially reduce undergraduate admissions. This would be to acknowledge today's reality: Makerere is no longer Uganda's only university. Unlike in the past, we now share responsibility for undergraduate education with a growing number of other tertiary institutions. At the same time, as the country's leading public university, our first responsibility is to provide *quality* undergraduate education. Where courses are over-subscribed, we must combine lectures with tutorials. Where classes are so overcrowded that lecturers feel compelled to distribute study notes, we risk fostering nothing more than students' dependence on similarly superficial solutions, whether from study notes or the internet. Is it not then but a short step to plagiarism? Instead, a solid reading culture must be inculcated in students at undergraduate level.

In addition, postgraduate education must become integral to the university, not a stand-alone facility that requires endless injections of external funding and input. In practice, all PhD students should be required to teach tutorials as part of their overall training. Post-doctoral fellows, too, should be required to combine teaching with research and writing. Every great university taps its doctoral students for a supply of tutors. MISR expects its PhD students to spend half of their third year tutoring undergraduates in different departments.

The development of quality students requires quality teachers. Good teachers never work only for the money, but they must be paid enough to be willing to work with diligence. Teachers are not business people; those with an eye on making money will look for work in Kikuubo (Kampala's business hub), not in a university. The important thing is to reform the motivational structure at Makerere so it attracts and rewards scholars, and discourages those who are there mainly for the money. For a start, this would mean paying meaningful salaries for teaching and research work, rather than allowances for attending endless meetings.

In fact, Makerere University should abolish all allowances for meeting attendance, as well as all payments for invigilating and marking. The money saved could be used to increase the salaries of those who teach and do research, as well as those whose services support these core activities. My guess is that this would do away with 90 per cent of meetings, and dramatically reduce the time spent in the 10 per cent of meetings that remain necessary. This strategy might not substantially increase salaries, but it would surely send the right signals to all concerned.

The starting point of any critique of neoliberalism in higher education is the recognition that a university is not a business but a place of scholarly pursuits. Its objective is to maximise scholarship, not profits. Of course, no one can afford to be blind to financial realities. Universities are no exception. But if promoting scholarship is our core mission, we must be prepared to subordinate all other considerations, including financial ones, to the pursuit of scholarship. To forget this is to lose our way.

## Clarifying the public interest

The Ugandan government shirks fiscal responsibility for the country's leading public university, yet continues to claim the right to define the university's policies and appoint its top management. How can this be? Of course, public universities should be substantially funded from the public purse, and their broad policies – including questions of fees and access – should be set by those who hold public power.

But who should be the custodians of the public interest in a public university? The tendency has been to see the state as holding executive power: Uganda's president was also chancellor of Makerere University before 2001. After the Universities and Other Tertiary Institutions Act of 2001, the country's president was named as the 'Visitor'. This keeps the university's top management, and thus the institution itself, on a short political leash. The alternative is to cast the legislature – not the executive – as the custodian of public interest when it comes to public universities.

It is commonly thought that if a government is going to pay a significant part of a university budget, it should have a significant say in the affairs of that institution. This is wrong for two reasons. First, in principle, government funds derive from taxation. Governments are therefore simply custodians of public resources; they cannot behave as if they own these. Second, in practice, a look at some of the world's great public university systems, such as the University of California in the US, or the nearby South African universities, is instructive. At least when these were great public systems, their financing was organised in ways that shielded them from the whims of the government of the day. Although the government was their major source of funds, their funding was determined by long-term formulas agreed on by all the key social actors; it did not fluctuate with the government in power or changes in state policy. In addition, the councils or trustees who shaped university policy were not instruments of any particular government. Even if the government appointed key members of these bodies, both the modes of their appointment and their tenures – and the legislation that specified these – ensured the autonomy of the university's policy-making bodies and its purse.

The public interest cannot be equated with the interests of any regime. The public interest is the interest of society, of which government is one part. This is why no university council should represent the government. Instead, such councils should represent all the different interests in society, providing a forum in which the public interest is discussed, debated and formulated.

## Notes

1     For example, see, Makerere vice-chancellor search process to cost Shs185m, *Daily Monitor*, 30 July. Available online.

2     See Chapter 1, this volume, for more on the World Bank's 'return on investment' position.

3     The report lists these as follows: 'participation in networks', 'translating findings into publications', 'promotion of PhD completers and of senior scientists', increased 'initiatives to seek external collaborators and research support', 'several units now sponsor journals', 'translation of researchers into research groups' (SIDA 2010: 36, emphasis added).

4     It is worth reading the SIDA report alongside another study that was published by Uganda's National Council for Science and Technology (UNCST) in collaboration with SIDA and the Embassy of Sweden in Uganda, entitled Research in Uganda: Status and Implications for Public Policy (Ecuru et al. 2008). The authors of this publication highlight three salient facts about the larger research environment in Uganda. First, in 2007/2008, the government contributed 42 per cent and donors 51 per cent of the country's research budget. However, as a percentage of GDP, Uganda's contribution in the preceding five years was low, between 0.2 and 0.5 per cent (Ecuru et al. 2008: 17).

    Second, Ecuru et al. noted that, 'The number of new research projects registered at UNCST almost tripled, from 109 in 1997/1998 to 335 in 2006/2007' and that 'much of the research in Uganda is undertaken through international collaborations and sponsorship' (2008: 9, 3). The questions that remain are: how many of these are research projects in Uganda by Ugandan researchers, and how many are projects on Uganda by externally based researchers? Obviously, once we have answers to these questions, we need to consider what this means for how and where our research agendas are set.

    Third, the largest proportion of research projects were in the fields of Social Sciences and Humanities (36 per cent), Medical and Health Sciences (31 per cent), and Natural Sciences (21 per cent). And further, 'In the field of Social Sciences and Humanities, most research projects were in the area of anthropology (40 per cent) and Governance (18 per cent)' (Freeman et al. 2010: 10, 12ff).

Ideally, SIDA's 2010 study team should have read this report and provided more detail, not only on how many PhDs were completed with SIDA support, but on their subject matter, and about what those candidates have done since they graduated.

5     Here is the full quote: 'Most [PhD students] expressed enthusiasm about PhD seminars at Makerere and in Sweden, but some expressed serious reservations about presenting their work, out of concern that colleagues could appropriate their ideas, citing little tradition of protection for intellectual property at Makerere' (Freeman et al. 2010: 22).

# References

Bako, Sabo (1993) Education and adjustment in Nigeria: Conditionality and resistance. In Mahmood Mamdani and Mamdou Diouf (eds) *Academic Freedom in Africa*. Dakar: Codesria

Ecuru, Julius, Leah Nawegulo, Richard Bosco Lutalo, Deborah Kasule, Edward Tujunirwe and Innocent Akampurira (2008) *Research in Uganda: Status and Implications for Public Policy*. Kampala: Uganda National Council for Science and Technology

Freeman, Phyllis, Eva Johansson and Jerker Thorvaldsson (2010) *Enhancing Research Capacity at Makerere University, Uganda, through Collaboration with Swedish Universities, 2000–2008: Past Experiences and Future Direction*. Stockholm: SIDA. Available online

Lugard, Frederick (1965) *Dual Mandate in Africa*. London: Routledge

Mamdani, Mahmood (2007) *Scholars in the Marketplace: The Dilemmas of Neoliberal Reforms at Makerere University, 1989–2005*. Kampala and Dakar: Fountain Press and CODESRIA

Mamdani, Mahmood (ed.) (2013) *Getting the Question Right: Interdisciplinary Explorations at Makerere University*. Kampala: MISR

Wallerstein, Immanuel (ed.) (1996) *Open the Social Sciences: Report of the Gulbenkian Commission on the Restructuring of the Social Sciences* (Mestizo Spaces/Espaces Metisses). Stanford: Stanford University Press

# CHAPTER
# 6

## South–North collaboration and service enhancements at Makerere and Bergen University libraries

*Maria GN Musoke and Ane Landøy*

Collaboration between Makerere University in Uganda and the University of Bergen in Norway began in 1999. In 2009, the two universities celebrated the first ten years of their ongoing relationship, which includes research collaboration, scientific competence-building, student and staff exchanges, and institutional development (Musoke and Landoy 2014). The relationship also extends to the libraries at the two universities, and the collaboration between Makerere University Library (Maklib) and the University of Bergen Library (UOBL) is the focus of this chapter, although their partnership has gradually expanded to draw in libraries at other universities in Uganda, Norway and South Sudan.

Makerere University was established in Uganda in 1922, making it one of the oldest public universities in sub-Saharan Africa. Initially, it was a College of London University, then it became the University of East Africa, and later Uganda's national university. In 1958, an Act of Uganda's legislature made Maklib the first legal deposit library in the country, and it carried out this function until 2002, when Uganda's national library was established. In 1972, in addition to its primary role of serving the primary academic institution in the region, Maklib became Uganda's national reference library. The institution has a main library and ten branch or college libraries.

By mid 2014, Makerere University's full-time student population had grown to about 50 000 undergraduates and postgraduates, about half of whom are female. The demand for library services is high, and Maklib has had to respond to the changing needs of its users (Musoke 2008; 2010). The University of Bergen has just over 14 500 students and 3 200 employees. With six faculties, covering most of the traditional university subjects, the institution is heavily involved in international co-operation in research and education. UOBL has approximately 93 staff members, and six libraries – one for each faculty. The staff include librarians with traditional librarianship training, academics with masters or doctoral degrees, and others with various high-school or lower-level university backgrounds. UOBL houses several special collections (including of pictures, old and rare books, and manuscripts), and also offers digital systems and services that include open-access institutional repositories.

Like Maklib, UOBL mainly serves the university's own academic staff and students, and its staff are active in initiating library-user and other forms of training for students. This has included collaborating with other national universities in Norway to create online courses such as 'Search and Write' (www.sokogskriv.no) and 'PhD on Track' (www.phdontrack.net).

Although there are similarities in the general challenges facing the two academic libraries, their different climates and economic situations have created some key differences. Uganda is a low-income country and the university is not well funded. This creates challenges for Maklib relating to the affordability of printed resources, IT facilities, furniture and the general ambiance of the library. The costs of bandwidth and internet connectivity in Uganda have also prevented the establishment of a fully automated and integrated library service. However, when it comes to influencing the universities' administrative structures, Ugandan legislation gives Maklib full membership of the university senate. UOBL, on the other hand, is governed by a board that has no direct access to the university senate committee.

## Academic libraries and changes in higher education

Given the ever-changing landscape of higher education, it is helpful to consider the ongoing role and relevance of academic libraries. The rapid changes in technology, paradigm shifts in research, as well as developments in areas such as scholarly communication, data management and pedagogy within the higher education arena, have led academic libraries to develop new resources and services that address the evolving needs and expectations of library users. To remain relevant, academic libraries have had to respond and adapt. However the libraries also have to balance the need to offer new facilities with continuing to provide their core services, while anticipating future user needs related to new technologies, growing data sets and further paradigm shifts in learning, teaching and research.

Michalak (2012) pointed out that some of the factors driving these changes are networked technologies with powerful search engines that are available to all, as well as social technologies and the digitisation of almost every piece of information. Factors supporting these shifts include collaborative relationships between academic and research libraries at national, regional or international levels, state funding, and pragmatic librarians who are transforming their workplaces from lumbering and old-fashioned facilities into agile, change-oriented units ready to respond to whatever the future holds. Budgetary constraints, rapid advances in technology, and demands that libraries continue to demonstrate their value have also played a role.

Raju (2014) highlighted the forces for change in academic institutions, and their impact on the relationship between universities and academic libraries. Specifically, new methods of scholarly communication, the expansion of the libraries' virtual space via knowledge portals or research commons, the proliferation of social media, and the explosive growth of mobile devices, such as tablets and related applications, have collectively altered traditional academic libraries beyond recognition. These changes have obviously also had a significant impact on the knowledge and skills requirements of library and information-science professionals.

Technology-influenced changes in teaching and learning, linked to new knowledge products such as subject portals and subject-specific websites, as well as new physical or virtual spaces, have greatly affected university libraries. At the same time, e-science has developed rapidly in the physical and medical sciences, which have traditionally been influenced by advancing technologies, but also within the humanities and social sciences. These developments have forced a dramatic shift in the way academic and research libraries serve the needs of researchers, and many have asked how academic libraries are coping with these advances (see for example Musoke et al. 2014).

Not only are libraries' traditional services (such as building collections and supporting teaching, learning, research and dissemination) becoming increasingly digitised, but technological changes have also created new tasks and roles for academic librarians. For example, large amounts of research data, sometimes referred to as 'big data', have to be collected and curated to ensure ease of access and use. Increasingly, academic libraries are expected to provide this service, and to be able to plan for and provide for future access, which is inevitably becoming more and more open.

To enable digital capture, curation, preservation, sharing and other knowledge-management tasks, academic libraries in the digital era have to embrace a wide range of new services. These include digitisation; electronic publishing; Web 2.0, Web 3.0 and beyond; Library 2.0, Library 3.0 and beyond; social media; big/open-data management and access; and a host of other fast evolving ICTs (Raju 2014). As research becomes more intense, and research information increasingly available via open access, libraries have to become more visible and relevant. Fortunately, the new technologies are opening up huge opportunities for academic libraries to support learning, teaching and research. Academic libraries are adapting in a myriad of different ways. Employing more staff, as well as retraining and retooling existing staff with new skills, changing physical spaces to serve new purposes, and restructuring to create new departments within the library, or merging with other university departments. Radical new forms of collaboration between libraries at different institutions are also emerging.

Saunders (2015) pointed out that the need for change raises concerns for academic libraries around the world, and emphasises the importance of collaboration between libraries. Areas of knowledge and expertise in different libraries may be exploited when such institutions work together, and solutions can be found either by transferring knowledge or by joint efforts. Worldwide, collaborations range from establishing consortia for the purchase of resources and joint storage of less-used collections, to setting up common portals and joint repositories.

In Africa, various organisations have echoed the need for change. For example, the New Partnership for African Development (NEPAD) has highlighted the need for universities in Africa to implement curricula that will produce a new generation of graduates who are capable of acting as nuclei for change. At another level, the *Trend Report* published by the International Federation of Library Associations (IFLA 2014) elaborated on anticipated changes following, among other things, the adoption of the Sustainable Development Goals by United Nations in 2015.

The theme of North–South collaboration implies strategic knowledge sharing and development, and this fits well with the shifts in library and information services outlined above. The term 'collaboration' is often used interchangeably with the term 'partnership'. In our view, there is a difference between the two. We concur with Carnwell and Carson (2009), who pointed out that a partnership refers to 'what something is' while collaboration describes 'something that is done'. Partnerships imply an equal commitment, accompanied by shared risks and benefits, and focus on a specific problem or outcome. They may be political, charitable or ideological relationships in which power is shared. Sometimes the focus of a partnership is strong enough for the boundaries between partners to fade and blur in deference to the overarching importance of shared goals. Collaborations share many of these characteristics, but collaborators contribute their expertise to the degree that is needed to solve a problem *with no expectation of reciprocity*. Collaborations can, therefore, be considered to be more project- or goal-focused, and when the goal is achieved and/or the project is implemented, collaboration may cease.

UOBL has collaborated with Maklib with no expectation of reciprocity, and, as subsequent sections of the paper show, the relationship has
enhanced service delivery.

## Collaboration and its effects

The collaboration between the two libraries has involved UOBL supporting Maklib in carrying out its various professional activities. This
includes training library staff, helping to manage interlibrary loans and
document delivery services, supporting catalogue conversion, and
establishing Makerere University's institutional repository – MAKIR
(this was formerly the Uganda Scholarly Digital Library).

One of the first activities that started in 2002 was a document delivery service between the two university libraries. Maklib's subscriptions
to electronic journal databases were then in an initial stage, and this
service offered a reduced subscription to much-needed print journals,
giving Makerere students and staff access to current literature at substantially reduced costs. At the time of writing, Maklib was subscribing
to over 20 000 full-text online journal titles, and has been able to do so
since 2009.

In 2003, Maklib began the long process of converting its manual
catalogue cards into an electronic library system. As part of the process,
a team from UOBL visited Maklib in March 2005, offering professional
support that included a well-articulated and mutually agreed work
plan. In 2006, Maklib launched its online public-access catalogue,
MAKULA (Makerere University Library Access). The word 'makula' also
means 'a gift' or 'something splendid' in one of Uganda's languages,
thus expressing something of how Maklib staff endeavour to maintain
and offer a 'splendid' catalogue as a 'gift' to library users (Musoke
2010). By 2010, all the old catalogue cards had been converted. Library
users, visiting librarians and scholars have described the change from
the wooden catalogue boxes to online terminals as a 'transformation'.

In 2009 and 2010, six additional university libraries in Nigeria and
one in Ghana joined Maklib in using the Virtua Integrated Library
System. Maklib staff have since shared their experience with librarians

at those libraries, offering training and support, and operating much like a 'help' desk, thus passing on some of the assistance they had received from UOBL.

Maklib's collaboration with the UOBL also expanded in 2005 to include a digitisation project. This was the beginning of setting up an institution-wide digital repository for the university. The repository was initially named the Uganda Scholarly Digital Library, and later renamed Makerere Institutional Repository (MAKIR); it runs on DSpace's open-source repository software. In addition to supporting the records conversion, librarians from UOBL assisted staff at Maklib in planning for MAKIR during their 2005 visit. A project plan was drawn up, which included the training of Maklib staff. Training was done in the use of DSpace and in hands-on scanning, and a first attempt was made to upload digitised documents to a DSpace server that was set up at the University of Bergen. By December 2014, over 5 000 full-text records had been archived in DSpace for access on the MAKIR site. Access limits were placed on some of the content (especially theses), giving authors the right to decide when their work is made fully accessible.

The training and support offered by UOBL inspired several Maklib librarians to pursue further studies in this field. For example, the head of Maklib's Digitisation section, who was also the key librarian in MAKIR, spent some time at UOBL and completed a PhD on the management of open-access institutional repositories in East Africa. In addition to building the capacity of librarians to manage an institutional repository in a low-bandwidth environment, digitising Makerere University's research output increased Makerere University's visibility on the internet. By sharing a high number of rich-text files, the institution has been able to continually improve its webometric rankings.

The establishment of MAKIR bore yet another fruit, when librarians at Sokoine University of Agriculture in Tanzania began to create their own institutional repository. UOBL recommended that they work with Maklib, and the experience of establishing MAKIR was then usefully shared.

Various departments at Makerere University have also benefited from the collaboration with UOBL in specific ways. For example, although the Department of Music, Dance and Drama was established at Makerere University in 1971, it was 2006 before the first digital music archive of Ugandan music was established.

To manage the collection, a music librarian had to be identified and trained to collect, organise and digitise the collection. Maklib and UOBL both worked with their respective music departments and researchers, and the University of Bergen's music librarian visited Makerere to help train Maklib's newly appointed music librarian. As part of this training, Maklib's music librarian and archivist both also visited UOBL. Maklib's archivist still supports the music librarian, and the music archive is hosted within the main library. While UOBL provided hands-on training, Makerere University supported the music librarian in enrolling for a masters in information science, and her research focused on the management of the music collection. Similarly, in training and sharing experiences with the MakLib music librarian, UOBL's music librarian also learned new skills, and was inspired to enrol for a masters degree, focused on copyright issues related to music materials held in academic libraries.

By 30 November 2014, 2 980 audio files had been uploaded, of which 1 577 were songs from the 1940s and 1950s (these included Klaus Wachsmann's and Peter Cooke's collections that were repatriated from the British Sound Library). In addition, 1 555 videos, 30 tapes and 28 phonographs – mainly related to ethnomusicology – had been digitised and preserved in the music archive, along with other digital recordings. In addition, 15 051 paper archives, 1 786 photographs (including 32 undigitised and 46 digitised photo albums) have been included in the collection.

As mentioned, various MakLib staff have been seconded to UOBL for periods ranging from two weeks to three months where they were able to get hands-on training and observe best practices. Between 2001 (when the Maklib–UOBL collaboration was first formalised) and June 2015, sixteen Maklib librarians visited UOBL, and six UOBL staff visited Maklib to conduct training in different aspects of academic librarianship, to prepare joint publications and to attend various planning meetings.

UOBL has also supported Maklib in introducing LATINA (Learning and Teaching in a Digital Era). Skills acquired by Maklib librarians who attended the initial LATINA training in Oslo have been applied in library activities and programmes. The course has introduced participants to new ways of approaching teaching, learning and digital librarianship. For example, the Maklib album in Picasa is continuously updated, and user guidelines and an OPAC video tutorial have been uploaded to YouTube, along with a photo story generated from pictures of branch libraries. The LATINA course aims to build capacity not only at Maklib, but to enable Maklib staff to facilitate similar training courses at their own or other institutions in future. In 2012, a LATINA course was held in Africa for the first time by Maklib, and was attended by participants from university libraries in South Sudan and various other East African countries. By 2015, LATINA had been held at Maklib three times.

Building on its collaboration with Maklib, UOBL was awarded two grants by the Norwegian University Cooperation Programme for Capacity Development in Sudan, which funded collaboration between higher education institutions in Norway and Sudan. The first new project was the Juba University Library Automation Project and the second was the Education of Librarians Project. Both focused on the automation of the library and the training of the library staff. As the projects had an academic training component, the East African School of Library and Information Science at Makerere University and the Norwegian School of Librarianship at the former Oslo University College were also involved.[1]

The sustaining of their relationship over many years is one of the major achievements of the collaboration between UOBL and Maklib; many similar projects have ended after just the initial phase. The ongoing collaboration has led to the relationship expanding into other East African countries, and particularly into South Sudan as Maklib has begun sharing the knowledge and experience it has gained (Musoke and Landøy 2014). The success of the Maklib–UOBL collaboration set a precedent for university administrators from both universities, particularly as they sought to expand their collaboration from two to five institutions, and this has benefited both institutions in various ways.

## Lessons learned

One of the lessons learned is that rapid advances in IT mean that automation is never complete. Librarians have to update their knowledge and skills constantly. Capacity building among librarians is therefore not only important to the implementation of IT library projects and activities, but also to the sustainability of entire institutions when the skills and knowledge acquired not only enhance access to knowledge *but* are shared with others in the region (Musoke 2010). This important benefit has informed subsequent phases of the collaboration.

Another lesson learned is the benefit of including 'neighbours' in library-development projects. That is, the partnership with Maklib was vital to the success of projects in South Sudan. The value of this was acknowledged by UOBL when they approached the Transilvania University of Brașov in Romania to became a partner in the development of an academic library in neighbouring Moldova.

Lessons were also learned outside the project, and the collaboration between UOLB and Maklib changed both partners in several ways. Both institutions faced challenges and had expertise in different areas of academic librarianship. UOBL had better access to electronic information and more technology, as a result of Norway's higher economic status and larger investment in staffing. Maklib had developed innovative approaches to lending as a result of books and other information resources being much less affordable for students. Maklib also had an impressive track record in fundraising, strategic planning and in implementing projects and strategies. UOBL learned from Maklib how to get library matters onto the agendas of university leaders, even though UOBL's director is not on the university senate in Bergen, as is the case at Makerere. UOBL also strives to emulate the culture of learning, improving and sharing that is a hallmark of Maklib.

## Conclusion and the future

In this chapter, we have highlighted the benefits of South–North collaboration in knowledge sharing and institutional development.

Although the activities described seem to focus on capacity building at Maklib with UOBL as the facilitator, the experience and knowledge sharing has been of significant benefit to UOBL librarians. This highlights the importance of strengthening and nurturing linkages, networks and collaborations as the higher education environment continues to change.

The fifth of the long-standing laws of librarianship developed by SR Ranganathan states that a 'library is a growing organism' (1931: 382). Accordingly, the imperatives of the new information environment require that competencies of knowledge organisation are developed and implemented with creativity or innovation and a sense of entrepreneurship. Continuing with business as usual at Maklib was never an option. Creativity and innovation have been key driving factors behind the collaboration between Maklib and UOBL since it began.

To continue to develop their libraries into the best possible scholarly information resource in ways that solidly support teaching, learning and research, Maklib and UOBL will have to remain true to their ideals of innovating within their ever-changing, albeit different, environments. Certain goals and activities are therefore relevant for both libraries, for example:

- Patrons and library users need to learn how to manage information overload, and the immense possibilities created by the internet. The libraries must, therefore, provide support through periodic information-literacy programmes that build search and retrieval skills in a scholarly and ethical way.
- Researchers have to publish, and funding agencies often expect researchers to make their research output available via open-access channels. Librarians can advise researchers on how to select the appropriate publishing channels, indicating which journals have the highest impact and widest outreach, and advising on portals for open access, including optimising their own institutional repositories. In this way, both the 'gold' and the 'green' publishing avenues can be catered for.
- Universities are required to show their 'output', in terms of graduates, research and publications. Libraries can play an important

role in contributing to bibliometrics/scientometrics by reporting into national research-information systems.

- A culture of mutual sharing and peer training is necessary if libraries are to succeed in developing relevant services of high quality for patrons/users and their institution.

Exchange visits remain an ongoing part of the collaboration. For example, UOBL hosted the librarian from Makerere University's Institute of Social Research for a two-week attachment in September 2015, and the MAKIR librarian spent a year in Norway from August 2015 on a NORHED-supported PhD programme focusing on digitising weather records. Furthermore, the collaboration continues to support joint research, publications and presentation of papers at conferences. To sustain such activities, grant-proposals are written jointly.

As Henry Ford observed, 'Coming together is a beginning, keeping together is progress, working together is success.' UOBL and Maklib have worked together successfully and plan to stay together as they build for the future of their respective universities.

## Acknowledgements

We gratefully acknowledge the support we have received from the administrations of the University of Bergen and Makerere University, as well as the staff of UOBL and Maklib, South Sudan, Oslo College and EASLIS. We also acknowledge the financial support of the Norwegian government. Maklib also acknowledges the support of various development partners including NORAD, SIDA, the Carnegie Corporation of New York and the Elsevier Foundation.

## Note

1    From August 2011, Oslo University College and Akershus University College of Applied Sciences merged.

# References

Carnwell, R and A Carson (2009) The concepts of partnership and collaboration. In: R Carnwell and J Buchanan (eds) *Effective Practice in Health, Social Care and Criminal Justice: A Partnership Approach.* Maidenhead: McGraw-Hill and the Open University

IFLA (International Federation of Library Associations)(2014) *Trend Report.* Available online

Michalak, SC (2012) This changes everything: Transforming the academic library. *Journal of Library Administration* 52(5): 411–423

Musoke, Maria GN (2008) Strategies for addressing the university library users' changing needs and practices in sub-Saharan Africa. *Journal of Academic Librarianship* 34(6): 532–538

Musoke, Maria GN (2010) Reconstruction @ Maklib with minimal resources. Paper presented at the International Federation of Library Associations conference in Gothenburg, 9–15 August

Musoke, Maria GN and Ane Landøy (2014) Building the capacity of librarians through collaboration: The experience of the University of Bergen and Makerere University libraries with their new partners in the North and South. In: Susmita Chakraborty and Anup Kumar Das (eds) *Collaboration in International and Comparative Librarianship.* Hershey, PA: IGI Global

Musoke, Maria GN, Andrew Mwesigwa and Timothy Sentamu (2014) The changing IT trends: Are academic libraries coping? *Qualitative and Quantitative Methods in Libraries* 342: 878–809

Raju, J (2014) Knowledge and skills for the digital era academic library. *Journal of Academic Librarianship* 40(2): 163–170

Ranganathan, SR (1931) *The Five Laws of Library Science.* Madras and London: Madras Library Association and Edward Goldston

Saunders, Laura (2015) Academic libraries' strategic plans: Top trends and under-recognized areas. *Journal of Academic Librarianship* 41: 285–291. Available online

# CHAPTER
# 7

## North–South research collaborations and their impact on capacity building: A Southern perspective

*Johnson Muchunguzi Ishengoma*

In this chapter I draw from the extensive literature, as well as some empirical data and my own personal experience of North–South research collaborations. I attempt to shed light on whether these collaborations contribute significantly to institutional and/or individual capacity building, or strengthen academic knowledge production and exchange in Southern (public) universities. For the purposes of this chapter, I define research collaborations as 'the working together of researchers to achieve common goal of producing new scientific knowledge' (Katz and Martin 1997: 7). I understand research capacity building to mean 'any efforts to increase the ability of individuals and institutions to undertake high-quality research and engage with a wider community of stakeholders' (ESSENCE 2014: 7).

My main argument is that, despite having the potential to enhance the research capacities of universities and individuals, North–South research collaborations have had limited impact because of the neocolonial nature of the donor–recipient framework within which most North–South research collaborations operate. This framework perpetuates power asymmetries and resource dependencies between both South and North, and between research and donor institutions. The funding of such collaborations is so often initiated by Northern research institutions and researchers because of their dependence on donor funding. Although this dependence is not well documented, my own observations and some of the literature show that Northern universities and researchers depend heavily on bilateral, multilateral and international donor organisations, foundations and governments to fund North–South research collaborations.

The major funders of North–South collaborations – such as NORAD, SIDA (and its research co-operation department, SAREC), the World Bank, the OECD and others, are in turn funded by their respective governments or member states. This creates a vicious cycle of dependency for universities and researchers, both Northern and Southern, while consolidating the donor–recipient framework that dominates research collaborations. It also means that when funds run out or funders change their priorities, capacity building, particularly in Southern universities, is sometimes quickly jettisoned and the sustainability of research collaborations totally compromised.

Essentially, the current donor–recipient framework is based on, and perpetuates, imbalanced relationships between collaborators, and it limits the potential for such relationships to enhance research capacities at Southern universities and research institutions.

Too often, North–South research collaborations apply to projects or programmes of limited duration. In addition, the synchronisation of effort between various project donors and actors is virtually non-existent (AFRODAD 2007). Both of these factors impact on the sustainability of research programmes and on their potential to build research capacity. In an evaluation of research projects in universities in Tanzania, Mozambique, Bolivia and Nicaragua, SIDA/SAREC acknowledged these problems, arguing that

> generally speaking, the financial sustainability of many SIDA/SAREC research activities is worrying. The incentives to carry out research at the institutions often remain heavily dependent on continued external support. (Boeren et al. 2006: 7)

Even where a single donor/funder supports several research projects at a single Southern university, these interventions are seldom synchronised and their impact in terms of capacity building at an institutional or individual level is very difficult to determine.

Despite the structural limitations of North–South research collaborations and the neocolonial divisions that continue to shape so many of the dichotomies that exist between North and South, research shows that some North–South research collaborations have promoted sustainable research networks. This implies that North–South barriers can melt away where real knowledge transfer occurs or where mutual research interests or common research goals between North–South researchers are forged. For example, Dean et al. (2015) identified a UK–Africa programme as one example of genuine North–South collaboration and capacity building between researchers.

It is also the case (as several contributors to this volume point out) that North–South research collaborations help to supplement Southern governments' inadequate expenditure and investment in research. For example, in 2011, African governments spent an average of 0.4 per cent of their countries' GDP on research and development. In the same year, several *single countries* in the North allocated several times more than Africa's total budget to this (Jowi and Obamba, 2011: 14). Citing NEPAD (2010), Jowi and Obamba have argued that 'the funding of research and innovation programmes remains a major challenge for African countries and universities and this could remain the same for foreseeable future unless particularly dramatic measures are taken' (2011: 14). As one report put it 'chronic underinvestment in universities and research institutions' is one of the many barriers that prevent researchers from low- and middle-income countries from fulfilling their research potential (ESSENCE 2014: 7).

Yet, despite the structural imbalances and inequalities historically embedded in North–South relationships, many argue that research collaborations are critical for research capacity building, as well as for knowledge exchange. For example, referring to the Irish–African higher education partnership model, Nakabugo et al. (2010) acknowledge that North–South partnerships on research capacity building (in the South) do have an impact, albeit more on individuals than on institutions. In my view, effective and impactful North–South research collaborations are characterised by:

- Mutual ownership of research agendas through processes of joint and collaborative agenda setting. That is, Southern universities should have an equal say or voting power, and should invest both financially and otherwise in research collaborations/projects. By making financial and material contributions, researchers and research institutions in the South would be able to transform their currently disadvantaged positions in which they are perceived to be recipients of aid, to being co-donors and co-sponsors. Co-sponsorship has the potential to enhance symmetry, mutual accountability, reciprocity, transparency and minimise self-censorship in the reporting of research results by Southern researchers.[1]
- Empowering research frameworks which enable Southern universities to initiate and design research projects on the basis of felt needs, and invite Northern collaborators (and possibly funders) to co-manage expenditure and collaborate in the research process.
- Strong institutional monitoring and evaluation mechanisms, which ensure that abuse of funds and benefits is minimised and financial transparency is guaranteed.[2]

## Neocolonialism and asymmetries of power

North–South research collaborations operate within a broader context of neocolonial structures and relationships. The Northern (high-income) countries tend to be former colonial powers that have strong economies and robust institutional structures. Their hegemony over the South remains largely unquestioned. The countries of the South are often former colonies, with weakened economies and embattled institutions. An inability to mobilise internal resources 'compels' Southern countries to depend on the North to finance their development agendas, including research and development. As Breidlid (2013: 358) observes:

Many countries in the Global South suffer from severe economic underdevelopment that is a legacy of their colonial history. Their fragile economic base means that their desire and goal to develop robust national higher education institutions cannot be put into practice. In such a perspective North–South collaboration is not unproblematic.

The neocolonial structure within which North–South research collaborations operate, limits their potential to impact on capacity building. In practice, Southern researchers are often the weaker partners as a result of their nations' weaker economic bases, and many Southern researchers are perceived to have little to offer in terms of research skills or other competencies.

## Paternalism and patronage

Linked to this neocolonial superstructure, relations of paternalism and patronage continue to operate within North–South research collaborations. Carbonnier and Kontinen (2014: 5), citing Lewis (1998) and Ericksson-Baaz (2005), explained how paternalism and patronage are based on colonial trusteeship in that the 'weaker partner requires guidance and help from the stronger in a spirit of paternal care'. Accordingly, researchers in the global South are perceived as requiring guidance, oversight and supervision from their Northern partners in terms of setting research agendas, spending and accounting for research funds according to certain rules and conditions, putting accountability and reporting mechanisms in place, and, at times, even in the designing of research projects and methodologies. In this way, Carbonnier and Kontinen (2014) argue, the capacity-building objectives, which are a hallmark of almost all North–South research collaborations, clearly echo the colonial enterprise of 'civilising' the South.

## Hegemony and power

Given contemporary hegemonic power structures and structural inequalities, North–South research collaborations are inevitably imbalanced, and mostly favour the agendas of Northern researchers and universities. To understand how this limits the impact of the research collaborations on research capacity building in the South, Maselli et al. (2004) developed a useful list of critical questions related to nine key factors that influence the balance of power in North–South partnerships (see Box 7.1). The answers to these questions provide a basis for understanding the hegemonic power relations and structural imbalances that are built into many research collaborations. As Maselli et al. (2004: 33) pointed out, the likely outcome of unbalanced partnerships is that 'the South merely presents a laboratory for the North, providing interesting scientific data'.

**Box 7.1:** Factors influencing the balance of power in North–South research collaborations

**Initiative**
- Who has the original research collaboration idea/agenda – a researcher in the North or South?
- Who designs the research project?
- Who sets the research agenda?
- Who makes conceptual inputs?
- Who selects research participants and who is selected?

**Interests**
- Who has what kind of expectations in the research collaboration project?
- Who has what kind of objectives in the research collaboration project?
- Who has what kind of stakes in the project?
- Are there any hidden intentions or agendas to be considered?

**Power**

*Funding*
- Who generates funds for research collaborations?
- Who negotiates with the donors that fund research collaborations?
- Who decides on how funds will be used?
- How transparent is the allocation of funds?
- How are the work, accountability and responsibility shared?

*Methodological competence*
- Who has the scientific and methodological competence?
- Who decides on the methodologies to be used?
- Who has contextual competence (contacts on the ground)?

*Roles/positions*
- Who is involved and in what kinds of roles?
- Who is where in the hierarchy?
- Who has the power to handle different perceptions, conflicts or differences?
- Who decides what kind of products must be delivered, to whom and by when?
- Who is seen as an expert?

*Operational responsibility and duties*
- Who is the lead researcher?
- Who is responsible for project management and co-ordination?

- Who has the authority to synthesise data and results?
- Who is responsible for supervision?
- Who invests how much time doing what kinds of work (conceptual, fieldwork, synthesis, discussion etc)?
- Who collects the research data?

*Interaction*
- Where and when do meetings take place?
- Who decides when the meetings will happen and who sets the agenda?
- Who takes part in what kind of meetings (steering, planning and reporting)?
- Who goes into the field and interacts with local stakeholders?
- Who meets official representatives, decision makers, donors etc.?

**Technical support**
- Who provides technical support?
- Who has access to what kinds of infrastructure and technology?
- Who provides training and support to the research team?

**Data**
- Who generates new information?
- Who collects what kinds of information?
- Where is the information stored?
- Who has access to what kinds of information?
- Who has control over the information?
- How is information disseminated or/ and exchanged?
- Who makes what kind of use of information/data collected?

**Capacity building**
- Which individuals can improve their capacities (knowledge, skills, empowerment)?
- Which institutions can improve their capacities? (structural aspects, empowerment)?

**Benefits**
- Who benefits in what ways (conference participation, publications, expertise/mandates, MSc/PhD degrees, scientific and social empowerment, bonuses, promotions, etc.)?
- Who gets scientific or academic credit (publications, awards, invitation to conferences, etc.)?
- How are the benefits shared?

*Source:* Adapted from Maselli et al. (2004: 35–36)

## Resource dependencies in research collaborations

The dependency of Northern research institutions on donors to fund North–South research collaborations further limits the impact of these research programmes. Northern research institutions depend on development agencies such as NORAD, SIDA, DFID and the OECD, as well as a plethora of private foundations (Ishengoma 2016). Northern governments and multilateral financial institutions such as the World Bank are also key, but this dependency undermines the long-term viability of North–South research collaborations, and feeds into other challenges such as the power asymmetries already discussed.

As argued by Pfeffer and Salancik (1978), access to and control over resources are sources of power in any organisation. Several chapters in this book describe the critical shortages of research and development funding that Southern universities and researchers experience and how they depend on external donors to cover their research and other core functions. Typically, this dependence tends to render Southern institutions and researchers powerless (Ali et al. 2006) as North–South research collaborations simply reproduce 'traditional patterns of economic and geographical dependency' (Jowi 2012: 51).

## Donor-determined research agendas and priorities

This powerlessness is directly related to the fact that research agenda-setting is so often donor driven. While it is difficult to provide empirical evidence on this, Bradley (2008a) suggested that research agendas in North–South research partnerships are dominated by the interests of Northern donors and researchers.[3] Bradley also observed that Southern researchers tend to encounter obstacles when attempting to set research agendas, and argued that North–South partnerships are not necessarily the best way to advance research agendas that reflect the priorities of countries in the South. Baud (2002) has also documented inequities in agenda-setting processes in North–South partnerships. Low-income countries allocate very few funds for research and development, creating a gap that international agencies now occupy, and in which they assume they have a right to dictate research agendas and priorities. Too often, donors fail to take local research needs and priorities into consideration. As Ali et al. (2006: 7) argued, Southern governments'

> inability to fund research leaves the scientists at the mercy of external funding agencies whose priorities determine the priority areas for research. A major challenge in the governance of research funding is agenda-setting given the fact that the priorities of the funding bodies largely dictate what ... issues are to be studied.

In other words, funding agencies fund what donors want information about, instead of what Southern countries need information on.

Various academic indicators for selected African and OECD countries are shown in Tables 7.1 and 7.2. A comparison of the two tables is instructive. The African Union has recommended that member countries spend at least 1 per cent of their GDP on research and development. As shown in Table 7.1, all 22 countries surveyed allocate less than this, including those that have relatively strong economies such as South Africa, Nigeria, Egypt and Ghana.

Research by Ali et al. (2006) showed that when research is funded primarily by Southern governments, Southern researchers are more likely to determine and own the research agendas. They cite the example of Cuba, which receives minimal support from international donors, and where local researchers have long determined the national research agenda and managed the country's research systems.

The Cuban example of funding research from their own resources, and thus determining their own research agendas, could be emulated by other low-income countries. Too few countries in the South *really* own their own national and strategic development agendas, despite publishing grandiose strategic plans and national visions from time to time. Too often, such grandiose visions are borrowed wholesale from some other country or are dictated by multilateral organisations without being adapted to local contexts. Tanzania's 'Big Results Now' programme is one example of such a scheme, and it is funded by external donors including the World Bank and the IMF.

Echt (2014) has also argued that the dominant research-funding model is linked to the control of research agendas, and suggested that the fact that sources of funding are generally limited to Northern countries threatens the autonomy and objectivity of research output. Echt also questioned whether donor-driven research agendas and priorities explains the failure of research to make any tangible impact in low-income countries, and recommended that institutions seek funding from a range of funding sources so as to reduce the influence of single donors on their research agendas.

**Table 7.1: Academic indicators for selected African countries, 2005–2014**

| Country | Expenditure on research as a percentage of GDP (2005–2014) | Full-time researchers per million citizens (2005–2014) | Articles published in scientific and technical journals (2011) |
|---|---|---|---|
| Botswana | 0.25 | 52 | 6 |
| Burkina Faso | 0.20 | 165 | 50 |
| Burundi | 0.12 | — | 3 |
| Democratic Republic of Congo | 0.08 | 21 | — |
| Egypt | 0.68 | 544 | 2 515 |
| Ethiopia | 0.61 | 45 | 170 |
| Gabon | 0.58 | — | 77 |
| Gambia | 0.13 | 34 | 13 |
| Ghana | 0.38 | 39 | 121 |
| Kenya | 0.79 | 231 | 290 |
| Madagascar | 0.11 | 51 | 33 |
| Mali | 0.66 | 29 | 29 |
| Mozambique | 0.42 | 38 | 38 |
| Namibia | 0.14 | — | 13 |
| Nigeria | 0.22 | 39 | 439 |
| Senegal | 0.54 | 361 | 79 |
| South Africa | 0.73 | 405 | 3 125 |
| Tanzania | 0.38 | 35 | 121 |
| Togo | 0.22 | 36 | 8 |
| Tunisia | 0.68 | 1 393 | 1 016 |
| Uganda | 0.48 | 38 | 158 |
| Zambia | 0.28 | 41 | 60 |

*Note:* Empty cells indicate that data was not provided.
*Source:* Adapted from World Bank (2014: Table 5.13)

**Table 7.2: Academic indicators for selected OECD countries, 2005–2014**

| Country | Expenditure on research as a percentage of GDP (2005–2014) | Full-time researchers per million citizens (2005–2014) | Articles published in scientific and technical journals (2011) |
|---|---|---|---|
| Austria | 2.83 | 4 704 | 5 103 |
| Australia | 2.25 | 4 335 | 20 603 |
| Belgium | 2.28 | 4 003 | 7 484 |
| Canada | 1.62 | 4 490 | 29 017 |
| Denmark | 3.06 | 7 265 | 6 071 |
| Finland | 3.31 | 7 188 | 4 878 |
| France | 2.23 | 4 153 | 31 686 |
| Germany | 2.85 | 4 472 | 46 259 |
| Israel | 4.21 | 8 282 | 6 096 |
| Japan | 3.47 | 5 201 | 47 106 |
| Netherlands | 1.98 | 4 303 | 15 508 |
| New Zealand | 1.25 | 3 701 | 3 472 |
| Norway | 1.66 | 5 576 | 4 777 |
| Sweden | 3.30 | 6 473 | 9 473 |
| United Kingdom | 1.65 | 4 055 | 46 035 |
| United States | 2.81 | 4 019 | 208 601 |

*Source:* Adapted from World Bank (2014: Table 5.13)

## North–South research collaborations as instruments of internationalisation

North–South research collaborations can also be understood as form-ing part of the internationalisation of higher education as advocated by multilateral international organisations such as UNESCO, the Association of African Universities (AAU), International Association of Universities (IAU) and others. For all the reasons already outlined, these agendas are still substantially driven by the North, perpetuating power imbalances and ensuring that countries in the South remain the weaker partners.

The fact that Southern countries, particularly in Africa, lack the 'baseline scientific and research capacities and infrastructure required to collaborate on a more equitable footing with their partners in the developed countries' (Jowi 2012: 51), is well illustrated by the number of scientific and technical journal articles published by academics at African universities (see Tables 7.1 and 7.2). Quite apart from the fact that so many of these journals are published by massive multinational companies based in the North and edited by Northern academics etc., this imbalance clearly highlights the limited impact that North–South research collaborations have on capacity building in the South.

Singh (2010) argued that the prospects of internationalisation yielding increasingly equal partnerships in higher education are bleak. While acknowledging that internationalisation is 'an important policy and strategy for most universities worldwide', even the IAU (2012) has expressed caution about its unintended consequences and tried to alert institutions (particularly in the South) of the need to ensure that its outcomes are positive and bring reciprocal benefits to all concerned. Possible unintended outcomes of internationalisation mentioned by the IAU include: uneven benefits arising from differential access to resources and the entrenching of asymmetrical power relations institutions based (again) on unequal access to the resources and capacities needed to successfully implement internationalisation strategies.

### North–South research collaborations and university development

Roseel et al. (2009) cited the example of the Flemish Inter-University Council-Development Cooperation in a study of how research collaborations form part of broader development programmes. The Flemish organisation supports both institutional co-operation between Belgian universities and selected/nominated universities in the South and research partnerships between individual professors and researchers. Roseel et al. show that, however, in almost all cases, collaborations are initiated by Northern countries and implemented by multilateral development agencies that are based in and effectively controlled by the North.

The concept of development co-operation is, as Alonso and Glennie (2015) observed, synonymous with official development aid. Apparently there are three types of development aid: i) financial (and in–kind) transfers whereby richer countries transfer financial resources and other support; ii) capacity development; and iii) policy development. In reality, 'university development co-operation' occurs within a donor-aid framework, making it much like food aid – where 'development partners' provide both financial and in-kind resources for research (such as books, lab equipment, computers etc.) to recipient countries in the South.

Furthermore, North–South research collaborations can be located in the broader context of international co-operation, whereby multilateral organisations, such as the IDRC, the World Bank, UNESCO, and the OECD, use research co-operation as a mechanism within their broader 'development' strategies. Perhaps especially in this context, 'asymmetry between partners remains the principal obstacle to productive research collaboration' (Bradley 2007: 2, quoted in Nakabugo et al. 2010: 1). In other words, because so many research collaborations depend on external funding, and 'because that funding is equivalent to foreign aid', research collaborations between North and South 'become linked to state-to-state relations' (Samoff and Carrol 2004: 53).

Despite years of advocacy and many calls for equality,[4] Carbonnier and Kontinen have pointed out that 'implementing equitable partnerships is difficult, money flows tend to determine decision making and actual division of labor' (2014: 4–5). As Carbonnier and Kontinen argued, unidirectional funding flows undermine genuine collaborations and partnerships. The donor–recipient relationship embedded in North–South research partnerships

> is clearly connected with the flows of money and is implicitly embedded in power relations. The donor sets the agenda and provides funds to the recipient with a set of rules, accountability mechanisms and an oversight right. (2014: 4–5)

Waardenburg (1997) has done a useful analysis of North–South research collaborations, examining their strengths and weaknesses, as well as the opportunities and threats they face (see Table 7.3).

My aim in the chapter so far has been to expose some of the erroneous assumptions underlying North–South research collaborations, namely that they:

- Promote knowledge-production and the sharing of knowledge;
- Pool financial and human resources across national and regional boundaries;
- Give rise to synergies and complementarities among the diverse participants to their mutual benefit (Obamba and Mwema 2009);
- Increase research productivity in Southern research institutions (Ordonez-Matamoros et al. 2011);
- Give researchers in the South access to advanced research facilities (Bradley 2007).

All of these assumptions are questionable. The literature and my own observations show that knowledge production in North–South research collaborations is dominated by Northern researchers via funding

**Table 7.3: An analysis of North–South research collaborations**

| Strengths | Weaknesses or challenges |
|---|---|
| Northern and Southern partners can both benefit if collaborations are mutually negotiated between equals and are based on principles of reciprocity and joint agenda-setting<br>Collaborations remain a reliable instrument for research capacity building in the South | Power asymmetries undermine relationships<br>Lopsided agendas prevent real collaboration<br>Partners have incompatible goals and objectives<br>Long-term perspectives and sustainability are lacking |
| **Opportunities** | **Threats** |
| Increasingly equal and balanced collaborations might emerge<br>People might develop more insight into the challenges facing both North and South | Over-dependence on financial and technical support from Northern donors imperils the sustainability and impact of collaborations, and ultimately undermines higher education in the South |

*Source: Adapted* from Waardenburg (1997: 14)

processes and the consequent agenda setting. Knowledge exchange is very limited because the skill sets of the Northern and Southern researchers are seldom complementary. The dominant mode of knowledge production is via more or less controlled laboratory settings in which Northern research partners and funders define the research problems, methodologies, objectives and deliverables. Also, because the research is so seldom led by the demands of people or nations in the South, it is difficult to determine how relevant the knowledge produced really is.[5] The power asymmetries involved also make it difficult to ascertain the extent to which collaborations promote the pooling of financial and human resources across boundaries or create synergies between participants that benefit both sides.

Furthermore, the claim that North–South research collaborations increase research productivity has been proven wrong by research at the Makerere University, which has received substantial research funding via North–South research programmes over many years. Musiige and Maassen (2015) found that Makerere University's research productivity levels remain low despite the university's status as one of Africa's flagship institutions and the relatively high levels of research funding it has received.[6] Musiige and Maassen identified four factors as responsible for this, which, in my view, apply equally well to many other Southern universities:

- *The nature and source of research funding*. At the time of the study, about 80 per cent of the university's research was donor funded, and the university had little control over what research was funded. In addition, the lack of local funding had created a dependency on donor income and made the university management unable or unwilling to invest in research to the extent necessary to strengthen the institution's research capacity.
- *Individual factors*. Qualifications, rank, ambition, a passion for and an interest in research, the confidence to engage in research and shape research agendas, years of experience, and time, were generally lacking.
- *Organisational factors*. These include research leadership and management, institutional incentives for research (financial and others), and the level of institutional clarity on matters such as

research policies, and the question of research dissemination and publishing in journals that are not open access.

• *The lack of a research culture.* The university has not become a research-oriented organisation despite its strategic plan's emphasis on research and innovation. The university (like many in Africa) remains primarily a teaching institution, where staff focus increasingly on private work to earn extra income. (Musiige and Maassen 2015: 112–113)

Although northern donors and academics often affirm that North–South research collaborations have 'the potential to revitalise African knowledge systems and reinvigorate research capacity in African universities' (Kot 2016: 3), unfortunately, there is little empirical evidence to support this. On the contrary, critical knowledge deficits and research gaps in African universities seem set to ensure that Africa remains 'a peripheral appendage to the global knowledge architecture for years' (Jowi et al. 2013:17).

Jowi et al. have also argued that the persistent deterioration of Africa's fragile higher education infrastructure is severely undermining any remaining capacity for research and knowledge production. However, Ordonez-Matamoros et al. (2011: 1) cite several different studies[7] to present a more optimistic view of North–South research collaborations, albeit in the context of Colombia. They argue that:

Research collaboration is commonly associated with [increased] creativity and scientific productivity, research quality, innovative capacity, and the creation of science and technology human capital, the consolidation of research agendas, the expansion of research areas and disciplines, and ultimately, the development of new or better [research] processes and services.

Ordonez-Matamoros et al. (2011) conclude that international research collaborations can be positively correlated with a research team's productive capacity and their ability to contribute to local knowledge. Whether these findings apply in the African context is debatable. The major limitation that emerges from almost every study on the issue (by both Northern and Southern researchers) is the problem of 'asymmetry' and 'the dominance of the partners in the North' (Gaillard 1994: 31). Nair and Menon (2002) recommend demand-led research as a panacea to this asymmetry and as a means to genuine capacity building in the South.

In the next section I present my own research on the impact of North–South research collaborations in the context of capacity building in state-funded Southern universities.

## Reflections from a Southern perspective

Despite their potential to contribute to enhancing Southern universities' research capacities, North–South collaborations often produce negative or undesired effects. Although difficult to quantify, in my experience North–South research collaborations perpetuate the dependence of Southern universities on the North for funding and Southern academics consequently lose control and ownership of research agendas.

The dependence of Southern higher education institutions on the North for research funds is a result of their own governments' declining investment in research and development, and more generally in higher education. With the possible exception of South Africa, Africa's contributions to the world's research and development budget is low. Bashour (2013) has argued that Africa's total contribution amounts to less than 1 per cent of global investment in research and development, and that scholarly publications from Africa constitute 'a mere 1.5 per cent of total scientific publications'. Bashour attributes Africa's low research output (despite the number of North–South research collaborations) to a lack of research infrastructure, adding that this also has implications for Africa's ability to collaborate and co-operate with other world regions in the fields of science and technology (Bashour 2013).

As UNESCO pointed out, in Africa, 'research and development (R&D) still attracts less public funding than the military, health or education sectors' (UNESCO 2010:1). Low levels of investment by

African governments has compelled (public) universities in Africa to aggressively seek external collaborators to fund research leading to the dominance of externally funded research in public universities (see Figure 7.1 for example). Like donor aid, donor-funded research collabo- rations are not based on the altruism per se of Northern collaborators. They are, *inter-alia,* designed to promote the strategic (and commercial) interests of Northern universities, research centres, and ultimately of the countries and regions in which they are located.

Politicians in Africa and other Southern regions often argue that investment in public universities is low because of the competition for resources with other sectors considered critical for development such as primary and secondary education, health, water and infrastructure.

**Figure 7.1** International and local collaborative research projects at the University of Dar es Salaam's main campus, 2000–2010

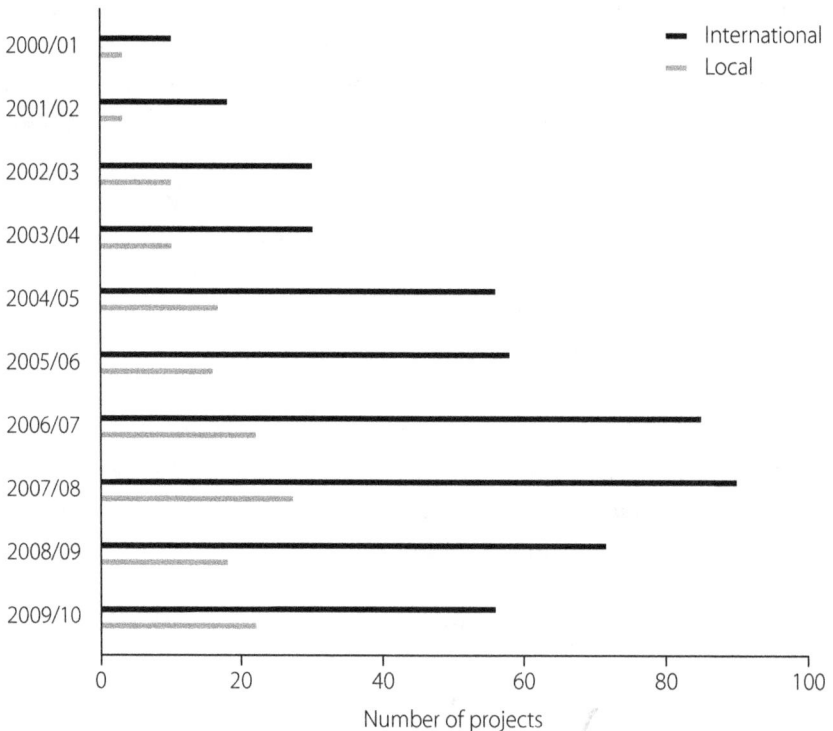

*Data source:* Directorate of Quality Assurance, Makerere University

Universities are also increasingly expected to compete for and generate their own research income. In my experience, policy makers and politicians fail to prioritise higher education because they see it as a 'private good'. For example, in 2010, at the University of Dar es Salaam, research funding suddenly dropped by almost 50 per cent (see Figure 7.1). This decrease happened in tandem with a decline in the number of international research collaborations from 53 to 40 between 2009 and 2011. Although reasons for the decrease are not provided in the data sources, the unsustainable and unpredictable nature of donor-funded research and collaborations might be part of the explanation. The decrease in funding levels might also be related to the fact that the government (the main financial sponsor of the university) only *partially* meets the budgetary requirements of the institution, thus making it impossible for the university to allocate adequate funds to research, thereby reinforcing donor dependence.

Rowlands (2008) and Lancaster (2007, cited in Warmerdam and De Haan 2011: 3) confirmed that commercial interests often influence the ways in which foreign aid policies are formulated. In many cases development assistance functions as an instrument of commercial market expansion and foreign policy. These commercial interests further consolidate and reinforce the growing economic disparities between North and South within which the donor-recipient framework operates.

Illustrating the ever-increasing economic disparity between North and South, Osama (2008) citing UNCSTD (2005) revealed that 86 per cent of the world's GDP, 82 per cent of its export markets, 74 per cent of its telecommunications infrastructure, and 86 per cent of foreign direct investment are controlled by countries that make up just 20 per cent of the world's population, and all of which are located in the North.

Similarly, in the context of universities, Northern institutions dominate and control knowledge production and dissemination. Their dominance derives from 'their huge resources, their role as international centres of innovation, their close relations with funding agencies, and from the intellectual socialisation of Southern decision-makers' (Girvan 2007: 2). Furthermore, as Girvan argued, Northern control over knowledge production creates power imbalances expressed in their dominance in knowledge construction, reproduction and in governance of international institutions, including universities and university ratings agencies.

Given the rise of the so-called knowledge economy, those who control knowledge production also control the world economy. In this context, public universities and other research institutions operate as instruments of state-to-state relations because they are funded by taxpayers' money and therefore have to advance and promote state interests. Despite the best intentions of certain academics and university leaders, Northern universities and research institutions still help to perpetuate the economic exploitation of the South.

## Why North–South research collaborations are still ineffective

### Lack of reciprocity and mutuality

As observed earlier, the donor-recipient framework that dominates the functioning of North–South research collaborations means that far too few collaborations are negotiated between equal partners who all stand to benefit. Certainly, in terms of financial or material resources, Southern 'collaborators' have very little (if anything) to contribute. This often ensures that relations between 'collaborators' are neither reciprocal nor equal. In formulating his theory of power-dependence, Emerson (1962) argued that the power of one organisation or institution over another emanates from its control of resources that are valued by the dependent organisation, and unavailable elsewhere.[8] Conversely, Emerson suggested that when based on equal relations of power, mutual dependencies bring people together; that is, people who are mutually dependent are more likely to form relationships that involve equal exchanges. He also pointed out that inequalities and power imbalances often lead to conflict. The implications of this for North–South research collaborations are obvious and have been discussed by Malatesta and Smith (2014) as well as Ordonez-Matamoros et al. (2011).

## Hidden carrots and sticks

Although not widely acknowledged in the research, my own observations point to the fact that research collaborations, like other forms of aid, come with disguised and entrenched conditionalities that stem from unequal power relations. Such conditionalities are expressed when Northern research funders create methodological rules and accounting procedures for example, or decide on budgetary allocations, and determine the nature of research outputs and the modes through which research findings will be disseminated.[9] These control mechanisms amount to what respondents in Carbonnier and Kontinen's study called the 'unilateral dictation' and 'pre-determination' of research agendas (2014: 10). Research funding often comes laden with conditions (sticks) that have major implications for the ownership of research agendas and research findings. Venner et al. (2009) defined the 'carrot approach' as respectful of the various powers and resources of each collaborator, and as seeking to identify and achieve common goals, while pooling all the available skills and resources. In my experience, such carrots are rarely used in research collaborations: as the English proverb goes: 'the one who pays the piper calls the tune'.

## Mismatched motives

The motives of research collaborators are often different. Of course, many researchers from the North genuinely wish to transfer knowledge and share international best practices with their Southern partners. However, the imperatives of internationalisation, as well as a desire to travel and contribute to development, thereby gaining access to unique data and fieldwork opportunities, undoubtedly also play a role (Bradley 2008b). Southern researchers collaborate for different reasons, and the major one seems to be financial rather than academic. In Africa, researchers often participate in research collaborations as a means of generating additional income and accessing research funds. As Samoff and Carrol (2004: 26) observe:

With low basic salaries, individual researchers are highly motivated to become consultants to the external agencies. The fees for a few weeks of consulting may surpass several months' salary in their home country. Their commissioned research enables them to acquire computers, cars, and cellular telephones, to travel overseas and participate in international meetings, and to escape overcrowded classrooms and empty libraries.

Bradley (2007: 675) adds that 'many Southern researchers enter into partnerships far removed from their own priorities, simply to generate the income required to stay afloat'.

As Osama (2008) pointed out, mismatched motives for collaboration can lead to dysfunctional behaviours and ineffective collaboration. The fact that many Southern researchers don't have or express clear priorities of their own when entering partnerships or research collaborations is a major concern. As Horton et al. (2009: 24) put it:

Although many Southern research organisations are best placed to maximize the benefits of collaboration, many of the organizations entering partnerships lack a clear sense of their own priorities and other key institutional capacities critical to successful agenda negotiation.

Oh the other hand, as Bradley (2007: 679) pointed out:

Although some donors certainly accept independent proposals from both Northern and Southern proponents, even prominent Southern institutions often struggle to secure funding when they compete against well-connected Northern organisations. Consequently, partnerships are a key source of funding for many Southern institutions, because their Northern counterparts are often better placed to secure large grants covering salaries and infrastructure.

Of course, there are exceptions (some of which are described in this volume) in which North–South research collaborations are driven by academic objectives, including capacity building through graduate training or joint publications, that enhance the academic status of all the institutions and individuals involved (Bradley 2008a, 2008b).

## Flawed models of collaboration

In 2005, the Overseas Development Institute (ODI 2005) identified five models of research partnerships along with their advantages and disadvantages (see Table 7.4).

A critical analysis of research collaborations indicates that the first model predominates in North–South research funding. Model 1 tends to exacerbate the power asymmetries referred to throughout this chapter. However, some Northern research institutes and donors adopt a *demand-led research approach* in which researchers and institutions in the South 'are able to bring about their own development with the objective of building up research systems to unleash the potential of the South' (Nair and Menon 2002: 2). Demand-led research approaches have emerged as awareness has grown about the asymmetries between North and South.

In general, this approach aims to generate knowledge that empowers the individuals involved to acquire capacities necessary to make informed development choices (Nair and Menon 2002). For example, all RAWOO-supported research collaborations adopted this approach. Donors from Scandinavian countries, although not applying this demand-led approach exactly, have also been credited as *ideal donors* in that their research funding and official development assistance seems to be far less driven by hegemonic political or commercial interests.

Model 2 is also quite common in African universities. A typical example is the World Bank-funded African Centres of Excellence (ACE) project. Through the Association of African Universities (AAU), the World Bank financed 19 university-based centres of excellence in seven countries in West and Central Africa through a competitive bid system, whereby eligible universities submitted proposals.

**Table 7.4: Dominant models in North–South research relationships**

| Model | Advantages | Disadvantages |
|---|---|---|
| 1. A Southern research institute is appointed and managed by a Northern research institute to carry out research activities as a sub-contractor | None | The Northern research institute has substantial influence over both the research agenda and output quality, often setting tight terms of reference for the research, and linking output and performance to the disbursement of funds |
| 2. A fund managed by a Northern research institute, and accessible by other institutions (including Southern) on the basis of competitive proposals submitted on a series of given research priorities | Competition can enhance research quality | The competitive nature of the bidding process encourages greater influence and domination by the well-resourced Northern research institutes in the research design |
| 3. Franchisees draw on financial resources from a Northern research institute and abide by its quality standards, to conduct research within a 'jointly agreed' work plan and governance structure | The Northern research institute has less influence on how research agendas and activities shift as research programmes unfold | The Northern research institute retains control of output quality, by, for example, quality performance to the disbursement of finances |
| 4. Franchisees choose to adhere to the quality standards of a Northern research institute and draw on financial resources from a third party | The Northern research institute is able to influence the research agenda only in so far as the Southern partners derive value from the (non-financial) competencies and assistance of the Northern partner | None |
| 5. A network of institutions with shared interests and complementary research competencies share information and co-operate when appropriate, but are funded independently and pursue research agendas established by stakeholders within their own country | The Northern research institute is unable to influence output quality | The Northern research institute may retain some influence in the research and uptake methods due to insight provided by the wider network. The Northern research institute may have some control over output quality if it hosts a secretariat offering publication or dissemination services, such as a website for research findings |

*Source:* Adapted from ODI (2005: 2)

This US$150-million project supports recipient universities to promote regional specialisations in areas that address challenges in science, technology, engineering and other related fields deemed critical for Africa's socio-economic development. The project also aims to strengthen the capacities of universities to deliver high-quality training and applied research. Initiated in 2014, the project expanded in 2016 to cover East and southern Africa. Participants include selected public universities from Burundi, Ethiopia, Kenya, Malawi, Mozambique, Tanzania, Uganda, Zambia and Zimbabwe, whose governments have previously been unable to negotiate singly with the World Bank. This project (dubbed ACE II) is co-ordinated by the Inter-University Council of Eastern Africa (IUCEA) and has similar objectives.

Although the World Bank claims that the ACE projects were derived from 'broad consultations' and collaborations with 'participating' African governments, they still operate within a donor–recipient modality in which the World Bank prescribes terms and conditions as well as criteria for eligibility. These are not negotiable and the Bank reserves the right to make a final decision on the participation of institutions, directly or through proxies. The World Bank is the sole donor. The fact that the funding is directed through the International Development Association (IDA) reinforces an argument I made elsewhere that World Bank-funded projects operate within a donor-aid modality (see Ishengoma 2015). The impact of the ACE projects on institutional capacity cannot be determined until the project ends in 2019.

Model 5 also applies to certain North–South research collaborations. One example of this was the Partnership for Higher Education in Africa (PHEA), which ran from 2000 and 2010. This joint initiative by seven US-based foundations (Carnegie, Rockefeller, the Ford Foundation, John D and Catherine T MacArthur, William and Flora Hewlett, Andrew W Mellon and Kresge) generally aimed to revive and revitalise African higher education. PHEA collectively invested about half a billion US$ in 'strengthening African higher education' in nine African countries (Ghana, Egypt, Madagascar, Mozambique, Nigeria, South Africa, Kenya, Tanzania and Uganda) in the following key areas: the use of ICTs; postgraduate training and research; research and analysis of the higher education sector; and developing and retaining the next generation of academics (Lewis et al. 2010).

PHEA ended its operations in January 2010, apparently because of donor fatigue. The Partnership faced a number of constraints revealed by Parker (2010: 30–34) that limited its impact on institutional capacity building. These can be summed up as:

- A lack of clarity about the mission, with clear goals and measurable outcomes;
- Cumbersome decision-making processes;
- The lack of strong co-ordinating structure;
- A lack of data showing the collective impact of the partnership, related to its single broad goal of 'strengthening higher education in Africa' but also because each foundation retained its own internal evaluation and monitoring systems;
- The lack of exit plan.

The lack of an exit plan is surprisingly common in North–South research collaborations in universities and impacts heavily on their long-term sustainability. Similarly, too many North–South research collaborations are set up without measurable outcomes or indicators being established to determine the extent to which they achieve their goals. Given this reality, donor fatigue seems likely to affect the sustainability of similar kinds of donor-funded North–South research collaborations.

One lesson we can learn from this is that Model 5 does not necessarily strengthen capacity in South universities. The PHEA still operated via the donor–recipient framework, in which the US-based foundations' presidents made most of the decisions through their programme officers. Furthermore, evidence from the 2004 and 2008 evaluations of the programme revealed that its engagement with (and therefore the support it received from) African governments and leaders was limited. It is likely that this undermined its impact (Parker 2010).

A model of North–South research collaboration, that is similar to Model 5, but seems to work better, was articulated by UNCTAD (1999) in a report titled, *Making North–South Research Networks Work*. UNCTAD defined research networks as 'voluntary associations of individuals and institutes [in both the North and the South] who share a common interest in exchanging information and in rendering support to advocacy and research programmes' (1999: 5). These associations were then classified into three categories on the basis of the functions they perform:

- Research networks that focus on sharing research information (they organise and facilitate exchange of information, ideas, and research findings among members).
- Research networks that try to co-ordinate research priorities and projects in specific fields (members focus their research on common priority themes).
- Research networks that concentrate on co-ordinating their research policies and strategies, and which pool their resources so that they can be more effective when engaging with international associations and donors.

Although these research networks are also donor-dependent, the usual power asymmetries are less potent because network members tend to meet as professionals and hence as equal partners in specific disciplines. Apart from securing donor funding, research networks are capable of generating their own income through membership fees and other activities. Research networks can be highly empowering of individuals in terms of building research capacity, but their contribution to institutional capacity building tends to be less significant because they essentially operate as social organisations.

Waardenburg (1997, cited in Rosseel et al. 2009: 15) identified another five models of research co-operation (see Table 7.5). In my view, if applied to North–South collaborations, some of these have great potential for empowering researchers in the South.

## The issue of a research culture

Although not well documented, the lack of a solid research culture (attributed to lack of resources as well as solid research competencies and skills) among Southern academics seems to be one of the major

**Table 7.5: Other models for North–South research collaborations**

| Modality | Advantages | Disadvantages |
|---|---|---|
| 1. Financial resources come entirely from the North; agenda setting and implementation is left entirely in the hands of the researchers from the South | Southern researchers own the research agendas and processes | Financial dependency on Northern research institutions which are likely to try to covertly control/influence research through the disbursement of funds |
| 2. Financial resources come from the North and both sides have a say in decision-making but Southern participants have a veto right in agenda setting, research expenditure, etc. | Asymmetry and power imbalance are counteracted | None |
| 3. Funding comes from the North but collaboration is symmetrical, with both sides having an equal say in agenda setting, financing, and management | As per Model 2 | North research institutions retain indirect influence over the research project via their control of funding |
| 4. Financial resources come entirely from and are mainly managed by the North. Collaboration without operational guarantees of symmetry or against the domination of the North partner | None | Power asymmetry with power in the hands of the North |
| 5. Participation of South researchers in research initiated, designed, managed, financed and largely implemented by the North collaborators | Some international research exposure can be gained by the South researchers | Asymmetry and power imbalance, lack of research ownership by the South researchers |

*Source:* Adapted from Waardenburg (1997)

factors that prevent North–South research collaborations from being more effective. As Carbonnier and Kontinen (2014: 14) argue:

> Lack of resources constrains the building of a research culture in developing countries, where leading researchers easily turn into consultants out of necessity and opportunism. Because of low salaries, the professors and researchers will not easily have the research culture found in northern institutions.

Cloete et al. (2011) and Musiige and Maasen (2015) have also acknowledged this problem, and acknowledged that it operates even in so-called flagship African universities.

## Conclusions

Drawing on the discussion above, I offer the following conclusions:

- North–South research collaborations can supplement the capacities and resources of individual researchers and higher education institutions, but are no panacea for capacity building or for the creation and utilisation of knowledge for development. As long as research collaborations remain grounded in a donor-aid framework, the modality of the collaborations will be flawed. In this imbalanced framework 'it is a fallacy to view North–South partnerships simply as exercises in Southern capacity building' (Bradley 2008a: 679). And, as Horton et al. (2009) point out, pervasive donor influence in research agenda-setting is probably not the best way to advance research agendas rooted in the Southern priorities.
- While North–South research collaborations remain overwhelmingly donor-funded and donor-dependent, they will be unsustainable and collapse when donor funding ceases. To an extent, North–South research collaborations perpetuate the dependence of Southern institutions on Northern partners for research funding.
- The factors that motivate academics from both sides of the North–South divide to enter into research collaborations can be so different, even opposing in some cases, as to prevent these relationships from being effective. For example, Northern researchers tend to seek out North–South research collaborations to gain access to unique data and fieldwork opportunities, and to contribute to development. The majority of (if not all) Southern researchers enter such collaborations for financial and other gains, such as access to professional resources and to be eligible for

opportunities such as attending international conferences and training programmes.

- Southern higher education and research institutions also seem to enter research collaborations and partnerships primarily for the financial benefits this offers. As Bradley (2008a: 679) reiterates:

> Partnerships are a key source of funding for many Southern institutions, despite the fact that direct donor support remains their preference. Partnerships may be particularly appealing as a funding avenue for Southern institutions, because their Northern counterparts are better placed to secure large grants covering salaries and infrastructure.

- Despite the plethora of North–South research collaborations between universities and researchers in recent years, the percentage share of world journal publications by researchers based in Southern institutions has not increased dramatically, South Africa being perhaps one exception. Mouton (2010: 3) noted that 'Africa's share of world science as measured by papers published in ISI indexes has been declining steadily over the past decades'. In fact, sub-Saharan Africa's percentage share of publication worldwide decreased from 0.9 per cent in 1980 to 0.4 per cent in 2004.

In closing, I would like to pose the following questions to those who are considering or involved in North–South research collaborations:

- Who *really* benefits from the collaboration and how? In my opinion, the material benefits that accrue to Southern researchers do not necessarily enhance research-capacities.
- Are North–South research collaborations managed democratically and transparently and are responsibilities equally shared between North and South?
- Is the collaboration sustainable after the donor funds are exhausted or when the research project comes to an end? Too often, the answer to this question is obviously, no. Examples abound, particularly in African universities, of research programmes that have been abandoned after funding dries up. The

University of Dar es Salaam's Research and Education for Democracy in Tanzania programme, and the AAU's Respond to HIV/AIDS Project are just two examples.[10]

- Do the Southern partners put monitoring and evaluation mechanisms in place to assess whether the objectives are achieved or not? In my experience, although almost all Southern research institutions have a directorate or a unit that focuses on co-ordinating links and partnerships at an institutional level, very little work is done on how such links and partnerships are implemented in different academic units, or on what effect they have.

## Notes

1    There is little concrete evidence of self-censorship among Southern researchers apart from reports by journalists, but my own observations and experiences indicate that self-censorship occurs where it is thought that this might please donors and thus elicit additional funding and or consultancies.

2    North–South research collaborations are often believed to be ineffective because funds and equipment are allegedly abused or misused by Southern (and especially African researchers), who apparently see such initiatives as opportunities to boost their meagre incomes. The inadequate remuneration of academics and researchers in Africa's public universities is widely documented; see for example Mihyo (2008) and Okello and Lamaro (2015). Samoff (1999) described the 'incentives' that entice African researchers in public universities to misuse or abuse North–South research collaborations, noting that international research grants make it possible for African academics to purchase computers, mobile telephones, access vehicles for site visits and undertake international travel to donor countries to present research findings or engage in consultations. That is, they gain access to all the kinds of 'luxuries' that many researchers in the North see as basic necessities.

3    There have been exceptions to this. For example, in some of the collaborations supported by the Netherlands Development Assistance Research Council (RAWOO), research agendas were determined by the Southern

partners. RAWOO operated on the principle that North–South research collaboration should be based on principles of co-operation and equality and strongly supported demand-driven research that considered locally (Southern) defined research priorities and needs (see Engel and Keijzer 2006). However, RAWOO was disbanded in 2007.

4   See for example, OECD–DAC (1996).

5   I refer here to Nair and Menon (2002: 2), who defined demand-led research as 'activities in which people are able to bring about their own development, with the objective of building up research systems to unleash the potential of the South'.

6   In the context of Musiige and Maassen's study, research productivity was limited to three components: the publication of articles in scholarly journals, presentations made to academic conferences, and the supervision of doctoral students. Researchers cited by Musiige and Maassen, such as Cresswell (1985), measure research productivity in terms of research publications in scientific journals, academic books and book chapters, conference proceedings, the gathering and analysing of original data, obtaining competitive research grants, as well as producing monographs and research reports. The findings of this study were also reported in *University World News*, 6 March 2015 (see Maassen 2015).

7   These include: Beaver (2001); Bozeman and Corley (2004); Bozeman and Lee (2005); Georghiou (1998); Landry et al. (1996); Rigby and Eldler (2005); Rogers (2000); Tsai and Ghoshal (1998).

8   Emerson developed his theory in relation to American businesses but it is now widely used to analyse power and dependence versus interdependence in a range of different organisations. An assumption on which the theory is based is that 'the key to organisational survival is the ability to acquire and maintain resources' (Pfeffer and Salancik, 1978: 2, quoted in Delke 2015: 3).

9   For example, Carbonnier and Kontinen (2014) argue that Northern donors and partners pressurise Southern partners to quickly publish their research outcomes via journals edited in the North.

10  This Tanzanian programme was funded by DANIDA, and the information about the AAU was disclosed to me by their director of Research Programmes at the Conference of Vice-Chancellors, Rectors and Presidents of African Universities held in Kigali, Rwanda in June 2015.

# References

AFRODAD (African Network on Debt and Development) (2007) *A Critical Assessment of Aid Management and Harmonization in Tanzania: A Case Study.* Harare

Ali N, C Hill, A Kennedy and C Ijsselmuien (2006) *What Factors Influence National Health Research Agendas in Low and Middle Income Countries?* Paper 5. Geneva: Council on Health Research for Development

Alonso J and J Glennie (2015) *What is Development Cooperation?* Development Forum Policy Brief, February 2015

Bashour NM (2013) Scant funding for research facilities is hurting Africa. *SciDev. Net*, 17 January. Available online

Baud ISA (2002) North–South partnerships in development research: An institutional approach. *International Journal of Medical and Dental Sciences* 1(3): 153–170

Beaver DD (2001) Reflections on scientific collaboration, (and its study) past, present and future. *Scientometrics* 52: 365–377

Boeren Ad, Tom Alberts, Thomas Alveteg, Erik W Thulstrup and Lena Trojer (2006) *SIDA/SAREC Bilateral Research Cooperation: Lessons Learned.* SIDA Evaluation 06/17. Stockholm

Bozeman B and E Corley (2004) Scientists' collaboration strategies: Implications for scientific and technological human capital. *Research Policy* 33: 599–616

Bozeman B and S Lee (2005, October) The impact of research collaboration on scientific productivity. *Social Studies of Science* 35: 673–702

Bradley M (2008a) On agenda setting: North–South research partnerships and the agenda setting process. *Development in Practice* 18(6): 673–685

Bradley M (2008a) *On the Agenda: North–South Research Partnerships and Agenda-Setting Processes.* Working Paper, International Development Research Centre

Breidlid A (2013) Collaboration in university development: North–South, South–South: A Norwegian case. *Postcolonial Directions in Education* 2(2): 355–380

Carbonnier G and T Kontinen (2014) *North–South Research Partnership: Academia Meets Development?* European Association of Development Research and Training Institutes Policy Paper

Cloete N, T Bailey and P Maasen (2011) *Universities and Economic Development in Africa: Pact, Academic Core and Coordination.* Cape Town: Centre for Higher Education Transformation

Cresswell JW (1985) *Faculty Research Performance: Lessons From The Sciences And The Social Sciences.* Washington, DC: Association for the Study of Higher Education

Dean Laura, Janet Njelesani, Helen Smith and Imelda Bates (2015) Promoting sustainable research partnerships: A mixed-method evaluation of a United Kingdom–Africa capacity-strengthening award scheme. *Health Research Policy and Systems* 13: 81

Delke V (2015) *The Resource Dependence Theory: Assessment and Evaluation as a Contributing Theory for Supply Management.* Faculty of Management and Commerce, University of Twente

Echt L (2014, 26 May) Defining a research agenda: Balancing internal and external influences. *Politics & Ideas.* Available online

Emerson RM (1962) Power dependence relations. *American Sociological Review* 27(1): 31–41

Engel PGH and N Keijzer (2006) *Research Partnerships: Who Decides? Review of a Design Process.* The Hague: RAWOO

Eriksson-Baaz M (2005) *The Paternalism in Partnership. A Postcolonial Reading of Identity in Development Aid.* London: Zed

ESSENCE on Health Research (2014) *Seven Principles for Strengthening Research Capacity in Low- and Middle-Income Countries: Simple Ideas in a Complex World.* Geneva

Gaillard JF (1994) North-South research partnerships: Is collaboration possible between unequal partners? *International Journal of Knowledge Transfer and Utilization* 7(2): 31–63

Georghiou L (1998) Global cooperation in research. *Research Policy* 27: 611–626

Girvan H (2007) Power imbalances and development knowledge. Paper prepared for the Southern Perspectives on Reform of the International Development Architecture Project, North–South Institute

Horton G, G Prain and G Thiele (2009) *Perspectives on Partnerships: A Literature Review.* Working Paper 2009–3, Department for International Development, London

IAU (International Association of Universities) (2012) *Affirming Academic Values in Internationalization of Higher Education: A Call for Action.* Paris

Ishengoma, JM (2007) Internal brain drain and its impact on higher education institutions' capacity building and human resource development in Sub Saharan Africa: The case of Tanzania. In: Association of African Universities *The African Brain Drain: Managing the drain, Working With the Diaspora*. Ghana: AAU

Ishengoma JM (2015) Emerging centres of excellence in Africa and the challenge of their financial sustainability and contribution to excellence in higher education. Paper presented at the Conference of Rectors, Vice-Chancellors and Presidents of African Universities, Kigali, 2–5 June 2015

Ishengoma JM (2016) Strengthening higher education space in Africa through North–South partnerships and links: Myths and realities from Tanzania public universities. *Comparative and International Education* 45(1): Article 3

Jowi JO (2012) Africa responds to internationalization: Redefining the terms of engagement between scholars worldwide. *SARUA Leadership Dialogue Series* 4(2): 49–58

Jowi, JO and M Obamba (2011) *Research and innovation management: Comparative analysis of Ghana, Kenya and Uganda*. Draft Report, Paris: OECD

Jowi JO, M Obamba, C Sehoole, M Barifaijo and G Alabi (2013) *Governance of Higher Education, Research and Innovation in Ghana, Kenya and Uganda*. Paris: OECD

Katz JS and BR Martin (1997) What is research collaboration? *Research Policy* 26: 1–18

Kot, FC (2016) The perceived benefits of international partnerships in Africa: A case study of two public universities in Tanzania and the Democratic Republic of Congo. *Higher Education Policy* 29: 41–61

Lancaster C (2007) *Foreign Aid: Diplomacy, development and domestic politics*. Chicago: University of Chicago Press

Landry R, N Traore and B Godin (1996) An econometric analysis of the effect of collaboration on academic research productivity. *Higher Education* 32: 283–301

Lewis D (1998) Development NGOs and the challenge of partnership: Changing relations between North and South. *Social Policy and Administration* 32(5): 501–512

Lewis SG, J Friedman and J Schoneboom (2010) *Accomplishments of the Partnerships for Higher Education in Africa, 2000–2010*. New York: Carnegie Corporation

Maassen, P (2015 March) Research productivity at flagship African universities. *University World News* 357. Available online

Malatesta, D and GR Smith (2014) Lessons from resource dependence theory for contemporary public and nonprofit management. *Public Administration Review* 74(1): 14–25

Maselli, D, J Andri and J Smid (2004) *Improving Impacts of Research Partnerships*. Berne: Swiss Commission for Research Partnerships with Developing Countries

Mihyo P (2008) *Staff Retention in African Universities and Links with the Diaspora*. Accra: AAU

Mouton J (2010) The state of social science research in sub-Saharan Africa. Background paper prepared for the 2010 World Social Science Report

Musiige G and P Maassen (2015) Faculty perceptions of the factors that influence research productivity at Makerere University. In: N Cloete and P Maassen (eds) *Knowledge Production and Contradictory Functions in African Higher Education*. Cape Town: African Minds

Nair KN and V Menon (2002) *Capacity building for demand-led research: Issues and priorities*. Policy Management Brief No.14, European Centre for Development Policy Management, Maastricht

Nakabugo MG, E Barrett, O McEvoy and R Munk (2010) Best practices in North–South research partnerships in higher education: The Irish African partnership model. *Policy and Practice: A Development Education Review* 10: 89–89

Obamba, MO and JK Mwema (2009) Symmetry and asymmetry: New contours, paradigms, and politics in African partnerships. *Higher Education Policy* 22 (30): 349-372

ODI (Overseas Development Institute) (2005) *North–South Research Partnerships: A Guidance Note on the Partnering Process*. London

OECD–DAC (1996) *Shaping the 21st Century: The Contribution of Development Cooperation*. Paris

Okello NG and G Lamaro (2015) Perceptions on remunerations and turnover intentions in public universities in Uganda. *International Journal of Development Research* 5(1): 3061–3068

Ordonez-Matamoros, G. et al. (2011) *North-South and South-South Collaboration: What Differences Does it Make for Developing Countries? The Case of Colombia*. Research report, Atlanta Conference on Science and Innovation Policy

Osama, A (2008) *Fostering South–South Research Collaborations*. Issues in Brief No. 002, Frederick S Pardee Center for the Study of the Longer-Range Future, Boston

Parker S (2010) *Lessons From a Ten-Year Funder Collaborative: A Case Study Of Partnership for Higher Education in Africa*. New York: PHEA

Pfeffer J and GR Salancik (1978) *The External Control Of Organizations: A Resource Dependence Perspective*. New York: Harper & Row

Rigby J and J Eldler (2005) Peering inside research networks: Some observations on the effects of the intensity of collaboration on the variability of research quality. *Research Policy* 34: 784–794

Rip A (2001) Utilization of research: A sociology of knowledge perspective. In: RAWOO *Utilization of Research for Development Cooperation. Linking Knowledge Production to Development Policy and Practice*. The Hague

Rogers J (2000) Theoretical considerations of collaboration in scientific research. In: S Haugher and C McEnaney (eds) *Strategies for Competitiveness in Academic Research*. Washington, DC: American Association for the Advancement of Science

Rosseel Peter, Erik de Corte, Jan Blommaert and Elke Verniers (2009) *Approaches to North-South, South–South and North–South-South Collaboration: A Policy Document*. Available online

Rowlands D (2008) *Emerging Donors in International Development Assistance: A Synthesis Report*. Ottawa: IDRC

Samoff J (1999) When research becomes consulting: Education research in Africa, the contemporary context. Paper presented at the Annual Meeting of the Comparative and International Education Society, Toronto, 14–18 April

Samoff J and B Carrol (2004) The promise of partnerships and continuities of dependence: External support to higher education in Africa. *African Studies Review* 47(1): 67–199

Singh M (2010) Re-orienting internationalization in African higher education. *Global Societies and Education* 8(2): 269–282

Tsai W and S Ghoshal (1998) Social capital and value creation: The role of intra-firm networks. *Academy of Management Journal* 41: 404–476

UNCSTD (2005) *Panel on Bridging Technology Gaps Within and Between Nations*. Paris

UNCTAD (1999) *Making North–South Research Networks Work*. New York and Geneva

UNESCO (2010) *UNESCO Science Report 2010: The Current Status of Science Around the World*. Paris

Velho L (2002) North–South collaboration and systems of innovation. *International Journal of Technology and Sustainable Development* 1(3): 171

Venner M, C Paulsen and F Gallivan (2009) *Incentive-Based Approaches for Environmental Stewardship*. American Association of State Highway and Transportation Officials. Standing Committee on Environment

Waardenburg G (1997) *Research, Developing Countries and EU-DC Research Cooperation*. Paper presented at a conference on Research Partnerships for Sustainable Development. March, Leiden

Warmerdam W and A de Haan (2011) *The Role of Aid in Politics: Putting China in Perspective, An Annotated Bibliography*. The Hague: International Institute of Social Studies

World Bank (2010) *Financing Higher Education in Africa*. Washington, DC

World Bank (2014) *World Development Indicators*. Washington, DC

CHAPTER

# 8

# Death on campus: Is academic freedom possible for students and academics at the University of Malawi?

*Joe Mlenga*

The *Encyclopaedia Britannica* defines academic freedom as 'the freedom of teachers and students to teach, study and pursue knowledge and research without unreasonable interference from the law, institutional regulations, or public pressure.'[1] Similarly, *Dictionary.com* says academic freedom is, '1. freedom of teachers to discuss or investigate controversial social economic or political problems without interference or penalty from officials, organised groups etc. 2. freedom of a student to explore any field or hold any belief without interference from the teacher.'[2]

Academic freedom can therefore be defined as the freedom and right to teach, learn and research at institutions of education any facet of human life without exception, be it social, political, economic or any other and without impediment from any individual, organisation, or agents of state. However, Shaffer (2007) argued that the principles of academic freedom apply differently to students because they are 'novices under the intellectual tutelage of faculty'. In my view, academic freedom is not for professors alone. Students, too, have the right to engage critically with the prescribed course materials and to be involved in extracurricular activities that enhance their experiences of tertiary education. In addition, both students and academics should be able to contribute to the well-being of a nation by conducting research that has the potential to influence state policy.

The importance of academic freedom cannot be overstated, especially in countries where social, economic and political development is a work-in-progress and where, in many cases, the ruling elite is averse to critique. Malawi is a case in point. Ranked at 173 of 188 on the 2015 Human Development Index, the country is among the poorest in the world (UNDP 2015). Over the years, several of Malawi's political leaders have had wrangles with academics, starting with the founding president Kamuzu Banda who held power from 1961 to 1994 all the way up to the incumbent president, Peter Mutharika. During his term in office, Banda jailed some and forced other academics into exile (see Kerr and Mapanje 2002). In May 2015, Mutharika advised university lecturers to stop commenting on what he called 'trivial issues' and instead do more research. He was reacting to critical comments from some academics on national issues (Nankhonya 2015a, 2015b).[3]

As Chirwa (2015: 14) argued, ties between academics and politicians in Africa tend to be uneasy:

> The history of African universities has been one of a constant tension between the state and higher education institutions, of a relationship of control and dependence that goes back to the very early days of independence … At the same time, seen as breeding grounds for political dissent, independence governments felt obliged to control the agenda and operations of universities.

However, the need to safeguard academic freedom is of particular significance in African countries, not just because the politicians prefer not to hear criticism of their policies, but also because many academic institutions are dependent on state funding. The University of Malawi, for example, is financed through annual government subventions, which have to be approved by parliament. This complicates relations between the government and academics. Although the authorities have not overtly stated that financial support is conditional, many academics practise self-censorship to avoid biting the hand that feeds them.

Considering that universities are meant to be hubs of research and knowledge generation that can help inform state policies, the lack of academic freedom and the suppression of analyses that are critical of the state, are a recipe for national stagnation. Where critical thinking is discouraged, it is difficult to envisage what active citizenship really means. In addition, when academics, who supposedly speak from the apex of the tower of knowledge, are silenced and prevented from being critical of government, the masses, who generally feel far less empowered, are much more likely to remain silent.[4]

## The death of a student

On 24 September 2011, the body of engineering student Robert Chasowa was found lying in a pool of blood at the Polytechnic, a college of the University of Malawi.[5] Chasowa had been politically active as the leader of a group called Youth for Democracy. The group's mission was to help entrench democracy and fight for youth empowerment, and its rise coincided with a downturn in the rule of law and good governance in Malawi. Earlier in that year, then-president, Bingu wa Mutharika,[6] had gone on the warpath against his detractors in civil society, the faith community, academics, the diplomatic corps and the opposition parties.

The Roman Catholic bishops issued a pastoral letter expressing concern about issues of governance and the rule of law, including the maltreatment of then-vice-president, Joyce Banda. The leaders of other large Christian and Muslim groups also wrote letters of protest on a range of issues that were negatively affecting Malawi, while civil-society organisations petitioned the president to repeal certain repressive laws, including those that gave government ministers the power to ban media organisations that the state deemed to be working against the public interest.

Around this time, Malawi was also facing tough economic problems, including fuel and foreign-exchange shortages. Motorists would queue for days or simply abandon their vehicles because of the lack of petrol, and many businesses had to scale down production because there was no fuel and no foreign currency for importing raw materials. Donors, who accounted for 40 per cent of Malawi's budget (Mzale 2015) threatened to freeze aid, raising matters related to human rights, financial prudence and governance. Britain withheld funding, alleging that the Malawian government was squandering money, and citing a US$22 million presidential jet purchased for Bingu wa Mutharika as an example. Germany and Norway, other key financiers, also withdrew aid based on concerns about human-rights abuses and poor governance.

On 26 April 2011, the president made Malawi's predicament worse by expelling the British High Commissioner Fergus Cochrane-Dyet who, in a leaked cable to London, had highlighted Mutharika's growing dictatorial tendencies. The expulsion was a suicidal move, as Britain was Malawi's key donor and was, among other things, propping up the health sector by supplementing doctors' salaries to try to prevent brain drain. In a tit-for-tat move Britain then withdrew funding from Malawi and expelled Malawi's ambassador to the UK. Normal relations were restored and aid resumed only after Joyce Banda replaced Mutharika as president in 2012.

The next key event in 2011 for Bingu wa Mutharika took place on 20 July when civil-society organisations had called for countrywide protests against his rule and these ended with 20 demonstrators being killed by the police. In addition, properties were looted and burned, including several that were connected to the government and ruling party. The president didn't help matters by insinuating that the victims who died were looters and thieves, and calling his critics, including opposition leaders and heads of donor organisations, 'foolish', 'stupid', 'drunkards', and other unsavoury names.

In this repressive atmosphere, Robert Chasowa and some fellow students published a newsletter criticising the president. Soon afterwards, however, Chasowa and his group changed direction in a shift that seems to have led to Chasowa's murder. Further details have been made public in a report produced by a Commission of Enquiry into Robert Chasowa's death (see Chasowa Commission 2012). According to the report:

At that point the focus of the group shifted to working with the government to stop further demonstrations which they had learnt were scheduled for 17th August, 2011. They became more concerned when they learnt that Government was preparing to confront the demonstrators during those demonstrations which would have meant more violence, loss of life and destruction of property. They feared the country would spiral into anarchy. The group then conceived a plan to work with the Police, a Government department which would be directly involved in handling the demonstrations. (Chasowa Commission 2012: 19)

Chasowa and his group apparently made contact with the leaders of the Malawi Police Service, claiming that they could halt the impending protests by talking to students at the University of Malawi and to leaders of civil-society organisations. The police then gave Chasowa and his followers some money to, among other things, rent offices, hire a car and bribe certain protestors. The group were also apparently promised a further large payment of 10 million kwacha (approximately US$60 200 at 2011 values) once it was clear that the protests had died down.

The plan seemed to be working. The group met with some of the protesters and the protests planned for 17 August didn't materialise. The police, however, suspected that Chasowa and his group were being dishonest, and terminated the 'contract' without handing over the final payment. Chasowa was apparently infuriated and again began publishing and distributing anti-government literature.

The regional police headquarters are situated just across the road from the Polytechnic, where police officers planned to arrest Chasowa in connection with the publications. On 23 September 2011, aware that the police were looking for him, Chasowa talked to some college officials about his impending arrest and was advised to surrender in the presence of a lawyer. On 24 September 2011, Chasowa's body was found at the Polytechnic lying in a pool of blood.

The national police spokesperson, Willie Mwaluka, soon appeared on national television, alleging that Chasowa had committed suicide by jumping off a building. Mwaluka went on to read a suicide note purportedly written by Chasowa. However, a post-mortem by Malawi's top pathologist, Dr Charles Dzamalala, showed that Chasowa had been bludgeoned to death. Apparently he was killed elsewhere, and his body was then dumped next to the university building to make it look as if he had jumped to his death.

Eventually, a number of people were arrested in connection with Chasowa's death, including police officers and several of the president's political cronies. By late 2016, however, no one had been convicted. Of the several people arrested, only two have been charged and are facing trial (Kapasule 2016).

For students, the patriarchal or neopatrimonial nature of Malawi society, which operates in various sectors of Malawi society, and especially in political and social settings, prevents them from standing up for academic freedom. Nicknamed the 'bigman syndrome', neo-patrimonialism encourages many officials (especially of political parties) to portray themselves as benefactors and treat ordinary people as lowly beneficiaries of their help. As Lwanda (2006) has argued, neo-patrimonial politics in Malawi has led to young people being dependent on 'bigmen' who offer money and other benefits in exchange for loyalty and to the detriment of democracy in the country.

Indeed, most political violence in Malawi is blamed on youths who, after receiving money and beer, wreak havoc in the lives of anyone their paymasters might see as opponents. Neo-patrimonialism is perhaps an after-effect of the rule of Malawi's first president, Kamuzu Banda, a dictator who ruled Malawi for 30 years. Banda emphasised loyalty, unity, obedience and discipline as the cornerstones of his reign under the Malawi Congress Party.

Chirambo (2004) has argued that Banda spread a type of political hegemony that he called 'Kamuzuism'. That is, Banda presented himself as divinely chosen to rule Malawi for his entire lifetime, and popularised the view that the people of Malawi wanted him to be president so much that anyone who opposed him was against the people. According to Chirambo, social relations and traditions in Malawi reflect the internalisation of 'Kamuzuism' and he cites special songs often performed by women's groups and the Malawi Army's brass band to support his view.[7]

Banda certainly seems to have seen himself as a 'bigman' who was indispensable to Malawians. In his speeches the former president spoke a lot about the importance of respect and obedience towards the authorities. Having ruled for three decades with a tight grip, Banda may have left a legacy of deference to authority that still reverberates in the present, even through the corridors of higher learning. At the University of Malawi, for example, a strict formality is maintained between students and lecturers. The staff must at all times be called 'sir' or 'madam'. This seems to indicate a power balance in which students feel that teachers are superior, know everything and are indispensable; it might well lead to students being overly dependant on lecturers instead of being independently creative, critical and investigative. In this context, it is crucial for students to have the right to engage in activities and express their views about the state, whether these take the form of research, active citizenship or even disseminating information about human rights or other pertinent issues via student media platforms.

## Factors that inhibit academic freedom in Malawi

The University of Malawi's governance system is probably the main factor impinging on the freedom of academics. When a national president takes office in Malawi, they automatically also become the chancellor of the university. Although the university council makes recommendations regarding the appointment of the vice-chancellor and chair of the university council (the institution's highest decision-making body), the president takes the final decision. It is evident then that the institution's senior management team is appointed by the president. In addition, legislation requires the national education ministry to play a supervisory role over the university.

As Mambo et al. (2016: 130) observed, 'This therefore creates a delicate balance between the state and universities when it comes to matters of autonomy. What autonomous rights can institutions claim when directions are given by the state, whose head is simultaneously their Chancellor?' In times of conflict, university managment tend to side with the appointing authority. This has been the case in pay disputes and more publically in a conflict over academic freedom that began in February 2011 and lasted much of that year.

On 12 February 2011, police chief, Peter Mukhito, questioned Blessings Chinsinga, a senior lecturer in the University of Malawi's Department of Political and Administrative Studies, about classroom comments in which Chinsinga seemed to draw parallels between Malawi's acute economic and social problems and the Arab Spring. Lecturers at the Polytechnic and Chancellor College (both part of the university) subsequently withdrew their teaching services in protest at being reported to the police by spies in lecture rooms.

In a saga that rumbled on for eight months, the president (and chancellor) backed the police and castigated university staff. The university council fired Chinsinga and three colleagues whom they saw as 'ring-leaders' in the protests. The courts later reinstated the sacked lecturers, including Chinsinga. It was clear, however, that the university council was doing the bidding of the president, and leaving the teaching staff to rely on court injunctions for protection.

In the end, the president gave some assurances regarding academic freedom. Nevertheless, it remains unusual for academics to openly criticise the president or the ruling elite, which suggests that many prefer to practise self-censorship rather than risk coming into conflict with, or being sanctioned by, the university council. Indeed, since 2011, the assurances made by the president have not been tested in any significant way. Nevertheless, as mentioned, in 2015, he seems to have felt riled enough by academics to remind them to focus on research, rather than comment on 'trivial issues'.

In fact, very little research is conducted on pertinent or controversial issues related to politics or governance at the University of Malawi. This could be because the university's budget is inadequate and no substantial funds are allocated for research. Even attending academic conferences can be a real struggle for teaching staff as college officials say there is no money for such trips.

Staffing levels and working conditions also contribute to low levels of research. The teaching load at the Polytechnic's Department of Journalism and Media Studies, where I teach, is often huge. Some lecturers teach as many as seven different classes a week, spending up to 21 hours in class. When time for lecture preparation and marking, as well as staff and other meetings are factored in, very little time is left for research or any other activities. Several lecturers work after hours and well into the night to manage their workloads.

The legal status of academic freedom in Malawi might also be a barrier. Malawi's constitution contains no clear-cut section that defines or guarantees academic freedom. Instead, academic freedom is included in section 33 alongside freedom of conscience, religion, thought and belief. The importance of academic freedom is also acknowledged in section 44 where it is included in the list of freedoms that cannot be limited, restricted or derogated. The constitution also recognises freedom of opinion and of free speech in sections 34 and 35.

In all likelihood, these factors all combine to create a social and economic fabric at the University of Malawi, and more broadly in society, that effectively limits academic freedom and freedom of speech.

## Comparisons with Nordic institutions of higher learning

Having studied at three Nordic universities, Orebro and Gothenburg in Sweden as well as Tromso in Norway, I have experienced some very different academic environments. My impression is that levels of academic freedom are higher at these institutions in that no overt or covert barriers limit those rights. In addition, order prevailed, university governance was de-linked from state governance, and relations between academic staff and students were less strait-laced.

I saw no implicit or explicit sign that the ruling party or the president interfered with the running of these universities. No Norwegian monarch or Swedish prime minister was the chancellor or rector at any of the institutions. I also studied at Roehampton University in England in 2007, during which time BBC correspondent John Simpson was chancellor. It is doubtful that Simpson would have tried to bring into the university any policies tainted by political partisanship towards the Conservatives or the Labour Party.

The University of Tromso was like an efficient and well-oiled machine. Chaotic struggles between its 2 500 staff or 12 000 students seem almost unimaginable; no strikes, rioting or sit-ins took place while I was there. The university showed discipline, order and focus on its goals. In addition, students observed no formalities in addressing staff. Students and lecturers certainly showed mutual respect for one another, but students were under no obligation to show deference to staff. In other words, no sense of inequality or hierarchy dominated student–staff relations, and a semblance of equality seemed to prevail.

## Repercussions from violations of academic freedom

Perhaps the most obvious consequence arising from the limits placed on academic freedom in Malawi is self-censorship. Academics do not venture to research or analyse areas deemed to be politically sensitive. As already indicated, the president made some statements apparently guaranteeing academic freedom in Malawi in 2012, as long as academics acted 'with responsibility'. From my own observation and reading, no topic serious enough to make the politicians' blood boil and test the strength of academic freedom has been tackled since then. The only exception was when Blessings Chinsinga, the lecturer who triggered the academic-freedom saga in 2012, published some research in 2016 indicating that Malawi's post-democratic era presidents have all been 'accidental' and did not fully deserve to be in power (see Chitsulo 2016). Middle-level politicians close to the ruling elite subsequently ridiculed and criticised his findings through the media, while more senior officials including the president remained silent.

This indicates that some quarters are ready to impinge on academic freedom for the sake of political expedience. As noted, the shadow of political interference looms large because of the university's funding and governance systems. Some academics may well be 'avoiding controversy' (and the attentions of party zealots in their lecture rooms) by choosing to turn away from research areas that might be politically volatile.

Given a campus culture that encourages acquiescence to lecturers, the chances of students producing research or knowledge that is critical of, or challenging to, the status quo in Malawi are minimal. Too many students feel they cannot contribute anything new, are overly dependent on lecturers and wrongly imagine that the academic staff are all-knowing.

Researchers, such as Mambo et al. (2016), have shown how research funding in African universities is determined by the agendas of its funders, including, in some cases, the private sector. This further limits academics, who are lured away from doing research into what they see as local or national priority areas, and persuaded to work on projects of interest to the private sector. This means that the relevance of much of the research itself might be questionable, let alone the 'knowledge' generated from it.

Although lecturers' job descriptions invariably indicate that they must teach, do research, run consultancies and participate in outreach programmes, the university provides neither the time nor the funding for research. The institution's low international ranking indicates that there is little respect internationally for the academic work being done by the University of Malawi, and with lecturers so overburdened with teaching, the university risks falling further down the ladder.[8]

## What must change?

As Mambo et al (2016: 131) say: 'Undue tension creates an environment unconducive for public universities to fulfil their mandates, undermining growth and their ability to become strong and responsive institutions.'

The first priority at the University of Malawi is to address the governance and funding system. The depoliticisation of governance and funding would free the University of Malawi to be more autonomous. Perhaps a concrete step towards this would be to break up the current federal system and make the constituent colleges into individual universities. Mambo et al. (2016) argue that such a move would enhance and speed up decision making. It might also encourage more academic freedom as the president might not be able to act as chancellor to all the delinked colleges, or the colleges could establish rules preventing senior political figures from being appointed to managerial positions.

Financing is also key. If the institution generated more of its own revenue by, for example, increasing fees, and offering more courses, the percentage of funding received from the state would decrease, and academics might feel less obliged to please the authorities. Similarly, collaboration with donors or the private sector in research projects must be undertaken on a more equitable basis so that the funders do not dictate research agendas.

Political will could also help 'free' the University of Malawi. The authorities should take steps to detach themselves from governance of the institution. Realistically, however, the politicians are unlikely to change until steps are taken to review the University of Malawi Act of 2008. If the legislation was re-drafted to ensure a lesser or no role for the president, it would certainly help.

Another matter that causes suspicion and tension is how often top university officials award honorary doctorates to the spouses of presidents.[9] Many wonder why the wives of presidents and of leaders of political parties deserve this honour, and who really proposes their names. It is speculated that there is arm-twisting behind the scenes to ensure that such degrees are awarded, possibly to impress the less-informed that the recipients have either made significant contributions to national development or are very highly educated.

Lecturers have a role to play by making the learning environment more free and responsive to critical and analytical thinking by students. More effort needs to be made to introduce learner- rather than teacher-centred approaches, both in how teaching occurs and how the university is run.

Steps should be taken to promote specialisation among academics. In some departments, lecturers have enough general expertise to teach any course. This is useful in the event of staff shortages but hardly promotes specialist knowledge in a particular field. In my view, this generalism tends to discourage research, as lecturers know a lot but have little specialist knowledge.

Colleges must also prioritise research in hotly contested areas such as academic freedom and political interference in universities.

## Conclusions

Academic freedom is a prerequisite for a vibrant university system that is focused on research, generating new knowledge and solving societal problems. It is important that academic freedom is entrenched not only in theory, but also in practice. The University of Malawi has suffered traumatic events, including the questioning of a lecturer by a police chief and the death of a student activist at the hands of suspected political figures.

Although the Malawian authorities claim to guarantee academic freedom, in practice the concept is not well entrenched. Steps must be taken to depoliticise the running of the University of Malawi so that it enjoys full operational autonomy. A freer environment would help the establishment improve the esteem in which its knowledge and research capacity is held, as reflected in better rankings.

Lecturers and students both have roles to play. Collaborative efforts could help entrench academic freedom in ways that would catalyse and enhance research activities, bearing in mind that it is through research that universities can help address societal problems.

## Notes

1    See www.britannica.com/topic/academic-freedomacademic freedom
2    See www.dictionary.com/browse/academic-freedom
3    Mutharika is Malawi's fifth president since the country achieved independence from Britain in 1964. In response to his advice, senior academic and law professor, Edge Kanyongolo, responded on his Facebook page as follows: 'On my part, may I suggest that presidents should focus on governance – for example, dealing with toxic bank "loans", mustering the courage to go to parliament to answer questions from MPs etc. – instead of wasting time commenting on comments.'

4    The CIA's *World Fact Book* (2015) estimated that 19 percent of males and 31 percent of females in Malawi were illiterate. Literacy levels tend to be especially low in rural areas.

5    The University of Malawi was established in 1965 under a federal system. It has constituent colleges in the southern and central regions of the country. The Polytechnic was originally inclined towards the commerce and engineering sectors; Chancellor College was dominated by the liberal arts. Programmes that do not follow either line of thinking are now run by both of these colleges. Meanwhile, the College of Medicine trains medical doctors, and Kamuzu College of Nursing is for aspiring nurses. Bunda College of Agriculture was delinked from the University of Malawi in 2013 and was merged with other institutions concerned with farming to form the Lilongwe University of Agriculture and Natural Resources.

6    The incumbent, Peter Mutharika, is the younger brother of former president Bingu wa Mutharika. The older Mutharika died in office in 2012. Joyce Banda succeeded him. Peter Mutharika won the general elections in 2014, thereby obtaining a mandate to rule Malawi until 2019 as head of the Democratic Progressive Party that was formed by his late sibling.

7    The army changed its name to the Malawi Defence Force to reflect a change in direction in the aftermath of multi-party democracy that was established in 1994. The police also changed their name from the Malawi Police Force to the Malawi Police Service at the same time. It is ironic that the military chose to retain the word 'Force' in their name, while the police rejected the word on grounds that it implied harshness or brutality, yet it was the police who were noted for overzealousness in carrying out Kamuzu Banda's wishes during his 30-year tyranny.

8    It is interesting to note that, in 2016, the University of Tromso was ranked 461 in the world. The University of Malawi was ranked at number 3 693 on the same list (see Webometrics 2016).

9    In February 2016, Gertrude Mutharika, the wife of the incumbent president, received an honorary doctorate in the Philosophy of Environmental Management, just a year after establishing the Gertrude Mutharika Beautify Malawi Trust. Not surprisingly, several academics and other observers questioned the motives behind the honoris causa.

# References

CIA (2015) Africa: Malawi. In: *The World Fact Book*. Available online

Chasowa Comission, Malawi (2012) Report of the Commission of Inquiry into the Death of the late Robert Chasowa. Available online

Chirambo, R (2004) 'Operation Bwezani': The army, political change and Kamuzu Banda's hegemony in Malawi. *Nordic Journal of African Studies* 13(2): 146–163

Chirwa, D (2015, 6 June) Mutharika's comments on Unima wide off the mark. *Weekend Nation*

Chitsulo, M ( 2016, 18 February) Accidental presidents leading Malawi since 1994. *Daily Times*

Kapasule, W (2016, 31 March) Robert Chasowa case must proceed – Judge. *Malawi Times*. Available online

Kerr D and J Mapanje (2002) Academic freedom and the University of Malawi. *African Studies Review* 45 (2): 73–91

Lwanda, J (2006) Kwacha: The violence of money in Malawi's politics, 1954–2004. *Journal of Southern African Studies* 32(3): 525–544

Mambo, MM, MS Meky, N Tanaka and J Salmi (2016) *Improving Higher Education in Malawi for Competitiveness in the Global Economy*. Washington: World Bank Group

Mzale, D (2015, 13 March) EU plans no budget support for Malawi. *The Nation*

Nankhonya, J (2015a, 1 June) Do more research, APM tells Unima colleges. *The Nation*

Nankhonya, J (2015b, 2 June) APM in trouble: Attracts wrath of academics over research. *The Nation*

Shaffer, FP (2007) *A Guide To Academic Freedom*. City University of New York, Available online

UNDP (2015) *Human Development Index: Briefing note for countries on the 2015 Human Development Report: Malawi*. Geneva. Available online

Webometrics (2016) *Ranking Web of Universities*: Malawi; Norway. Available online (accessed 23 September 2016)

CHAPTER
# 9

# The crisis of higher education in Sudan with special reference to the University of Khartoum, 1956–2014

*Fadwa Taha and Anders Bjørkelo*

In this chapter, we focus on higher education in Sudan, directing attention to the internal political and ideological factors that have shaped its
development and the crisis it is facing. Our focus is on the history of
the University of Khartoum since it was founded in 1956. We describe
how the political regimes that have held power, and the legislation they
enacted from the mid 1950s to 2014, have impacted on the university's
independence and integrity, as well as on its attitudes to academic
freedom and North–South collaboration. Although we touch on key
developments from 1899 to 1956, our emphasis is on the period after
June 1989, when the National Islamic Front (NIF) seized power in
Sudan through a military coup d'état.[1]

Zain Ibrahim (2002: 134, 138) identified three models relevant to
university governance in Sudan, which he called: the 'control or military
model', the 'autonomy model' and the 'ideological commitment model'.
The period we focus on has witnessed the implementation of all three
models, with each one clearly related to the nature of different regimes.
While we acknowledge that no form of governance is ideologically
neutral, these models help summarise what each regime saw as the
primary role of higher education, and form our basic tool of analysis.

Essentially, the University of Khartoum was founded in 1956, within the framework of an autonomy model. The control or military model became dominant after the country's first military regime took over, and ruled from November 1958 to October 1964. From October 1964 to May 1969, democracy was restored, and the autonomy model was re-introduced. After a second military coup on 25 May 1969,[2] the military rule was reinstated, but this briefly shifted towards the ideological commitment model, until an exclusively military model (albeit with an Islamic orientation) was reverted to, until this regime was overthrown via a popular uprising in April 1985. The autonomy model was briefly dominant again during Sudan's second short period of democracy from 1986 to 1989. However, since the National Islamic Front took power in June 1989, the ideological commitment model has been zealously enforced under the banner of the Inqaz (or Salvation Revolution), which is based on the NIF's strict interpretation of the tenets of Islam.

Our work relies on both primary and secondary sources. However, as El Tom (2006) mentioned, few records or statistics have been published on higher education generally in Sudan. Accordingly, little information is available on the number or qualifications of staff, student enrolment rates or library holdings at the University of Khartoum. Nevertheless, Ibrahim's book, *A Hundred Years of the University of Khartoum 1902–2002: The Making of a University,* is very detailed and has informed much of our chapter. In addition, Ali Abdalla Abbas's paper, 'The political and ideological bases of the trends and policies of the National Islamic Fronts in the sector of higher education in the Sudan', touches on several points that we discuss and remains pertinent, even though it was published in 1998.

The chapter has three main sections. First, we describe the development of the University of Khartoum before 1989. Then we examine the implementation of the Inqaz and its policies of Arabisation and Islamisation, as well as crises that have emerged in Sudan's higher education system since 1989. Finally we briefly touch on the history and current status of academic collaboration between universities in Sudan and various international institutions, before offering some conclusions.

## The University of Khartoum before 1989

### 1899–1956: The birth of a university

The history of modern higher education in Sudan goes back to the era of the Anglo-Egyptian Condominium, which administered the country between 1899 and 1956. The University of Khartoum's predecessor, the so-called mother of higher education in Sudan, was established in 1902 as the Gordon Memorial College. At first, this was basically a primary school, but in 1937 the college began offering post-secondary courses. The Gordon Memorial College became the University College of Khartoum in 1951.[3] The period from 1951 to 1956 was a transitional one as the college evolved into a university. According to university calendars published between 1952 and 1954, the institution sought to develop in its students the qualities of mind and character judged necessary for future good citizenship and professional competence. The Act by which the University of Khartoum was established was proposed and drafted by the University College, and the name of the institution was changed to the University of Khartoum in 1956. The university was modelled on British examples, and, for the first few decades, it adopted British curricula and examination systems, and regularly imported teachers and examiners from the UK.

### 1956 to 1958: Autonomy

When Sudan achieved independence in 1956, a brief period of democracy prevailed in Sudan until the end of 1958. In this time, the University of Khartoum adopted the autonomy model. A statutory research committee was established to design research programmes under the supervision of the university senate, and the university was generous in allocating funds to this committee and in giving it wide discretion in many respects (Ibrahim 2002).

Meanwhile the government relied on its own research capacity and did not expect the university to provide it with services in this regard. This gave the university the freedom to design and conduct its own research programmes. The university's financial affairs, and the allocation of government funds, were handled by the Ministry of Finance rather than the Ministry of Education, indicating the importance accorded to the country's only tertiary education institution (Ibrahim 2002). Meanwhile, links with universities in the UK were maintained, and scholarships were given to masters and doctoral students who wished to study abroad.

### 1958 to 1964: The military model

On 17 November 1958, Sudan's armed forces staged a coup d'état, suspended the country's constitution and assumed political power. The military government introduced relatively minor amendments to the University of Khartoum Act. However, they gave the education ministry authority over the university and reduced the size of the university council to guarantee that government representatives would form a majority. No member of staff was denied the right to teach or to do research, and postgraduate training in the UK continued. In addition, staff considered extended debates held at the Students' Union Club as an integral part of the teaching, practical training and preparation for a responsible life offered by their institution (Ibrahim 2002).

In this instance, military rule was relatively short-lived. The first signs of resistance came from University of Khartoum students, led by the Students' Union (El Tayeb 1971). The Union organised demonstrations and strikes and opened its doors to critics of military rule in a bid to promote a return to democracy. After two years of confrontations with the students, the military rulers decided to intervene and impose state control over the university (Ibrahim 2002). During this period the institution's external collaborations were allowed to continue because the regime's position on foreign policy was to enhance relations with both the East and the West. The military regime was deposed by a popular uprising on 21 October 1964.

### 1964 to 1969: Autonomy returns

After military rule was brought to an end, the University of Khartoum's autonomy and independence was quickly enshrined in the National

Charter of October 1964 and the University Act of 1956 was reinstated (Council of Ministers 1964). Nevertheless, the academic community remained concerned about academic freedom, so the university's new council formed a sub-committee to revise the Act, with a view to including additional guarantees of university autonomy and academic freedom. The sub-committee's proposals were endorsed in 1968 by the University of Khartoum council (University of Khartoum 1968), but before their recommendations could be turned into law, another military coup took place in May 1969. According to Zaki El-Hassan (n.d.), before the coup,

> an uneasy understanding was observed where universities were allowed to operate 'freely' and their sanctity was observed. Political interference was minimum [sic], and normally covert, and freedoms were allowed to flourish. The appointment and dismissal of staff, appointment to heads and deans, and other decisions were left to the University and its senate and political correctness was not an overt factor in recruitment.

## 1969 to 1985: A military–ideological model

The situation described by El-Hassan stands in stark contrast to how things developed after what became known as the May Regime, led by Jaafar Numayri, took power. Political interference in higher education was clear and political compliance was expected. Political upheavals spilled onto campuses, and staff were dismissed for political reasons. Academics on both the left and the right were purged at different times, 'depending on the prevailing political mode' and Numayri's 'fleeting alliances' (El-Hassan n.d.). On 2 July 1969, barely two months after the coup, the ruling Revolutionary Council appointed itself as the 'custodian of the University'.[4]

Four months later, on 4 November 1969, Numayri set up a ministerial and technical committee to look into the structure, objectives and laws of the University of Khartoum with a view to making it participate effectively in the national drive for socialist transformation (Ibrahim 2002). In a statement about the establishment of this committee, Numayri stated that the university in a socialist state 'is destined to play a vanguard role as a nursing home for socialist leaders and progressive thinkers,'[5] and that the University of Khartoum should be transformed in ways that would enable it to perform this role. The main feature of this transformation was the orientation of the university's educational activities towards socialism, pan-Arabism and pan-Africanism. It was evident that the government's aim was to control the university.

The ministerial committee appointed by Numayri decided to divide its work into two major tasks. The first task was to tie the university into the state machinery, which required the urgent drafting of a new Act. Accordingly, the University of Khartoum Act of 1970 gave the state tighter control over the university. The new Act also decreed that one of the university's primary objectives would be to organise, extend and improve university education with special emphasis on subjects and activities that were of direct relevance to the needs of the people of the Sudan, and to their aspirations for socialism, national unity and close ties with Arab and African nations.[6] The second task was to find ways of fully identifying the university with the state. To this end, radical amendments were made to the workings of the university council and senate, and to find ways of bringing the university closer to society (Ibrahim 2002).

The final report and recommendations of the ministerial committee were submitted to Numayri in February 1971.[7] By this time, however, the communists and Arab nationalists had fallen out of favour with Numayri, and lost influence entirely after an aborted military coup in June 1971. This marked the end of the regime's first attempt at imposing an ideological model of governance on the university (Ibrahim 2002).

Meanwhile, the Muslim Brotherhood (which was formed in Egypt in 1949 and had been active in Sudan since 1954) were also opposed to the changes happening at the university. Their relations with the state became strained early in January 1970 when they protested against the dismissal of university lecturers known for their Islamic leanings.[8] At that time, the Brotherhood held 19 of the 40 seats in the Student Union, and the Union's president was a Brotherhood member.[9]

Amidst these upheavals, the university's vice-chancellor established another committee composed of the deans of all the faculties to draft another new university Act. The University of Khartoum Act of 1973 was then adopted (Ibrahim 2002). Although support for socialism, pan-Africanism and pan-Arabism was removed from this Act, it was never really implemented because both the Act and the regime encountered severe opposition. Members of the Muslim Brotherhood organised strong demonstrations against the May Regime on 19 August 1973,[10] and the government responded harshly, not only towards the students but towards the university and the higher education system as a whole (Ibrahim 2002). Three-hundred students from the University of Khartoum were expelled, 90 of them permanently. Some lecturers, members of the Muslim Brotherhood were also dismissed. The University of Khartoum was closed for more than three months and the Students Union was dissolved.[11]

Numayri then formed a committee to define the role of higher education in Sudan.[12] A new Act was adopted in 1975, under which the University of Khartoum was defined as a centre of learning that had to perform its functions within the limits of the national constitution and state policy. Under the new Act, the chairperson of the University Council was to be appointed by the president of Sudan in consultation with the chairperson of the Higher Education Council. The university's vice-chancellor and deputy vice-chancellor were also to be appointed by the president. The university was thus transformed into an organ of the state.

The 1975 University Act was promulgated along with the Higher Education Act of 1975. The two Acts covered the higher education system as a whole, and worked together to curtail academic freedom in all universities, including the new University of Gezira which was established in 1975 and the University of Juba in South Sudan which opened in 1977. Seen as a hub of political opposition, the University of Khartoum was often a primary target of the regime. While few of the previous University of Khartoum Acts had lasted, the 1975 Act remained in force for a full ten years, much to the detriment of the university, until a popular uprising eventually toppled Numayri and his regime in April 1985.

To sum up this period, in the 1970s, all universities in Sudan were placed under strict state control. As Numayri's May Regime moved from the left to the centre and then to the right, the military control model replaced the ideological model of university governance. Following a reconciliation between the Muslim Brotherhood and the May Regime in 1977,[13] Sudan's Islamists were integrated into the country's ruling elite, and Islamist students became a dominant grouping on university campuses. According to Abbas (1991), the Muslim Brotherhood, which later became the NIF, knew exactly what they wanted from Numayri: influence over the economy and education. Numayri's decision to introduce sharia law and 'Islamise' the banking system later paved the way for the NIF to take control of certain levers of economic power in the country (Abbas 1991). In fact, as shown below, after a brief respite, the NIF seized the opportunity presented by the need for national reconciliation to impose its ideological model of governance on higher education institutions generally, and the University of Khartoum in particular.

### 1985 to 1989: Autonomy returns

After the May Regime was ousted, national elections were held in 1986, and democracy was briefly reinstated. From 1986 to 1989, Sudan experienced a resurgence of more liberal views on academic freedom and less political interference in the internal workings of the universities.

At its first meeting, the new state's Council of Ministers tabled the 'independence of universities' as a prime agenda item. It resolved that the state should not only respect the autonomy of universities, but should also staunchly guard and protect all their traditional liberties (Abbas 1991). The autonomy model of governance was reintroduced at higher education institutions, and the University of Khartoum's Staff (Faculty) Union pushed for a new Act to be developed to replace the 1975 University Act. In particular, they wanted clauses that infringed on the autonomy of the university, and on freedom of thought and research to be reviewed. A system of elections for the university's top administrative positions was also proposed.

A new University of Khartoum Act was drafted and passed in 1986, turning the university council into a strongly representative body. The vice-chancellor and the deputy vice-chancellor were to be elected by an electoral college, comprised of the council, the senate and the academic staff, with the votes of the council and the senate having a weighting of 30 per cent each, and the staff vote counting 40 per cent.

Three further stipulations were included in the 1986 Act. The first was the redefining of the university as a scientific and cultural organisation. This transcended the crippling provisions of the 1975 Act, which had defined the institution as a centre of learning, performing a function within the limits of the constitution and state policy. The second was the reformulation of the university's objectives such that it was designated as a centre committed to the acquisition, importing and development of learning. The third stipulation related to the independence of the university. Article 6 of the Act clearly stated that 'no police or armed forces are allowed to enter the University precinct for the purpose of or under pretext of effecting orderly behaviour on an accusation of freedom of thinking, scientific research and political action, other than with the permission of the vice-chancellor.'

The democratic inclinations of this period meant that North–South co-operation was approved of in principle, but the Act was in effect for too short a time to allow solid foundations for such co-operation to be laid. However staff-to-staff relationships and co-operation blossomed and flourished at the individual and interdepartmental levels.

## 1989: The turning point for higher education

The brief revival of the autonomy model at the University of Khartoum ended in 1989, when the army and the NIF seized power through yet another coup led by then-brigadier Omar al-Bashir. The new regime installed itself as the Revolutionary Command Council for National Salvation, and announced a highly ambitious political, economic and social programme aimed at transforming Sudanese society under the banner of the Revolution of National Salvation or Inqaz. Still in operation today, this programme has included the transformation of higher education following the principles of the revolution, and motivated by an Islamist ideology (Abbas 1998). In line with this, the state considers centres of learning as incubators for the 'fundamentalisation' of knowledge and has enshrined this in legislation and policy documents. It is important to note that Islamist influence on education policy did not emerge overnight in 1989. It had been on the rise since the 'national reconciliation process' that took place between Numayri and his Islamist political opponents in 1977.

## A new vision for higher education

After a conference on higher education held in Khartoum in 1989, the NIF spelled out their vision in the Higher Education and Scientific Research Act of 1990.[14] The Act introduced various reforms that were widely referred to as the 'higher education revolution' in Sudan, and were designed to Arabicise, Islamise and expand the country's higher education sector in unprecedented ways. As far as the University of Khartoum was concerned, the 1990 Act defined the objectives of the university as 'asserting the identity of the nation' and 'observing religious values'. In an amendment to the Act passed in 1995, these objectives were literally repeated. The Act also confers on the country's head of state the power to appoint the chairperson of the university council, as well as the vice- and deputy vice-chancellors (Ibrahim 2002).[15] The Act also alludes to the strengthening of relations between higher education institutions and the research centres outside Sudan on both regional and international levels, and mentions the need to request aid from different countries and institutions to support higher education and scientific research (Ibrahim 2002).

The aims of the 1990 Act, and the 1995 amendment, can be summarised as follows:

- To embed the higher education system within the Islamic faith, and within Arab and African traditions.

- The Islamisation of knowledge, and the preparation of ideological leaders who believe in God and affirm their faith and their cultural heritage.
- To foster an interest in Arabic, and in religious and cultural studies at all higher education institutions. This includes the adoption of Arabic as the language of teaching and the development of Arabisation programmes in each institution.
- The amendment of higher education legislation to confirm the identity of the nation and its authenticity.
- To establish Islamic studies departments in all university colleges of education.
- To double the number of students admitted to public universities.
- To provide for the establishment of new universities under the banner of a university for each state.
- To encourage the establishment of new private universities and colleges.
- To provide for the conversion of existing colleges and technical institutions into universities.
- To abolish student accommodation and subsistence allowances, and introduce university fees.
- To encourage scientific research and publishing.
- To redirect teaching and research programmes towards the interests and needs of the local environment and local communities.[16]

## Arabisation

The 'higher education revolution' has consistently aimed to change university curricula in Sudan in ways that reflect the core policies of the Inqaz, that is: to promote Islamic and Arabic values and norms.

In effect, an 'Arabic only-policy' was introduced in the early 1990s at all public universities. Some years later, article 3 of Sudan's 1998 Constitution made Arabic the country's official language, but noted that the state would permit the development of local and other world languages.[17] Then, after the Nivasha Agreement between the government and the Sudan Peoples' Liberation Movement, the 2005 Interim

National Constitution upheld both Arabic and English as languages of teaching in higher education.[18] Nevertheless, lectures have to be held in Arabic and Arabic textbooks have to be prescribed as far as possible.

Academic staff were not consulted about the Arabic-only policy and opinion among them is divided, not so much about the principle of using Arabic as a medium of instruction, but about the timing of its introduction and the preparatory work necessary for its effective implementation. The government's approach to the issue has never emphasised the pedagogical arguments commonly advanced by advocates of Arabisation (that students learn better in their own language); nor does the state seem to have reflected on the need to improve the standard of education offered throughout the country, or on the educational and pedagogical challenges involved in this. Instead, the need to inculcate in students the state's version of Sudan's 'culture and traditions' seems to be of paramount importance.

Of course, the use of Arabic as the medium of instruction in higher education was on the agenda at Sudan's older universities well before 1989. In fact, Arabisation was first introduced into secondary schools in 1965, when the then-minister of education decreed that Arabic should be the medium of instruction, noting that, as a matter related to culture and identity, this was considered vital to national sovereignty (Isa 1996).[19] At that time, English was the medium of instruction at the University of Khartoum, and the decree on secondary education was issued without any co-ordination or consultation with university authorities. Consequently, the University of Khartoum was compelled to introduce English as a subject in a preparatory year, to help new students to undertake their university studies in English (Isa 1996). Then, in the early 1980s, the University of Khartoum set up a translation and Arabisation unit. Now a fully-fledged department, this unit has concentrated almost exclusively on teaching translation, not because the members of faculty concerned are averse to Arabisation, but because the university has no clear policy on the issue (*Sudan Update* n.d.).

Arabisation was introduced despite the fact that few textbooks or reference books are available in Arabic (see *Sudan Update* n.d.). In science and technology, especially, almost all the primary academic reference works are in English, and few Arabic translations or equivalents are available.[20] The problem is not so much that teaching has to be conducted in Arabic, but that students have been denied access to English textbooks, thereby reducing their opportunities to learn to read and write in English. This has affected, in turn, research because few postgraduate students are equipped with the English skills they need to be able to grapple with much of the existing research, or with the key reference materials, many of which are available only in English.[21] After some protests, the University of Khartoum's medical faculty was largely exempted from teaching in Arabic, but the humanities faculty, in particular, has suffered from the effects of the Arabisation policy.

## Islamisation

Islamisation has transformed the content of higher education curricula since the early 1990s, with major consequences for universities and society in Sudan. The move towards Islamisation began before the June 1989 coup. In January 1987, the Department of Islamic Studies and Psychology at the University of Khartoum and the Washington-based Institute for Islamic Knowledge held a conference on the Islamisation of knowledge.[22] With the implementation of the Inqaz, two institutes for the Islamisation of knowledge were set up, both in 1991: one at the University of Khartoum and the other at the University of Gezira. Subjects such as Islamic economics and Islamic accounting were introduced, and it became compulsory for students across all disciplines to pass a course on Islamic civilisation.

A department for the Islamisation of knowledge was established within the Ministry of Higher Education, and in May 1995, Ibrahim Ahmed Omar (who was minister of higher education from 1990 to June 1996 and from December 1996 to 2000 and has since been a presidential advisor on higher education) made a statement indicating the government's attitude towards higher education and the centrality of Islamic knowledge. Omar argued that science 'ought to stem from religion in the first place. We want to see the universe as it is described by the Qur'an because the Qur'an's vision is the basis for building Islamic sciences.'[23]

In May 2012, at a conference on the Islamisation of education curricula organised by the National Ribat University in Khartoum, Omar denied that the state had any plans to move away from or deviate from policies of Islamisation and Arabisation (Khalifa 2012). Omar added that Arabisation is crucial for Islamisation because the Qur'an 'as a source of knowledge needs a language that enables its understanding'. At the same conference, the deputy director of Ribat University added that the humanities, as well as the social and applied sciences, must be built on Islamic foundations and be 'entrusted with new purposes' (Khalifa 2012).

Since the 2011 referendum, and the division of the country into Sudan and South Sudan, the government of the north has proceeded further down the Islamist path, intensifying its Arabisation and Islamisation programmes.

## Academic freedom in teaching and research

Academic freedom is integral to the culture of universities in many parts of the world. Like Kilase (2013), we define academic freedom as the liberty and obligation to study, investigate, present and interpret findings, and to discuss facts and ideas concerning people, society, and the physical and biological world in all branches and fields of learning. In our view, the policies pursued under the Inqaz, including Arabisation and Islamisation, violate this definition.

The Dar es Salaam Declaration on Academic Freedom and Social Responsibility of Academics of 1990 defines academic freedom as 'the freedom of members of the academic community, individually or collectively, in the pursuit, development and transmission of knowledge, through research, study, discussion, documentation, production, creation, teaching, lecturing and writing'.[24] As Teferra and Altbach (2004) have noted, ideally, academic freedom ensures that academics are able to teach freely, as well as undertake research, and communicate their findings and ideas, openly and without fear of persecution.

In terms of legislation, article 6 of the University of Khartoum Act of 1995 stipulates that: teaching staff and their assistants, and students 'enjoy freedom of thought and scientific research within the limits imposed by the law and the constitution'; and that 'no Sudanese shall be forbidden to belong to the university, as student or employee, on the basis of belief, race or gender'.[25] Article 25 of Sudan's 1998 Constitution provided for freedom of opinion and expression as long as this was done without prejudicing public order or security.[26] The 2005 Interim Constitution stated that the government would provide for academic freedom within the higher education institutions, and protect the freedom of researchers as long as they complied with the ethical regulations related to research.[27] Thus the only piece of legislation that placed no limitations on freedom of research was the University of Khartoum Act of 1986. Article 6 of that Act states that the university is an independent body enjoying freedom of thought and scientific research.

In his paper, 'Promoting academic freedom in the Sudan: Constitutional daydreams and legal nightmares', Mustafa Babiker (2008) examined the issue of academic freedom and university autonomy in Sudan since 1989. He stressed that the reforms included in the 2005 Interim Constitution never became legal realities. He described the University of Khartoum and Ahfad University for Women as being 'nightmares' as a result of the Inqaz, and noted that there has been no political will to address the deplorable state of affairs that has developed since 1989. He argued that references to academic freedom and university autonomy in the Interim Constitution were simply empty promises that were never meant to be implemented, and pointed out that, since 2005, academic freedom has been severely restricted by several other laws, Acts and amendments to Acts. For example, the constitutional right to register staff associations was severely restricted. In addition, Sudan's police and the security forces have also continually undermined the Interim Constitution by subjecting academics and students to threats of beating, arrest and torture.

As noted, social scientists, who conduct fieldwork among society at large, are subject to tighter controls than natural scientists who conduct research in laboratories on university premises. Babiker (2008) cites stories of undergraduate and postgraduate students attempting to conduct fieldwork for projects or dissertations being denied access to sensitive research sites (such as camps for people displaced by war), or having their questionnaires confiscated by security officers.

In the early years of the Inqaz, academics had little freedom to design their own teaching programmes. Just a month after the 1989 coup, Dr Farouq Mohamed Ibrahim, a biologist in the science faculty at the University of Khartoum, was imprisoned and tortured for 12 days for teaching Darwinian theory. He was told by his captors that the theory of evolution is inherently anti-Islamic. Days after his release, on 20 January 1990, Ibrahim lodged a complaint with the Sudanese president. He drew attention to the fact that the university senate is the only body legally authorised to decide on the content of courses taught and their suitability. On 13 November 2000, Ibrahim sent another letter to the presidency asking for justice and redress in respect of his complaints. When this went unheeded, he lodged a case with Sudan's constitutional court, challenging the legality of the immunity and prescription laws that blocked investigations and prosecutions in his case. The constitutional court dismissed the case on 6 November 2008. On 6 May 2010, Redress, a human rights organisation based in the United Kingdom, lodged an application to the African Commission on Human and Peoples' Rights on behalf of the applicant, alleging a violation of articles 1, 5, 6 and 7 of the African Charter on Human and People's Rights (Redress 2010).

Another example of the limits placed on academic freedom was the intimidation of a professor of veterinary science after he wrote an article for one of Sudan's daily newspapers entitled, 'Rift Valley fever and the prospects for meat and livestock exports'.[28] State security officials considered the article to be potentially damaging to the country's meat export industry and arrested the professor. In another episode, a fatwa was issued by 14 prominent members of the Muslim community, including two University of Khartoum faculty members, decreeing that all members of the leftist students' organisation, the Democratic Front, are 'apostates'. The background to this was an article that appeared on the university campus that some found insulting to Islam (El Tom 2006).

Of the tertiary institutions that have persevered with research in this context, the University of Khartoum has long been the main one. From 1973 to 1999, almost 90 per cent of the research findings published by Sudanese universities emanated from this one institution. And from 2000 to 2004, the Institute for Scientific Information (ISI) recorded a total of 448 publications from Sudanese universities; the University of Khartoum's share of these was 293 publications (66.8 per cent) (El Tom 2006: 81). Nevertheless, the quality of research has deteriorated as access to periodicals and books has become increasingly limited. Funding for resources such as equipment and infrastructure, as well as technical assistance, has also declined. In addition, opportunities for Sudanese academics to communicate with (and take sabbaticals in) other countries have been reduced.

In addition, declining levels of proficiency in English among (especially younger) university staff has drastically diminished their chances of publishing their research in English-language journals. The University of Khartoum's ranking among international research institutions has declined accordingly. However, this means little to a government that takes no interest in international standards or ranking systems.

## Massive increases in student numbers and the growth of new universities

Another reason for the crisis in higher education in Sudan has been the massive increase in student enrolment. Before 1976, the country had three universities: the University of Khartoum, the Omdurman Islamic University (which was founded in 1912 as the Institute of Religious Studies and developed into a full university in 1965) and the University of Cairo's Khartoum Branch, which was founded in 1955. In 1975 and 1977, the University of Gezira and the University of Juba respectively were established to serve the needs of the rural areas in which they were located (El Tom 2006).

Since 1989, Sudan's higher education sector has expanded phenomenally. By 2012, there were 31 public universities, 54 private colleges, 15 technical colleges and 11 private universities – 111 institutions in all (MOHE 2000–2001, 2004, 2005, 2009). Most of the colleges and universities outside Khartoum operate from buildings that had formerly housed high schools (Kilase 2013). According to the International Association of Universities' World Higher Education, the number of higher education students in Sudan rose from 6 080 in 1989 to 38 623 by 2000 – (quoted in Watson et al. 2011: 142). By 2010, this figure had apparently risen to more than 159 000 (MOHE 2009).

Although the expansion of education provision above the secondary level was undoubtedly needed in Sudan, the sudden proliferation of universities in a country that does not have the resources to sustain more than a few universities, has caused the quality of higher education provision to plummet. The opening of new universities, and the increase in student numbers, led to a radical change in the ratio of teachers to students. For example, in 1997, the ratio of teachers to students in the science faculty at the University of Khartoum was as follows: Botany 1:58; Zoology 1:67; Chemistry 1:72; Geology 1:18 (Mohammed and Jiha 1998: 429–431).

Amidst deteriorating working conditions, high inflation and low pay, academics left the universities in droves. Our research indicates that around 1997, an average of 50 University of Khartoum academics were emigrating annually. For the academic year 2004/2005, the number of teaching staff (from assistants to full professors) in all of Sudan's public and private higher education institutions was 9 299. By 2011/2012, this number had decreased to 3 344 (MOHE various). With too few staff to fill new posts, senior (and even junior) officials from the public service have been appointed as lecturers and professors in some of the regional universities (Nyaba 1998). According to Kilase (2013: 183), nearly 26 per cent of faculty members in 2013 were teaching assistants, and only about 40 per cent were lecturers. Both groups generally held masters degrees or less, which means that almost two-thirds of faculty members at university level do not have doctorates.

Supporters of the Inqaz often claim that they expanded higher education in Sudan to meet the needs of the country and enhance its economic development. Yet, the regime's decision to increase student enrolments and to create new universities at a time of dire economic crisis seems to have been designed more to broaden the ruling party's support base, and to increase its share of adherents among future members of the elite, with the aim of eventually controlling professional unions and associations (Abbas 1991). In fact, the expansion of higher education has done nothing to boost employment in Sudan, and has simply meant that many of the people now looking for work are graduates who hold degrees and diplomas. Several of the new universities occupy buildings smaller than a secondary school, the students now have to pay fees, and subsidies for board and lodging are no longer available. Essentially, therefore, the proliferation of higher education institutions, with a new university established in every 'state' in Sudan, has more to do with an attempt to enhance the government's image than with changing economic realities for the country's citizens.

The opening of new universities had a highly negative impact on the University of Khartoum as the country's financial and human resources were redeployed to the new institutions.[29] As Linda Bishai (2008: 203) put it: 'The creation of so many new institutions of higher education resulted in scarcer resources for all, even the country's premier institution and national pride, the University of Khartoum.'

Furthermore, because the University of Khartoum had been a focal point for political opposition over several decades, the state's decision to establish many more public universities and to sanction the development of several new private universities throughout the country, can also be seen as an effort to undermine the university, while introducing a more practically oriented (high-school type) education into the higher education sector. El-Hassan (n.d.) notes that the

> University of Khartoum was, and continues to be, an anathema for the fundamentalists. The university was viewed as the bastion of secularism in the country and its demise and disintegration was viewed to be important for the Islamic Project. Several of the leading fundamentalists made statements to such effect and some of them today are in positions where they can effectively strangle the university.

In fact, the higher education revolution undermined the university in terms of governance, funding and academic freedom. As noted, some staff were arrested and fired, many chose to leave, and others were expected to take up positions at the many new universities. Several departments lost more than three-quarters of their academic staff. Fewer staff and reduced funding led to a deterioration of research capacity; this in turn added to the severe brain drain, making it virtually impossible to maintain academic standards.[30]

## Policy stagnation

As shown, the government of Sudan radically restructured the higher education sector to advance its political programme, giving no consideration to the disastrous consequences this has had for the quality of learning and for the country's economy. Although various government ministers have expressed reservations, these have been quickly silenced and the regime has made no attempt to revise its policy.

The most serious critique of the Inqaz came in August 1998, ten years after it began, when a conference on 'The State and Future of Higher Education in Sudan' was organised by the Association of Sudanese Academics and held in Cairo (see El Tom 1998). The following observations appear in its report on the proceedings:

> A number of decisions were taken including the decisions to double the intake in Sudan's public universities, Arabicise university studies and transform Khartoum Polytechnic into a traditional university. Then other decisions followed. The regime decided to set up a large number of public universities, do away with board and lodging for students at the old public universities, substitute new university Acts for the old ones, force a large number of Sudanese students who were pursuing their studies abroad to come back to Sudan before finishing their studies, allow the private sector to invest in the field of higher education, and force students to enlist in its militia, which is known as the Popular Defence Forces (PDF) and, consequently, to do what it called national service. Furthermore, it decided that students would not get their Sudan School Certificate results or gain access to

> institutions of higher education unless they did their one-
> year stint at the PDF or national services camps or at the
> front in the South ... Some papers presented at the confer-
> ence show clearly that these decisions were motivated by
> political and ideological considerations and that they had lit-
> tle or nothing to do with the welfare of the students or
> Sudan's needs with regard to trained manpower [*sic*]. (El Tom
> 1998: 125)

The conference noted that the government had: completely politicised
the education process; imposed its policy of Islamisation and
Arabisation; rejected the most important values of higher education (as
exemplified by the need to approach knowledge critically, to doubt, and
ask probing questions); encouraged a herd mentality among young
people; and alienated many of the country's best academics (El Tom
1998). Delegates at the conference also pointed out that 'The NIF's
philosophy of education is based on a narrow vision of religion (theol-
ogy) and goes contrary to the essence of modern science' (El Tom 1998:
133).

According to the conference proceedings, the situation at the
University of Khartoum had become alarming enough by 1994 to cause
administrators and students to launch an appeal for rehabilitation,
both inside and outside Sudan. The conference also noted that the
universities of Khartoum, Gezira, Juba and Sudan lost between 41 and
70 per cent of their academic staff between 1989 and 1994. Even government reports showed that the new universities were ill conceived,
poorly funded and terribly understaffed (El Tom 1998).

There is no documentation or literature on student-led criticism or
protests about higher education under the Inqaz.[31] However, since
June 1989, at least 17 students from universities around the country
have paid with their lives for peacefully practising or demanding their
basic rights (Haj-Omar 2014). What is clear is that conditions for students in Sudanese universities have deteriorated dramatically. Although
the University of Khartoum's student union was intensely involved in
overthrowing two dictatorships (in 1964 and 1985), it has not func-
tioned since 2010. Nevertheless, and despite the collapse of their

union, students at the university went on strike in April 2014 in a courageous protest against the murder of a fellow student, and to demand justice and a violence-free campus. The authorities responded by closing the university for five months (Haj-Omar 2014).

Signs of dissent within the state were evident in 1996, when Abdel Wahhab Abdel Rahim was appointed as minister of higher education, and seemed to be quite critical of aspects of the higher education policy. Three committees were formed: one to study the situation at the new universities, another to examine the private universities, and the third to examine state policy on scientific research and identify how it could be enhanced. Rahim then used the recommendations from the three committees to draft a comprehensive report that was critical of many aspects of the higher education revolution. The report was presented to to the National Assembly in December 1996. Rahim was promptly sacked, and the former minister, Ibrahim Ahmed Omar, was reinstated (see El Mubark 2008).

More than a decade later, the then-minister of higher education, Peter Adwok Nyaba, criticised the Inqaz in a statement made to Sudan's daily newspaper *Al-Rayaam* on 20 October 2008. Noting that the revolution had produced 'students of little use', he described the general situation as 'miserable' (see Abu Shouk 2008). In 2011, Nyaba informed the National Assembly that the higher education budget was less than 2.5 per cent of total government expenditure. He emphasised that the disruption of universities was linked to the emigration of university staff, and revealed that 625 staff members had emigrated in 2011, allowing Saudi Arabia's universities to absorb 180 Sudanese university staff in just one month of that year. He noted also, that despite rising living costs, the salaries of staff at public universities had not increased since 2007.[32]

Nevertheless, in 2009, Sudan's Ministry of Higher Education and Scientific Research published a report about its achievements for the period 1989 to 2009, in which not a single reference is made to any disadvantages or shortcomings of the higher education revolution (MOHE 2009). The report does mention that one of the problems with the higher education sector before the Inqaz was meagre resources.

The Inqaz has also affected the schooling sector, and was designed to change the outlook of Sudanese children to encourage them to value their Arab and Muslim identity (Breidlid 2005). This should have meant that the universities would then be able to recruit students who had the 'right' knowledge, values and attitudes, and little interest in politics. As Beny (1998) has noted, however, a good higher education system must be able to rely on policies and plans that help to strengthen primary and secondary schooling.

## International standing

Until the mid 1980s, the University of Khartoum was among the top ten universities in Africa and the Arab world. Since 1989, the institution has been terribly undermined and its international ranking has suffered accordingly. Of course, international organisations rank the world's universities using criteria that may not always be appropriate. Even so, the University of Khartoum's decline is undeniable (Abdel Rahman 2011). Webometrics, for example, measures the quantity of research, scientific and academic information made available via university websites.[33]

Table 9.1 shows selected Webometrics rankings for the University of Khartoum and the Sudan University for Science and Technology. Although some improvement is evident, the rankings are low, and the improvements probably reflect an increase in research being published, rather than increased resources, staffing levels or international

Table 9.1 Rankings of two Sudanese universities for 2008, 2012, 2014 and 2015

| Ranking | 2008 | 2012 | 2014 | 2015 |
|---|---|---|---|---|
| Among African universities | UoK: 41 | UoK: 13 SUST: 24 | UoK: 24 | UoK: 27 SUST: 56 |
| Among Arab states | UoK: 51 | UoK: 11 SUST: 35 | UoK: 20 | UoK: 18 |
| Worldwide | UoK: 6 213 | UoK: 1 216 SUST: 2 517 | UoK: 2 070 | UoK: 1 918 SUST 3 176 |

Note: UoK = University of Khartoum; SUST = Sudan University for Science and Technology
Data source: Webometrics

collaborations. No other Sudanese universities featured in the top hundred Arab or African universities or anywhere in the first 10 000 universities worldwide in the years shown.

## North–South collaboration

From 1956 until the early 1980s, the University of Khartoum sent its junior lecturers abroad to obtain masters and doctoral degrees, and their costs were covered by state funding. During these years, the university enjoyed strong relations with international institutions, and particularly with several British universities. As mentioned, European academics (again, mainly British) were also employed at the university during this time. Others, including anthropologists, archaeologists and historians, often used their holidays to carry out fieldwork in Sudan (Boe 2009). In this way, solid links were established between individual academics and institutions, and Sudanese researchers were often given scholarships by universities abroad. Capacity building was seen as a key element in more formal institutional relationships.

In the case of the University of Bergen in Norway, formal co-operation agreements were set up, and European funding was used to the benefit of both institutions (Boe 2009). From 1976, the two universities launched a number of joint research projects, including the Red Sea Rescue Programme, which was initiated in the 1980s. Relations also developed between the dentistry faculties of the two institutions. Naturally, findings were published jointly where possible (Boe 2009).

This atmosphere of mutual co-operation and trust changed dramatically after 1989. Some Sudanese academics who had been involved in projects with the University of Bergen were removed and replaced, and several staff at the University of Khartoum, who were critical of the new regime, were fired and/or jailed. This made the Norwegian government reluctant to continue supporting projects in Sudan, and in 1991, official collaboration between the University of Bergen and the University of Khartoum came to a halt. Since then, contact has been maintained mainly via academic fellowships and student scholarships, several of which were made possible via Norway's Quota programme (Boe 2009).[34]

Various other Western universities also withdrew from formal co-operation agreements with institutions in Sudan. What remains is limited staff-to-staff and some intra-departmental collaboration. For instance, the anthropology department at the University of Khartoum is involved in two collaborative projects with the University of Bergen's anthropology department.

The first is a project funded by the Norwegian Programme for Capacity Development in Higher Education and Research for Development (NORHED), which began in 2014 and is expected to run until 2018. NORHED brought together the anthropology departments at the universities of Khartoum, Bergen, Addis Ababa (in Ethiopia) and Makerere University (in Uganda). The prject aims to build capacity by providing post-doctoral fellowships, PhD and MA scholarships, and by organising refresher courses for supervisors, student and staff exchanges, as well as national and regional conferences. By early 2016, the project had supported two post-doctoral fellowships (both from Sudan), seven PhDs (four Ugandans and three Ethiopians) and 13 masters students (three Sudanese, five Ugandans and five Ethiopians).[35]

The second project, known as ARUSS (Assisting Regional Universities in Sudan and South Sudan), has created links between the anthropology departments at the University of Khartoum, the University of Bergen, the Chr. Michelsen Institute and the Ahfad University for Women.[36] ARUSS grew out of an earlier project called Micro-Macro Issues in Peace Building, which ran from 2006 to 2012. It organises training for junior staff members at regional universities in Sudan (Kassala, Red Sea, Gedarif, Diling, Blue Nile and Nyala universities), and provides modest funding to help junior and senior academics to conduct research and publish their work. According to the University of Khartoum's Professor Manzoul Assal, who is involved in ARUSS, very little happened between 1989 and 2005 in terms of collaborative projects, although some individual initiatives continued during this period. It was only after the Comprehensive Peace Agreement of 2005 that this began to shift.[37]

Ahfad University for Women is an interesting example of the potential for North–South collaboration. In January 2010, Ahfad University was involved in the Regional Institute of Gender, Diversity, Peace and Rights, funded by the Norwegian Agency for Development Cooperation. The university has partnerships with gender institutes at Makerere University in Uganda and Addis Ababa University in Ethiopia to build capacities in higher education in Africa, and to promote gender equality and human rights in a range of contexts.[38] This point is mentioned here to show that although international collaborations are declining at Sudan's public universities, Ahfad University has stepped into the vacuum and made some gains.

In 1997, the US imposed comprehensive economic, trade and financial sanctions against Sudan, claiming Sudan's support for international terrorism, ongoing efforts to destabilise neighbouring governments, and the prevalence of human rights violations. Since then, Sudan's relations with China have strengthened, but we do not have any reliable data about academic co-operation between Sudan and China.

## Conclusions

Between 1956 and 1989, the University of Khartoum survived a series of legislative and administrative experiments, all related to regime change, few of which had time to take root. Sudan's three military regimes (from 1958 to 1964, from 1969 to 1985 and from 1989 to the present) have all imposed strict controls on the higher education sector, aimed less at improving academic standards than at curtailing and preventing the growth of political opposition. The model of university governance adopted after the 1989 coup was a major turning point for higher education in Sudan. Reforms implemented in the higher education sector since 1989 have been designed to bring tertiary institutions in line with the Islamist ideology adopted by the government, and have done little to improve academic institutions or enhance education levels.

Sudan's experiments with higher education affirm that expansion in the tertiary sector must be done cautiously and gradually. The rapid expansion of the number of higher education institutions and student numbers has resulted in the collapse of existing infrastructure, the use of untrained teaching staff, little staff development and low levels of motivation. While the expansion of higher education was important, and an increase in the number of universities with a fair geographical reach was essential, this should have been carried out after careful study of available resources and the use of sound methods to ensure the most effective deployment of those resources.

For decades, the government has, to a great extent, succeeded in implementing its policy. The crisis in higher education in Sudan is the direct result of a carefully planned policy inspired by Islamist ideology. The government has turned a deaf ear to calls for change, and universities have been forced to comply with state decrees. For universities to function at high levels of excellence, academic staff require the freedom to think, research and teach, while enjoying job security. For much of the period under discussion in this chapter, Islamised knowledge has been taught in Sudan to legitimise the regime and discourage citizens from questioning authority. Unless the University of Khartoum is freed from the state's ideological straitjacket, it cannot be expected to play a leading role in the development of the country.

Research-based knowledge contributes to a deeper understanding of the world around us, of both the physical world and the socio-cultural world; in principle, no area should be excluded from the scrutiny of research. And new knowledge should not be rejected or censored a priori on moral, religious or political grounds. If truth is the goal, then who can decide which truths people should and should not hear? Of course, many regimes around the world, past and present, have been afraid that scientific, historical or political truths will undermine their hold on power. Authoritarian regimes are particularly vulnerable to criticism from the academic community.

In the Republic of Sudan, tension between the universities and the regime have grown since Sudan's independence in 1956. More than once, student demonstrations have contributed to the fall of an unpopular military regime. This is why students and staff are kept under strict surveillance. In this context, the combination of academic freedom and democratic values is seen as politically dangerous.

The Inqaz set about creating a new generation of Sudanese with an Islamist world view. To achieve this, the education system had to change from bottom to top. Secularism in society and in the schools was out. This had many consequences, not least of which was to intensify the conflict between the north and south of the country. The bold project of Islamising knowledge has created severe restrictions on freedom of research and freedom of speech. Islam was made the guiding principle of research and teaching, and because Islam is believed to have already provided many truths, the fields left open to legitimate and serious research have been limited.

What were the practical effects of Islamisation, Arabisation and the other reforms? First, because academic freedom became restricted, and many academics were thrown into jail or just disappeared, many others chose to leave the country – an option that remains relevant today. The loss of nearly half of the professors from the old universities, combined with the rapidly increasing numbers of students, put pressure on the authorities to fill the vacuum. They did this by appointing a small number of professors from other Arab countries, along with many locals who are loyal to the regime, even if they hold no more than a bachelors degree and have no experience of teaching at or administering a university.

Secondly, the value placed on Islamised and Arabised knowledge and research has prevented postgraduate students from consulting much of the Western literature, from obtaining scholarships to Western universities, and from communicating with universities and colleagues at the forefront of research worldwide. In addition, low budgets and a lack of proficiency in English mean that literature and course material that is available only in English is no longer accessible in the public universities. As Nyaba noted, the Arabisation and Islamisation of higher education added another dimension to the downward plunge of education standards, and this has been exacerbated by the acute shortage of textbooks and reference material in Arabic. The exodus of able Sudanese academics to universities abroad is partly attributable to the phenomenal decay in the state of higher education but it has also contributed to that problem (Nyaba 1998).[39]

Thirdly, the reforms have tended to exclude non-Arabic speaking and non-Muslim Sudanese citizens from obtaining a university education. Students are forced to learn classical Arabic (to be able to read the basic academic texts) and in this way, education has become an instrument of identity construction, with Arab–Muslim identity portrayed as the most genuine and the most useful of the many Sudanese identities for anyone wishing to pursue a career. Furthermore, the removal of subsidies (particularly board and lodging) means that many students from lower-income families have been deprived of higher education.

If Sudan's public universities and colleges are to have any hope of functioning effectively and helping to build a knowledge society, they desperately need additional financial and human resources, new infrastructure and organisational restructuring. Wide-ranging reforms are needed in all aspects of academic and student academic life. However, the Inqaz look set to continue to shape Sudan's higher education sector for the foreseeable future, and the road ahead for the country's universities is unlikely to be easy.

## Notes

1   As the bulk of this chapter deals with the period from 1956 to 2014 when Sudan was one country, its separation into two states in 2011 is not covered in any detail. The effects of the war on higher education institutions in Sudan are also not discussed because no higher education institutions were established in areas such as Kordofan, Darfur, eastern Sudan and the northern provinces before the Inqaz higher education revolution. The University of Bahr el Ghazal and the Upper Nile University were established in 1991, and these were temporarily housed in Khartoum.

2   The regime that followed has become known as the May Regime.

3   The change was gazetted in the *Sudan Gazette* No. 833, Supplement No. 1 of August 1951, which brought the University College of Khartoum Ordinance (Ordinance No. 13 of 1951) into effect.

4   Revolutionary Command Council Decree No. 41, University of Khartoum General Archive, National Records Office, Khartoum.

5    Address of the President of the Revolutionary Council on the occasion of the Setting up of the Ministerial and Technical Committee on the Revision of the Structure, the Objectives and the Laws of the University of Khartoum, 1969, p 2. Copy available in the Sudan Library, University of Khartoum.

6    The University of Khartoum Act was Act No. 1 of 1970. See *Sudan Gazette* No. 1093, 15 January 1970, Supplement No. 1, Khartoum.

7    The Final Report and Recommendations of the Ministerial and Technical Committee of the University of Khartoum, February 1971, Khartoum University Press, 1971.

8    Republican Palace Archive (2), 15/3/8, Security Report, 4 January 1970, National Records Office, Khartoum.

9    Republican Palace Archive (2), 16/4/5, Analysis of the Election Results of the University of Khartoum Students' Union, National Records Office, Khartoum. See also Ahmed (n.d.).

10   This was known as the Sha'ban uprising – Sha'ban being the eighth month in the Islamic calendar.

11   Republican Palace Archive (2) 5/4/16, University of Khartoum, General, National Records Office, Khartoum.

12   This was reported in the daily newspaper, *Al Sahafa*, No. 4208, 13 September 1973.

13   For more information on this, see Aloub (2010).

14   The Higher Education and Scientific Research Regulation Act of 1990 (as amended in 1993 and 1995) is available online in Arabic on the Republic of Sudan's government website.

15   It is interesting to note that, in 1991, the chair of the National Council of Higher Education was given to Ibrahim Ahmad 'Umar, a high-ranking and long-standing member of the ruling party, and professor of philosophy at the University of Khartoum. 'Umar later became the minister of higher education.

16   Article 12 of the Higher Education and Scientific Research Act 1990. The Act is available online in Arabic at http://www.moj.gov.sd/content/lawsv4/5/3.htm.

17   The 1998 Constitution of the Republic of Sudan is available online in Arabic at http://www.aproarab.org/Down/Sudan/Dostor.doc

18   Sudan's Interim National Constitution of 2005 is available online.

19   For more on the issue of choosing a national language, see Coombs (1985).

20   By 2009, the University of Khartoum had published only 123 Arabic text-books (Adam 2009); see also *Sudan Update* (nd.).

21   Postgraduate studies have been possible at the University of Khartoum since 1958. In 1972, the university also established a graduate college, to promote postgraduate studies related to national development and to train people in high-level skills.

22   Human Rights Watch 1992: 6.

23   This statement appeared in *Ataseel Magazine*, No. 1 of 1995, which was published by the Administration of Islamization of Knowledge, Ministry of Higher Education and Scientific Research, in Sudan. See also MOHE (2009).

24   On 19 April 1990, 12 delegates from autonomous staff associations of six higher education institutions in Tanzania adopted the Dar es Salaam Declaration on Academic Freedom and Social Responsibility of Academics. The Declaration was formulated at a time when African higher education systems were in a serious, multi-dimensional and long-standing crisis. Chapter 1 of the declaration stated that institutions of higher education should be critical of political repression and violations of human rights.

25   The University of Khartoum Act of 1995 is available online in Arabic at http://www.moj.gov.sd/content/lawsv4/7/5.htm.

26   The Constitution of the Republic of Sudan of 1998 is available online.

27   The Interim National Constitution of the Republic of the Sudan, 2005 is also available online.

28   The article was published in *Al Sahafa* on 10 October 2000 (cited in El Tom 2006: 27).

29   As Isa (1996: 161) points out, this was a repeat of what had happened when Juba University and Gezira University opened in the late 1970s.

30   After the country split in 2011, the universities of Juba, Bahr el Ghazal and the Upper Nile were absorbed into South Sudan. This has had little impact on funding and student numbers in Sudan as these institutions were rela-tively small. In addition, the new University of Bahri has taken the place of Juba University's campus in Khartoum. The establishment of Bahri University reflects the willingness of Sudan's government to absorb aca-demic staff, students, and other employees who wish to transfer from institutions in what is now South Sudan (Kilase 2013).

31   Balsvik (1998) tackled the issue of student protest in Africa but she did not refer specifically to Sudan.

32   This was reported in *Huriyyat Online*, 6 June 2011 . After the separation of Sudan in 2011, Nyaba served as minister of higher education in South Sudan until 2013.

33   For more information, see http://www.webometrics.info/en/Methodology.

34   The Norwegian government's Quota scholarship programme covered expenses for students from collaborating institutions in the South who wanted to study in Norway. Sudan was never excluded from the programme, and the Sudanese institutions that took part in it included the University of Khartoum, the Ahfad University for Women and the Sudan University of Science and Technology. The aim of the programme was to build capacity in the South, so students were encouraged to return home when they had completed their studies. The programme was terminated in 2015, and alternative programmes are now being explored.

35   This information is derived from personal communication with Professor Manzoul Assal, of the Department of Anthropology, University of Khartoum on 6 March 2016. Prof Manzoul is the co-ordinator of the NORHED project. The ARUSS project is co-ordinated by Abdel Ghaffar Mohammed Ahmed, who was also the first Sudanese scholar to obtain a PhD in anthropology from the University of Bergen in 1973.

36   Personal communication with Prof. Manzoul Assal, University of Khartoum, 6 March 2016.

37   Personal communication with Prof. Manzoul Assal, University of Khartoum, 6 March 2016.

38   For information on Afhad University's masters programme on Gender and Governance, see http://www.ahfad.net/index.php/gag.html

39   Interestingly, Nyaba was made minister of higher education in 2005 within the Government of National Unity but, while he made one or two statements that were critical of government policy, he implemented no reforms while he was in office.

# References

Abbas, Ali Abdalla (1991, September/October) The National Islamic Front and the politics of education. *Middle East Report* 172. Available online

Abbas, Ali Abdalla (1998) The political and ideological bases of the trends and policies of the National Islamic Fronts in the sector of higher education in the Sudan. In: Mohamed El Amin Ahmed El Tom (ed.) *Proceedings of the Conference on the State and Future of Higher Education in Sudan*. Cairo: Aramis

Abdel Rahman, Abdel Malik Mohammed (2011) *University of Khartoum Present and Future* (in Arabic). Omdurman: Abdel Karim Mirghani Cultural Centre

Abu Shouk, Ahmed Ibrahim (2008) Higher education in the Sudan: Revolution and Reality (in Arabic). Available online

ACFYS (A College for Yasmine Stigting) (2004) *Jaarverslag 2004* [Annual Report]. Available online

Adam, Bashir Mohammed (2009) *The Contribution of the University of Khartoum to the Arabization of University Books* (in Arabic). Khartoum: Khartoum University Press

Ahmed, Hassan Mekki Mohammed (n.d.) *The Students' Movement Between Yesterday and Today* (in Arabic). Khartoum: Dar al-Fikr

Aloub, Hashim Babikier (2010) National reconciliation in the Sudan 1972–1985 (in Arabic). Masters thesis, University of Khartoum

Babiker, Mustafa (2008) Promoting academic freedom in the Sudan: Constitutional daydreams and legal nightmares. In *Proceedings of the Workshop on Rethinking Academic Freedom in East African Universities*. British Council Ethiopia, Ethiopian Forum for Social Studies, and the Organisation of Social Science Research in Eastern and Southern Africa, Addis Ababa, 21–23 October

Badri, Arena and Lee Burchinal (2004) The Ahfad University for Women: A Sudanese educational experiment. *SlideShare* post. Available online

Balsvik, Randi Rønning (1998) Student protest: University and state in Africa, 1960–1995. *Forum for Development Studies* 2: 301–325

Beny, Ambrose A (1998) Education policies/plans and access to Higher Education in the Sudan. In: Mohamed El Amin Ahmed El Tom (ed.) *Proceedings of the Conference on the State and Future of Higher Education in Sudan*. Cairo: Aramis

Bishai Linda S (2008) *Sudanese Universities as Sites of Social Transformation.* USIP Special Report No. 203, United States Institute of Peace, Washington, DC. Available online

Boe, Marianne (2009) The Bergen–Sudan connection. In: Henriette Hafsaas-Tsakos and Alexandoros Tsakos (eds) *Connecting South and North: Sudan Studies from Bergen in Honour of Mahmoud Salih.* Bergen: BRIC

Breidlid, Anders (2005) Education in the Sudan: The privileging of an Islamic discourse. *Compare* 35(3): 247–263

Coombs, Philip H (1985) *The World Crisis in Education: The View from the Eighties.* Oxford: Oxford University Press

Council of Ministers (1964) The National Charter of the October Revolution (in Arabic). National Records Office, No. 149/11/1 (5), Khartoum

El-Hassan, Zaki (n.d.) Instability of higher education in the Sudan: The effect of Al-Bashir's higher education policies. *Sudan Update.* Available online

El Tayeb, SE (1971) *The Students' Movement in the Sudan.* Khartoum: Khartoum University Press

El Tom, Mohamed el-Amin Ahmed (ed.) (1998) *Proceedings of the Conference on the State and Future of Higher Education in Sudan.* Cairo: Aramis

El Tom Mohamed el-Amin Ahmed (2006) *Higher Education in Sudan: Towards A New Vision for A New Era.* Sudan Currency Press

El-Mubark, Waleed Mohammed (2008, 24 December) The higher education revolution (in Arabic). *Sudanese.com.* Available online

Haj-Omar, Dalia (2014, 23 April) Sudanese university students demand a campus free of violence. *Open Democracy 50.50.* Available online

Human Rights Watch (1992, 7 November) Sudan: Violations of Academic Freedom. *News from Africa Watch.* Available online

Ibrahim, Zain A (2002) *A Hundred Years of the University of Khartoum 1902–2002: The Making of a University.* Khartoum: University of Khartoum Press

Isa, Suad Ibrahim (1996) *The Process of Higher Education in the Sudan 1898–1987* (in Arabic). Khartom: Khartoum Publishing House

Khalifa, Mohammed (2012, 24 May) The Fudamentalisation of Knowledge: Conference report (in Arabic). *Sudaress.com.* Available online

Kilase, Mohamed Eid (2013) Academic freedom and state control on universities: Lessons learned from Sudan experiences. *International Journal of Humanities and Social Science* 3(10): 180–186

Ministerial and Technical Committee (1971) *The Final Report and Recommendations of the Ministerial and Technical Committee of the University of Khartoum*. Khartoum: Khartoum University Press

Mohammed, Buthaina Hamid and Nawal Mohammed Ahmed Jiha (1998) The exodus of university teachers from the Sudan: Reasons and factors. In: Mohamed El Amin Ahmed El Tom (ed.) *Proceedings of the Conference on the State and Future of Higher Education in Sudan*. Cairo: Aramis

MOHE (Ministry of Higher Education and Scientific Research, Sudan) (2000–2001) *Guide to Higher Education Institutions in Sudan*. Khartoum

MOHE (2004) *Guide to Non-Government and Foreign Higher Education Institutions*. Khartoum

MOHE (2005) *Guide to Admission to Higher Education Institutions*. Khartoum

MOHE (2009) *Achievements of the Higher Education Revolution in the Period 1989–2009* (in Arabic). Available online

MOHE (various) *Reports and Statistics*: 2009 to 2015. Available online

Nyaba, Peter Adwok (1998) Politico-ideologisation and regionalization of higher education in the Sudan: A prelude to its destruction and irreversible decay, The case of Juba University. In: Mohamed El Amin Ahmed El Tom (ed.) *Proceedings of the Conference on the State and Future of Higher Education in Sudan*. Cairo: Aramis

Redress (2010, 6 May). Complaint filed by Dr Farouk Mohamed Ibrahim against the state of Sudan. Available online

*Sudan Update* (n.d.) *Report on Education in Sudan: Education and Art*. Available online

Teferra, Damtew and Philip G Altbach (2004) African higher education: Challenges for the 21st century. *Higher Education* 47: 21–50

University of Khartoum (1968) Report of the Sub-Committee of Council for the Revision of the University of Khartoum Act (unpublished)

Watson David, Robert Hollister, Susan E Stroud and Elizabeth Babcock (2011) *The Engaged University: International Perspectives on Civic Engagement*. New York: Routledge

# CHAPTER
# 10

## Knowledge generation through joint research: What can North and South learn from each other?

*Ishtiaq Jamil and Sk Tawfique M Haque*

Contrary to widespread opinion, co-operation between Southern regions is neither novel nor new. Centuries ago, the Egyptian, Arab and Persian empires, the Hindu and Mayan cultures, and the African kingdoms, all had dynamic centres of civilisation. Various kinds of exchanges occurred via the movement of emissaries, students, merchants, explorers and military contingents between these centres of influence. The rise of European imperialism and its expansion undermined these relationships, as the slave trade, mercantilism and capitalism progressively created the basis for contemporary inequalities between South and North. The real divisions between North and South began with the Industrial Revolution and the rise of colonialism, with the subjugation of autarchic units forcing Southern nations into economic, educational and cultural dependency (Greene 1989). So much has been lost in this process.

Contemporary scholars of post-colonial studies often refer to the strong Eurocentrism (or Westcentrism) in mainstream theories of international relations and in social and political theory more generally. Global power hierarchies seem to be stuck in post-Second World War configurations of a modern West and a traditional South. Admittedly, many social science theories originated in the West, but this does not mean that no theorising is done elsewhere. Edward Said's *Orientalism* (1978), for example, is a foundational text for post-colonial studies that exposes patronising Western perceptions of the 'Orient' and other parts of the world.

Although Said's work was published decades ago, paternalistic attitudes and behaviours remain. Many academics in and outside the West are still arguing for the cultural and academic histories of the Middle East, Asia, Latin America and Africa to be properly acknowledged and studied. This kind of inclusivity, however, demands the deconstruction of prevailing discourses about ourselves and others. As Grovogui (2007) suggested, post-colonial discourse on science and knowledge should inform development theory, as well as analyses of international relations and development.

In the twenty-first century, geopolitical shifts away from bipolarity (East–West/Russia–USA) to unipolarity (US hegemony) and multipolarity (many global powers in the East and West, North and South) have occurred. Against this background, while many recipients of development co-operation still criticise the paternalism of donor agencies, power relations and normative orientations are gradually changing. According to Waltz (1990), the old configurations are moving towards a new balance of power, albeit within an anarchic system.

Of course, most of the world's wealthier states still promote their strategic foreign-policy interests through dispensing development aid (which is not necessarily the same as development co-operation) as they attempt to enhance their power and influence in other regions. Co-operation on development issues mainly serves these countries' self-interests on the international stage. Certainly, such power plays remain intrinsic to many North–South and South–South co-operation programmes. Altruistic, normative and morally motivated rhetoric about development abounds but, in the end, co-operation is still primarily a tool of foreign policy (Piefer 2014).

Nevertheless, since the early 2000s, South–South and triangular co-operation are two important and emerging forms of development-aid management that can be quite far removed from the typical 'Northern donor–Southern recipient' model. In 2008, signatories to the Accra Agenda for Action affirmed that:

> South–South co-operation on development aims to observe
> the principle of non-interference in internal affairs, equality
> among developing partners and respect for their independ-
> ence, national sovereignty, cultural diversity and identity
> and local content. It plays an important role in international
> development co-operation and is a valuable complement to
> North–South co-operation.[1]

South–South co-operation allows for an exchange of knowledge and
resources in the political, economic, social, cultural, environmental or
technical domains, between governments, organisations and individuals. It can take place on a bilateral, regional, sub-regional or interregional
basis and can involve two or more countries. Trilateral co-operation
promotes partnerships between various actors including donors, multilateral agencies, public organisations, private sector, academic
institutions and civil society organisations. It does not necessarily
involve just three partners, but rather three groups of actors: donors,
recipients and providers of technical assistance (CUTS 2005).
Triangular or North–South–South co-operation usually involves two or
more low-income countries in collaboration with a third party, typically
a government or organisation in a high-income country that contributes its own knowledge and resources to the exchange (ITUC-CSI 2012).

It is often assumed that Southern researchers benefit most from
North–South partnerships. In fact, Northern academics and research
institutions also need relationships with Southern countries and institutions to facilitate the development of new knowledge. This is
especially true in the fields of natural, medical and social sciences. In
this regard, the local and indigenous knowledges of Southern countries
remain largely ignored and untapped. Research collaborations between
North and South could help unlock some of this knowledge if the challenges facing these kinds of partnerships are overcome, and if Northern
researchers acknowledge that their capacities are often significantly
enhanced through such partnerships. Southern researchers provide
access and hands-on experience that can help Northerners to engage
with different cultural contexts, and adapt their research methods to
unstable or complex conditions (Bradley 2007).

This means that capacity building is not a need experienced by low-income countries alone. In many cases the policies and positions of high-income countries may not be appropriate in other countries because their policies are based on a particular perspective. Increasingly, agencies are beginning to emphasise the need for sensitisation and capacity building in high-income countries to give some perspective to researchers and other stakeholders there. Awareness is finally growing that the kinds of technical and consultancy services provided by actors from high-income countries are not always appropriate to the needs of countries in the South (CUTS 2005).

Similarly, huge gaps exist between universities and research institutions in the North and the South that are related to the very nature of scientific and technological advances (World Bank 2000). Such gaps and inequalities present a major challenge to effective and fruitful collaboration in joint research and knowledge-generation initiatives. The creation of a 'level playing field' for both the partners is essential.

## Objective and research questions

Our objective is to assess the potentials and challenges of knowledge generation through North–South collaboration in the arena of social-science research. The questions we try to address are:

- What are the major constraints and opportunities that impact on the extent to which individual academics and institutions in the South and the North learn from one another?
- Are universities adequately prepared for North–South and South–South collaborations?
- How much does organisational culture and local context matter in research collaboration?

## A brief review of old North–South partnerships

Binka (2005) has noted that, in any relationship between North and South, the Northern partner is usually considered the 'giver' and the

Southern partner the 'receiver', and the benefits that accrue to the North receive little attention. This implies that inequality is inevitable, and that research collaborations are a form of 'scientific colonialism', whereby the Northern collaborators dictate research agendas, method-ologies and budget allocations. Wollfers et al. (1995, cited in Binka 2005) have argued that if Southern partners wish to conduct any research at all, they often have little choice but to accept the priorities and interests of Northern donors.

Although research collaborations have evolved at different times between North and South, control has generally remained in Northern hands. Too often the labour and expertise of Southern researchers is exploited during the data-collection and data-processing phases of research and then results are analysed and published in the North with no acknowledgment of the contributions made by researchers or their institutions in the South.

Binka (2005) has also argued that this trend is changing, and that Northern partners are increasingly showing a willingness to transform what were fairly dubious collaborations into 'true partnerships'. However, a major obstacle to the evolution of 'true partnerships' are the huge gaps that exist between researchers and research institutions in the North and South. The World Bank's Task Force on Higher Education and Society identified some of these as involving: laboratory facilities, equipment and supplies; the availability of well-trained teach-ing staff; the proportion of well-prepared and motivated students; links with the international scientific community; and access to the global stock of up-to-date knowledge (World Bank 2000).

Implicit in these differences is a range of challenges that face poten-tial research partners. These include:

- Unequal power relations whereby the Northern partner is viewed as the 'giver' and expects to have more say in key decisions that need to be made.
- Incompatible goals and different opinions about working methods and processes; this issue is related to conflicting priorities, and often means that Northern agendas and preferences are imposed on the South.

- Conflicting expectations about the longevity and sustainability of research projects.
- Different levels of access to relevant infrastructure and training.
- A lack of clarity about authorship, who controls data, and how research findings will be disseminated, that leaves Southern partners feeling exploited and excluded.
- A scarcity of resources and basic infrastructure in the South that can make projects ineffective.

## Reducing the gaps

The economic and geopolitical might of the North has dominated international relations for a long time. The asymmetries within the global economy are so massive that any meaningful convergence will need considerable effort and could take a very long time. Among scholars and researchers, the divergence is expressed in income levels, research budgets and patterns of specialisation, as well as in structural and institutional conditions. Nevertheless, research collaborations between North and South have the potential to create spaces in which the world's finest minds can work together to help dismantle these imbalances.

New kinds of North–South relationships are moving away from the donor–recipient dynamic into partnerships with shared ownership and decision-making (see Nossum, this volume). Interestingly, many NGOs in the North and the South have already made significant progress in forging new and more equal partnerships, transforming previously unequal relationships with donors into authentic partnerships involving mutual trust and respect, mutual accountability and shared ownership in decision-making. All parties to these relationships have helped to restructure, reskill and renew their organisations to better meet the challenges of engaging with one another on a more equitable footing, and have valuable experience to offer to North–South initiatives in the research arena.

Equal partnerships in scientific collaborations between North and South have always been a challenge. One way to address this is to delegate management and financial responsibilities of projects to the South. This is likely to promote confidence in the South in its own capabilities to learn how to manage a project, while enhancing their confidence that their Northern partners are serious about equality. As described below (and in Nossum, this volume), the Norwegian Programme for Capacity Development in Higher Education and Research for Development (NORHED) has some experience to share in this respect.

## North–South–South research co-operation: Three case studies

In this section, we provide a brief description of three projects as case studies of North–South–South co-operation in knowledge generation and dissemination. The key actors in the North are the Norwegian government (as donor)[2] and the University of Bergen's Department of Administration and Organisation Theory (as the co-ordinating institution). The Southern partners are the Central Department of Public Administration at Tribhuvan University in Nepal, the Department of Political Science and Sociology at North South University in Bangladesh, and the Department of Political Science at the University of Peradeniya in Sri Lanka. The four universities have a longstanding and active relationship that aims to enhance their teaching and research capacities and to contribute to the dissemination of new research-based knowledge.

Tribhuvan University and the University of Bergen began their relationship in 1998, when two graduate students from Nepal enrolled for their MPhil in Public Administration at Bergen under a NORAD-funded fellowship programme. A partnership was established between 2007 and 2011 when a joint PhD programme was established between the two institutions, still in the field of governance and public administration. Under the auspices of this ongoing project, known as 'Governance Matters: Assessing, Diagnosing, and Addressing Challenges of Governance in Nepal', several PhD candidates have graduated, some joint research has been undertaken and some publications have been produced.

From 2008 to 2012, all four institutions were involved in establishing a masters programme in public policy and governance in the Department of Political Science and Sociology at North South University in Bangladesh. Students enrolled in the programme came from Bangladesh, Nepal and Sri Lanka and the majority were junior-level civil servants. These development professionals wrote their theses on issues of policy and governance related to their respective countries. The research-based two-year masters programme draws on some of the teaching and learning methods and aspects of the core curriculum used in the University of Bergen's MPhil degree; some graduates of the Bergen course played a catalyst role in this North–South collaboration.

In 2013, the four institutions launched their 'Policy and Governance Studies in South Asia: Regional Masters and PhD Programme'. The programme aims to strengthen teaching and research capacity in public administration at all the universities involved. Staff at each institution are working together to develop and provide quality education and training researchers to conduct research of an international standard on public policy and governance.

The project has three major components. The first is educational and includes a PhD programme based at Tribhuvan University in Nepal as well as a masters programme based at the North South University in Bangladesh. The second is the promotion of evidence-based research. This is covered by post-doctoral fellowships that involve the conducting of research and surveys in topics such as accountability and trust in public institutions, post-conflict management, multi-level governance and politics, gender in governance and politics, administrative culture, and the role of NGOs in development. The third is about the publication and dissemination of research and knowledge with the aim of improving policy advocacy and extending academic networks and collaborations. The knowledge sharing and joint research, the publication of findings, and the exchange of staff and students are all significant aspects of the ongoing collaboration between these organisations.

Another important feature of their relationship was that the Southern institutions remained independent and assumed management and financial responsibilities. They are therefore empowered to make decisions and set priorities in relation to curriculum content, research topics, and the publication of research findings. The Northern partners acknowledge and value the fact that the local contexts and research priorities of the Southern institutions and countries take precedence, but also that *all* the partners, Northern and Southern, benefit from all the projects.

Between 2007 and 2015, a range of different outputs contributed to knowledge sharing between the institutions and the wider community. A few of the more significant ones are:

- Three PhD candidates graduated and 65 masters students produced theses and graduated;
- The bi-annual *Nepalese Journal of Public Policy and Governance* was renamed the *South Asian Journal of Policy and Governance* under the ongoing partnership;
- Three books, edited by individuals closely associated with the partnership have been published, namely: *Understanding Governance and Public Policy in Bangladesh,* edited by Ishtiaq Jamil, Salahuddin M Aminuzzaman, Steinar Askvik and Sk Tawfique M Haque (North South University, 2011); *In Search of Better Governance in South Asia and Beyond*, edited by Ishtiaq Jamil, Steinar Askvik and  Tek Nath Dhakal (Springer, 2013); and *Governance in South, South East and East Asia: Trends, Issues and Challenges*, edited by Ishtiaq Jamil, Salahuddin M Aminuzzaman and Sk Tawfique M Haque, (Springer, 2015). Many of the contributors to these books were also linked to this partnership programme.
- Four countrywide surveys were conducted in Nepal and Bangladesh on citizens' trust in public institutions and on the idea of a citizens' charter. The survey results have also been published;
- Similar surveys on governance and citizens' trust in public institutions are now ongoing in Bangladesh, Sri Lanka and Nepal;

- Special issues of two international journals have been published, namely: Administrative Culture in Developing and Transitional Countries and Contexts, *International Journal of Public Administration,* (November/December 2013); and Policy and Governance in South and South East Asia, *Public Organisation Review* (December 2013);
- Three international conferences have been convened (two in Kathmandu, Nepal and one in Dhaka, Bangladesh). In total, 120 papers were presented at these conferences, and conference proceedings have been published;
- More than a hundred journal articles, research reports and conference papers have been produced by students and faculty members involved in the programmes from Nepal, Norway, Bangladesh and Sri Lanka;
- Although difficult to quantify, there can be little doubt that the partnership has contributed significantly to expanding the academic community and research networks in the fields of public administration and governance in South Asia and beyond.

## What we have learned

In terms of the preparedness for collaboration, the Southern universities were clearly not as well equipped in terms of infrastructure and has been a drawback. Library and laboratory facilities, access to electronic journals, well-trained researchers and enumerators, as well as the availability and proper use of quantitative and qualitative software, are some of the hurdles that have had to be addressed. One of the Southern institutions' academic and research activities has also been seriously constrained by electricity load-shedding and poor internet access.

Conflict, war and natural calamities have also played a role in obstructing collaboration efforts. The civil wars in Sri Lanka and Nepal, as well as periods of political chaos and unrest in Bangladesh, posed serious threats to the conducting of quality research and data collection. The earthquake in Nepal in 2015 also disrupted academic and research activities.

The level of academic competence and knowledge related to research design and methodology was not at the same level among all the partners. It was a challenge to minimise these gaps and to design research instruments suited to comparative studies across the different countries. In addition, the theoretical and conceptual understandings of Southern academics about research methodology can differ from those of many Northern researchers. Research evidence in the South tends to mostly be derived from historical accounts, secondary sources and observation methods. Many Southern researchers are both less inclined and lack the skills to manage primary quantitative data. These differences can create a level of conceptual mismatch in collaborative research.

The delegation of management and financial responsibilities has been crucial in ensuring that the Southern partners can set their own priorities for educational, research and publication activities. The launching of the MPhil and Bachelor of Public Administration programmes at the Central Department of Public Administration at Tribhuvan University is a testimony to their confidence in running and managing academic activities. Similarly, the hosting of an international seminar on 'Public Sector Human Resource Management in South Asian Countries' at Tribhuvan University in 2016 was an example of a research-related activity initiated by the Southern partners.

### Organisational culture and research context

In relation to the scope for research, as well as the training necessary for knowledge production and dissemination, challenges prevail at both the individual and structural or institutional levels. In Southern institutions, few researchers have the skills and leverage to shift the system from description-based knowledge produced through essay writing to analysis-based knowledge produced through the systematic collection and interrogation of data. In some contexts, legal and/or bureaucratic barriers act to prevent the conducting of evidence-based research. At one of the Southern institutions, for example, one researcher was not permitted to conduct research for a PhD because of state-imposed regulatory and bureaucratic hurdles.

Although the Southern partners are from same geographical region and share much common history and culture, the differences between them are also quite significant. Nepal is one of the most diverse countries in the region in terms of ethnicity, language, caste and religion. Bangladesh is much more homogenous. These differences make comparative studies across the three countries more interesting, while also giving rise to some cultural and contextual difficulties.

Variations in administrative culture between North and South are also interesting. Administration in Southern institutions is strongly based on hierarchy. Symbolism and ritual are seen as important, and relationships between senior and junior academics can be described as following a kind of patron–client model. The working environment in Bergen is very different. The rule-based administrative culture that prevails in Southern institutions does not merge seamlessly with the results or outcomes-based approach of Northern colleagues.

Moreover, the Southern partners tend to take a parallel approach when trying to accommodate different preferences, that is, they pursue a range of interests and arguments simultaneously. Since official and private lives are quite often blurred, this culture of diverse interests being pursued in parallel characterises not only academic life, but almost all activity in the South. This tends to mean that attention and focus can be quite diffused, as several issues are attended to at the same time. In the North, tasks tend to be arranged according to priorities, and tackled in a more linear and sequential way, with time and resources allocated accordingly. Where Northern researchers might see the parallel approach as resulting in tasks being half done or taking too long to reach resolution, Southern researchers tend to see the linear approach as overly simplistic and dismissive of the many social implications and consequences of specific activities.

In addition, North–South collaborations provide a cultural meeting point. For example, a Northern partner will often delegate project rights and responsibilities to one or a few individuals, but the collective culture of the Southern partners makes it difficult for individuals to accept exclusive rights. Because international projects provide access to resources, they confer status and prestige, attract the attention of institutional leaders, and have the potential to eventually be a source of institutional power. Preventing professional jealousy among peers and colleagues is a real concern, and makes the careful inclusion and accom-modation of diverse interests a priority for Southern partners. On the one hand, this ensures that inclusion of a wider range of academics develops their collective commitment and research interests, and even-tually fosters collective capacity building. This benefits the whole institution. On the other hand, if inclusion becomes a goal in itself, it can prevent progress, thus undermining the building of new research capacity and blocking a wide range of other positive outcomes.

For the most part, representatives of all four institutions have decided research agendas consultatively, taking into consideration the research interests and expertise of faculty members and students at each organisation. We suspect, however, that this might be an excep-tion rather than the rule in the majority of international research collaborations.

## Dissemination and publication

Many of the findings from research conducted as a result of the part-nerships described here have been disseminated in the South through local and regional seminars, international conferences, and through publication in journals and books. A range of publications including *South Asian Journal of Policy and Governance* and student theses are available online.[3]

In general terms, the Northern partners have benefited from access to new knowledge generated through joint research and publications, but it is difficult to measure precisely how this knowledge has helped the Northern institutions. The outcome of research and innovation in the natural sciences, engineering and life sciences is universal and beneficial for all. Research in the social sciences seems more culture and context bound – its implications and usage are probably different in different contexts. Social science theories and knowledge developed in the North have filled Southern textbooks and literature for decades. It is still rare to see Southern knowledge and theories discussed in journal articles by Northern scholars or used in teaching and learning materials. The dissemination of new knowledge created through joint academic and research projects remains limited in the North, as journals and publishers remain focused on knowledge production from the North.

## Conclusions

Levels of preparedness in both Northern and Southern universities and higher education institutions are still not equal when it comes to facilitating partnerships in joint research programmes. Organisational culture and local context significantly influence the outcomes of joint research projects. Nevertheless, North South research collaborations offer both opportunities and challenges. Joint initiatives have the potential to gradually improve the preparedness of Southern and Northern institutions as they plan and carry out research together. The inclusion of cultural and contextual realities in research design has the potential to improve the quality of future research and research projects in the social sciences and help advance advocacy efforts related to evidence-based research. Our recommendations are as follows:

- Northern partners need to develop a more accommodating approach to knowledge generation by acknowledging and recognising the importance of indigenous and local knowledge in the South.
- Southern partners (faculty and researchers) need to enhance their methodological skills, while taking local cultural uniqueness into account.
- Faculty members and researchers need to realise that their active engagement in developing clear understandings of project goals plays a significant role in the susutainability of collaborative research projects. Similarly, managers and project leaders need to formulate strategies to address the sustainability and mainstreaming of project goals and activities.

Strong levels of committment, rapport and understanding between and among Southern and Northern partners are crucial for the successful implementation of collaborative research projects. Existing collaborations are developing deep roots and unique features that need to be carried forward by future project leaders. Key resource persons will be important in ensuring that this occurs. In this regard, trust building, mutual respect and close rapport between key persons in the North and in the South are critical for the further advancement of knowledge and capacity building in both regions. Project management and financial responsibilities entrusted to the South are crucial in enhancing their confidence and faith in their own abilities to make sound independent decisions regarding academic, research and publication priorities. At the same time, the support of institutional leaders remains crucial for the success of any long-term collaboration.

## Notes

1   This quote is from Article 19e of the Accra Agenda for Action. The Agenda was endorsed during the third High-Level Forum of government ministers and heads of multilateral and bilateral institutions involved in development. They met in Accra, Ghana, on 4 September 2008 to attempt to accelerate and deepen implementation of the 2005 Paris Declaration on Aid Effectiveness.

2   At different times, Norwegian government funding to higher education and research has been channelled via NOMA (the Norwegian Medicines Agency), NORAD (the Norwegian Agency for Development Cooperation) and NORHED (the Norwegian Programme for Capacity Development in Higher Education and Research for Development).

3   See http://pgs-southasia.org/

## References

Binka F (2005) North–South research collaborations: A move towards a true partnership? *Tropical Medicine and International Health* 10(3): 207–209

Bradley M (2007) *North–South Research Partnerships: Challenges, Responses and Trends: A Literature Review and Annotated Bibliography*. Working Paper 1, IDRC Canadian Partnerships Working Paper Series. Ottawa: IDRC

CUTS (Centre for International Trade, Economics and Environment) (2005) *Trilateral Development Cooperation: An Emerging Trend*. Briefing Paper 1. Jaipur

Greene, JE (1989) Developing centres of excellence through North/South linkages in higher education. *Social and Economic Studies* 38(2): 37–67

Grovogui, SN (2007) Postcolonialism. In: T Dunne, M Kurki and S Smith (eds) *International Relations Theory: Discipline and Diversity*. Oxford: Oxford University Press

ITUC-CSI (International Trade Union Confederation) (2012) What are South–South and Triangular Cooperation? Briefing Note, 3 August. Available online

Piefer N (2014) Triangular cooperation: Bridging South–South and North–South cooperation? Paper prepared for a workshop on South–South Development Cooperation, University of Heidelberg, 26–27 September

Said, E (1978) *Orientalism*. New York: Pantheon

Waltz, KN (1990) Realist theory and neorealist thought. *Journal of International Affairs* 44(1): 21–37

World Bank (2000) *Higher Education in Developing Countries: Peril and Promise*. New York: Task Force on Higher Education and Society

# CHAPTER
# 11

## Into the great wide open:
## Trends and tendencies in university
## collaboration for development

*Jorun Nossum*

I am a development worker in the field of higher education and research. I look at competing and future priorities for development aid. In particular, I focus on the arguments for and against supporting higher education and research. In my work, numerous dilemmas arise in relation to priorities, principles and models of development co-operation. In this chapter, I present some stories, examples and experiences gathered from encounters with university partners and colleagues. I reflect on the recent history of Norwegian support to higher education and research, and build on some of the ideas put forward by Göran Hydén in his chapter.

Hydén's typology of academic collaboration, mostly funded by donors, captures much of what has happened in the past. His chapter also clearly illustrates the contrast between norms that have dominated the higher education sector and what I see as new ways of designing programmes and interventions that aim to support the sector. I explain why the Norwegian Programme for Capacity Development in Higher Education and Research for Development (NORHED), which I discuss in some detail, can be seen as an example of this new way of doing things.[1]

Individual academics, departments, faculties and universities support a multitude of academic networking arrangements across the North–South divide, in ways that tie in with their own strategic priorities. When donors enter this arena to offer support, they often choose to support 'capacity development' programmes. Here, too, a range of different approaches and models apply, depending on whether the programmes aim to strengthen individual, organisational and/or institutional capacities.

The notion of capacity development is widely used, and has been defined as

> the process by which individuals, groups and organisations, institutions and countries develop, enhance and organise their systems, resources and knowledge; all reflected in their abilities, individually and collectively, to perform functions, solve problems and achieve objectives. (OECD 2006: 83)

Today, initiatives and programmes for capacity development in higher education and development-related research projects are included in the priorities of many Northern donors (see Adriansen et al. 2016). Donor support for the higher education sector often relies on the existence or establishment of partnerships between universities in the respective donor and recipient countries. This is certainly how support from Norway to the higher education and research sector has been channelled over the last few decades.

Support for university collaborations, *for the sake of* 'capacity development', takes various forms and, while there is some agreement on what research capacity is, there is little consensus on how it can be improved. Different pathways include supporting scholarships and infrastructure development, establishing centres of excellence, and training senior staff. Initiatives involving scholarly networks and/or academics in the diaspora in processes that aim to improve the quality of research and teaching offer another route with the same goal.

How 'capacity' is conceived often depends on the partners involved, and on the political contexts in which they work. For this reason, I offer a brief reflection on the broader contexts that shape contemporary ideas about capacity development.

## Ideals, experience and knowledge: Essential or elitist?

In 2000, the World Bank (in collaboration with UNESCO) published its report, *Higher Education in Developing Countries: Peril and Promise*, stating that: 'Higher Education is no longer a luxury: it is essential to national social and economic development'. Nevertheless, higher education and research in Africa is often still perceived as a luxury, an elitist project for a privileged few. Thus, what is seen as essential for wealthier societies is viewed as elitist for others.

A story often told about Norway is how investment in knowledge and technology was key to the development of the country's oil and gas sector. When oil was first discovered off the country's coast in the late 1950s, the technical expertise needed to exploit oil and gas deposits was lacking. State policies and priorities were then deliberately developed to ensure that, rather than simply selling fossil fuels to the big oil companies, Norway remained in the driving seat in terms of both ownership and knowledge. An independent oil industry gradually emerged, so one of the world's smaller countries has retained control over its own resources in a sector that is controlled almost everywhere else by huge multinationals.

This illustrates the value of knowledge in the development of natural resources of all kinds. Obtaining knowledge and competence can be about gaining the means to independently define, describe and develop. Why should this be different for poorer countries? Shouldn't every country have opportunities to harness their own natural resources and potentials, and to take ownership of their own development?

Africa's long history of exploitation also makes knowledge development crucial for social, cultural and political change. As the African Union's chairperson, Nkosazana Dlamini-Zuma, stated in her address to the Higher Education Summit in Dakar in 2015: 'Africa needs to develop its own knowledge. Only then can we be completely free.' In my view, this kind of freedom involves countries owning their own histories, defining their own challenges and deploying their own resources and energy for their own development.

## Higher education and development

Since the mid 1990s, Norway's Ministry of Foreign Affairs (working with the country's Ministry of Education and Research) has considered support for higher education and research crucial for development. More recently, higher education and research have regained prominence in the wider development agenda. They are increasingly seen as key drivers of social and economic change, and therefore feature in the list of Sustainable Development Goals (SDGs) adopted in 2015.[2] In fact, many of the SDGs will be achievable only if the higher education and research sector contributes to their realisation, and is transformed by them. That is, curriculum content and research priorities must change, while postgraduate throughput rates must improve so that more people can contribute to knowledge production and innovation.

In 2016, NORAD commissioned a review of the literature on the relationship between higher education and development. The study underlined a key shift in understandings of the sector that occurred in the 1990s:

> The 1990s signalled the start of a big change in the focus of external financing for education. The donors were adopting an economic lens through which they looked at the value of providing financial support to different education sub-sectors. This was influenced by a journal article by a leading World Bank staff member on rates of return to education (Psacharopoulos, 1985) which stated that the economic rates of return to primary education were much higher than those for higher education. (Ndaruhutse and Thompson 2016: 5)

Combined with a strong focus on primary education, and inspired by UNESCO's Jomtien Conference in 1990 where the declaration on Education for All was adopted, the World Bank's rate-of-return analysis influenced both the policies and the budget allocations of donors and governments in many parts of the world. For a decade or more, support for higher education and universities was drastically curtailed. Academics and university leaders have shared experiences and research findings on how cost-benefit thinking shaped education policies at a national level and donor interests internationally, shifting support towards primary education and neglecting higher education and research (see Mahmood Mamdani's chapter in this volume, for example).

This imbalance was also influenced by an atomistic view of education. Competing priorities overshadowed the understanding that the different educational levels depend on and relate to one another in complex ways. As Mamdani noted in a keynote speech made to NORHED's 2016 conference in Oslo:

> In the process, the World Bank lost sight of the big picture: that primary, secondary and higher education are not isolated islands. Key to understanding the significance of each is the relations between them. If you ask the right questions, you will understand that the pivotal link in this three-way relationship is university education: Who will train teachers? Who will produce the curriculum, one that will respond to the needs of society, the demand for citizenship, the need to think of a future in a rapidly changing world?

In the literature review mentioned above, Ndaruhutse and Thompson (2016) described the broader dimensions and impacts of higher education beyond merely its capacity to stimulate economic growth and provide a decent return on investments. Quoting Oketch, McCowan and Schendel's rigorous 2014 report, Ndaruhutse and Thompson (2016: 9) noted that:

> Tertiary education was found to have an important impact on development in low- and middle-income countries. Higher education provides measurable benefits to graduates, relating to health, gender equality and democracy. It contributes

to the strengthening of institutions, and the forming of professionals who are vital for sectors such as education and health. Universities should be acknowledged and supported for the diverse range of functions they offer in addition to contributing directly to economic growth.

Mamdani also highlighted the role of universities in his 2016 speech, when he explained:

> The basic challenge lies in our conception of the university. Let me begin with those who would like to think of the university as an economic unit. A university is less like a business enterprise, more like a road, a power station. You do not measure the returns on a power station by dividing the investment made with the numbers employed at the station. Or the returns on a road or a bridge by dividing the investment with numbers employed. The returns are also social, sometimes mainly social – say if the region in question had been economically marginal and socially isolated. That the university is not just an economic unit means that its returns are not just economic, quantitative, measurable – they are also social, qualitative, not always available for measurement ... And, the returns are not just social, they are also in the realm of ideas, thought – ideological, philosophical, spiritual.

To sum up, priorities and funding for higher education and universities have shifted since the 1990s. The shifts have been influenced by different ways of thinking about universities and of measuring their impact on society and on other development goals and priorities. Some of these debates are ongoing, some should perhaps be over by now. However, as concluded by the Education Development Trust, 'Nowadays there is little doubt that research and tertiary education are main drivers of economic development' (Ndaruhutse and Thompson 2016: 15).

## Norway's support for capacity building in higher education and research

The three main programmes in this sector run by Norway and funded by the Norwegian Agency for Development Cooperation (NORAD) are the Norwegian Programme for Development, Research and Education (NUFU), the Programme for Masters Studies (NOMA), and the Norwegian Programme for Capacity Development in Higher Education and Research for Development (NORHED).

- Established in 1991, the NUFU programme represented a major effort by Norway to build sustainable capacity and competence in research and research-based higher education institutions in low- and middle-income countries. The aim was to establish close and mutually beneficial partnerships between academic institutions in the South and those in Norway. In its fourth and final funding period (from 2007 to 2012), NUFU supported 69 projects in 19 countries in Africa and Asia. These involved research collaborations, the training of masters and PhD students, the development of study programmes and courses, and the training of technical and administrative staff.
- NOMA was set up in 2006, and provides financial support for the development and running of masters programmes at Southern institutions via collaborative relationships with higher education institutions in Norway. The overall aim is to enhance staff training in all sectors of partner countries, through a focus on improving masters-level programmes at higher education institutions in the South.
- NORHED was launched in 2012. Its aim is to strengthen the capacity of higher education institutions in low-and middle-income countries to better educate more postgraduates, and to enhance the quality and quantity of their research. The theory of change adopted by NORHED is that stronger higher education institutions will help to enrich their countries' intellectual resources, the competence of their workforces, the quality of their leaders, while increasing gender equality and respect for human rights. In the longer term, NORHED aims to contribute to

evidence-based policy and decision-making that enhances sustainable economic, social and environmental development. In 2016, NORAD was supporting 46 university partnerships through NORHED, which was involved in 60 universities in Africa, Asia and Latin America, and 12 in Norway. More than 300 academics are involved in these partnerships.

## Capacity building and Norway's track record

For those involved in NORHED, it is important that the overall objective of capacity development for the university sector is based on an understanding that capacity development is not a goal in itself, but a means towards a higher goal – outlined in the theory of change mentioned above. This theory of change was discussed in the first evaluation of the NORHED programme, albeit in more technical terms (see DPMG 2014). The evaluators questioned whether NORHED's theory of change was in line with the existing theory and literature on capacity development in higher education institutions. In analysing the presuppositions built into the NORHED programme, the evaluators took the following levels at which capacity development occurs as their point of departure:

- The individual level (knowledge, technical skills, motivation, etc.);
- The organisational level (policies, processes, systems, structures, incentives, resources, practices);
- The environmental level (enabling policies, legislation, social and economic contexts, and other external factors).

Further, they considered how these different levels are related to one another, and how substantial and sustainable capacity can be developed. They argued that:

> While capacity development efforts may sometimes focus on only one of these levels, in most cases they involve activity at multiple levels. For example, while building individual's knowledge and skills on a particular technical issue may be

necessary to improve capacity, steps may also need to be taken to change how the wider organisation functions to enable these skills to be put into practice. Likewise, changes in the organisation may only be possible with shifts in the wider enabling environment. Sustainable capacity development often requires working simultaneously across these levels. (DPMG 2014)

As the evaluators suggested, when looking at capacity as a means to other ends (namely, societal development), all the social spaces within which academic work occurs – from individual capabilities to organisational support to socially 'enabling environments' – as well as factors influencing these spaces, have to be considered.

In higher education and research, it is reasonably easy to see results at the level of individuals. However, success at an institutional level is more difficult to measure, and even more so at a social level. The relationships between individuals and institutions – that is, how individuals affect institutions and how institutions shape individuals – is worth exploring further.

The evaluators concluded that the NORHED programme is largely in line with recommendations made in the existing literature, but that its work addresses the wider environment in which the universities operate to a limited extent. The authors of the report defined an 'enabling environment' as one that has adequate funding and supports good governance, as well as meritocratic, transparent and fair staffing practices (DPMG 2014: 24).

Scholarship programmes have long been a major part of global efforts to widen access to higher education and research (again, indicating a belief in developing capacity at the individual level). Numerous challenges and dilemmas related to such initiatives have been identified, including the brain-drain effect, and the relevance, usefulness and cost-effectiveness of non-localised education and qualifications. How investing in individuals might impact on the expansion of enabling environments, beyond enhancing an individual's own career and productivity, also merits further consideration.

A 2016 study of a large scholarship programme focusing on alumni of international fellowship programmes, is one example of research that is being done on individual versus institutional impacts (see Martel 2016). Martel's study looked at people who have accepted scholarships, and examined the effects of this on their communities and society at large. Martel concluded that programmes that target individuals can have significant multiplier effects for communities, societies, and organizations (Martel 2016).

This is highly relevant for NORHED, and other similar initiatives. Exploring the effects that individuals have on their workplaces, communities, and society at large might be one way to assess their impact, but we also want to know how the institutions individuals work for and with are shaped by their employees' conceptions of themselves and the value of their work. We want to know how individuals see their work as contributing to changing institutions.

The Norwegian Centre for International Cooperation in Education (SIU) conducted a tracer study in 2015. It's main objective was to assess whether, where and how masters graduates who had been supported by NOMA and NUFU were able to apply the skills they had acquired within the remit of national or regional workforces in the South. Their main finding was that:

> Graduates from both the NOMA programme and the NUFU programme have been highly successful in obtaining employment within the first 12 months following graduation, and close to 70% of the NOMA graduates and approximately 90% of the NUFU graduates have obtained employment relevant to their masters degrees. The majority of the graduates are employed in their country or region of origin, with the public sector and higher education institutions being the sectors employing the highest share of graduates. (SIU 2015: 83)

Additional information on issues like this, which are related to capacity building at different levels, and to the impact that individuals have on the institutions they work for, will be crucial for informing future programmes and initiatives. In this respect, NORHED aims to be a laboratory from which new knowledge about what works in capacity development can emerge.

## Questionable motives

Models of capacity development differ depending on their motives – from imperialist to altruist – and they tend to foster either economic exploitation or knowledge production accordingly. Clearly, different development agendas create a variety of consequences for universities and research. Justifications of support for higher education and research vary from idealism to utilitarianism, from development aid to meeting the needs of business and industry. These justifications have also shifted over time. Historical mapping of how higher education and scholarships were used by the former colonial powers, as well as by the old and emerging superpowers, and by the Scandinavian countries, shows that support for universities has served many purposes.

The NORHED programme is attempting to walk a new path. For decades, the support offered to individuals through scholarships meant they had to travel to a foreign country and enrol in full-time study at one of their universities. The most talented or privileged (or both) few were selected and educated in the North. Many never returned. The differences between what they were offered abroad, and what they could return home to, were often overwhelming. Some returned home and succeeded as academics, or government and business leaders. Others returned, but did not succeed. Although they had obtained a good education from reputable universities, their knowledge was not what was needed in their countries; the solutions they offered or their ways of working were inappropriate. Often, this inability to fit in car-ried political overtones, particularly within the politics of knowledge, and the variety of factors related to 'not fitting in' again highlights the importance of understanding the institutional preconditions for capac-ity development; that is, how institutions and individuals interact.

Mahmood Mamdani was among the first group of 12 students who left to study abroad after Uganda achieved independence. Now director of Uganda's Makerere Institute for Social Research, he is also co-ordinating a NORHED programme in the region. When I interviewed him in Kampala in February 2015 about his own education experience, he observed: 'Half of us never returned. The other half of us became misfits within our societies.'

The issue of what we learn and how adaptable our knowledge is to where we work remains critically important. Internationalisation is now higher on the agenda than ever before, and stories about the brain drain abound: about the number of African doctors in Britain and France outnumbering doctors in the countries they come from; about graduates who went home full of hope and enthusiasm to find that their knowledge was irrelevant to their country's needs. Nevertheless, the extent to which internationalisation and education across borders have provided individuals with opportunities and experiences that they would never have had otherwise should not be underestimated.

Leben Moro at the University of Juba is a living example of this. He shared his story with me during an interview I had with him in Juba in November 2016. Leben was a refugee for much of his youth. In primary school, he fled from South Sudan and became a refugee in Uganda. From there he went to high school in Khartoum and then to university in Cairo. Eventually, this young man from a poor background in wartorn South Sudan, obtained a doctorate from Oxford University. With his certificate in hand, plenty of opportunities opened up for him, but he wanted to go home. He explained:

> I have been given so many opportunities, in Cairo, England and Canada. I needed them, but I never felt that they needed me. There, I am only one of many, I wouldn't make much of a difference. But here in South Sudan they need me, here I can make a difference.

Moro is not unusual. Many African academics choose to stay at their own institutions, in their own countries, despite having fewer publication opportunities, poorly equipped laboratories and difficult environments in which to conduct critical or independent research. Many have returned, and continue to return, thus changing the institutions within which they work. Yet more returns are hoped for and expected. In his keynote speech at the African Higher Education Summit in Dakar in 2015, Kofi Annan expressed this fairly unambiguously, noting: 'Africa has exported some of its brightest minds. I am waiting for them to return.'

Moro returned, and so did Mamdani. Mamdani has had an impressive academic career in a number of countries. He shares the ideal of building strong academic communities in his homeland, Uganda. The number of people who have PhDs from the US and other Western countries is rising in Uganda and elsewhere in Africa, and the number of students studying abroad is higher than ever. Their experience is, however, still varied, both internationally and at home. We therefore have to question the value of current models promoting the 'internationalisation' of knowledge.

Adriansen et al. (2016) comprehensively addressed the debates around the politics and geography of knowledge. As they explain, although higher education institutions in the North look to expanding their recruitment in Africa and elsewhere, it is important to note that opportunities abroad will never be a solution for more than a few. And, as the experiences of Mamdani and others indicate, there is a growing realisation that study programmes in the South need to be developed to a level and quality that enables them to meet and engage with international standards. Externally obtained PhDs should be less of a necessity for individuals to achieve academic status. For all cultures, going abroad always has value, but this should not be forced on aspiring academics for lack of local alternatives. Nor should international study opportunities be available only to the well-resourced or well-connected.

Establishing study programmes is thus not only about offering programmes for students, it is about developing the knowledge base within countries in ways that make knowledge emerge from, and remain connected with, local cultures, so that while study programmes take into account global debates, their priorities remain relevant and responsive to local needs.

To some extent, however, this creates a conflict of interest between the aid community and the education sector in the North. Supporting in-country education programmes makes perfect sense for donors that are inspired by principles of ownership, involvement and Southern-based initiatives. However, this does not help prestigious higher education institutions that are being encouraged to recruit the world's most talented students and draw them into their universities in accordance with their own internationalisation agendas. When universities become 'talent catching machines', and act primarily to enhance their own reputations and better serve the economies they sustain, it is difficult to see how aid money provided to facilitate student mobility is serving its real purpose. It should be noted, however, that many academics and higher education institutions have strongly altruistic motives for their engagement in international academic collaboration and student exchanges.

## University partnerships: Focusing on institutions

Norwegian programmes that aim to support the development of higher education and research in the South have gradually shifted their focus away from the Norwegian universities. Instead, they focus on supporting partner institutions in Africa, Asia or Latin America. A key issue is, however, not only about where education and research takes place. More importantly, the shift aims to influence who has the initiative, the power and the ideas to define curriculum content and shape joint research projects.

Much research and debate has focused on the inherent asymmetries in the partnership models that so far have prevented Southern universities from 'truly owning' the research that donor aid has supported (see Ishengoma, this volume). This 'non-ownership' is clearly undermining the sustainability of such research, and preventing the formation of independent academics who are empowered to shape curricula and research agendas.

The model of partnership that lies at the core of the NORHED programme means that each project has to build a collaborative partnership between higher education institutions in Norway and institutions in Africa, Asia and Latin America. In addition, regional collaboration within or between countries in the South is strongly encouraged. Wanni et al. (2010: 18) defined effective educational partnerships as:

> A dynamic collaborative process between educational institutions that brings mutual though not necessarily symmetrical benefits to the parties engaged in the partnership. Partners share ownership of the projects. Their relationship is based on respect, trust, transparency and reciprocity. They understand each other's cultural and working environment. Decisions are taken jointly after real negotiations take place between the partners. Each partner is open and clear about what they are bringing to the partnership and what their expectations are from it. Successful partnerships tend to change and evolve over time. (quoted in Ndaruhutse and Thompson 2016: 8)

Indicators, such as improved curricula, increased publication rates and additional research projects are often used to establish the effectiveness of a higher education partnership. These are in line with the indicators developed for the NORHED programme. However, as highlighted in the study by Ndaruhutse and Thompson (2016: 8), we also need to be aware of the institutional contexts within which these numbers are produced:

> Evidence exists that shows the effectiveness of partnerships through quantifiable outcomes. However, such evidence does not always reflect the complex, ongoing processes that underpin effective partnerships. The design and implementation of a partnership must be analysed to understand the conditions that support mutuality, ownership and sustainability.

In NOMA and NUFU's standard programme documents, the idea of equal partnership was set out as follows: 'The cooperation shall be based in the principle of equality between the partners and should be characterized by transparency at all levels.' In practice, however, the model proved to be asymmetrical, from the formal administrative requirements to limitations placed on programme scope and focus. As long as such projects are required to include a Norwegian partner, they will also be limited by what expertise the partner can offer or has an interest in developing. This can conflict with the principle that development projects should be based on the needs of the country being supported. An evaluation of NOMA and NUFU conducted in 2009 pointed to this when recommending stronger 'emphasis on demand-driven forms of collaboration, rather than the prevalent supply-driven nature of cooperation' (COWI AS 2009: 16).

Interestingly, this viewpoint was shared by both the Norwegian partners and the partner institutions in the South. According to the same NOMA/NUFU evaluation:

> Although most partners in the South were reluctant to express sharp standpoints or requests for change, they nevertheless often gave the impression that the asymmetries in programmes were in need of revision. Some would like to see more decentralized administrative and decision-making structures, with much greater influence given to the partners in the South ... Partners in the North generally agree with the view from the South that the existing asymmetries within the NOMA and NUFU programmes are counterproductive and run against overall objectives of creating capacities in the South which are sustainable and carried forward by competent local ownership. Further, it is recognized by Northern partners that the programmes should be demand driven, and less supply driven'. (COWI AS 2009: 47, 48)

The authors of the NOMA/NUFU evaluation point out that asymmetry is present from the outset of a project, in the sense that partnerships seldom originate from the South. This, of course, presents a challenge for any Southern partner who might wish to take real ownership, responsibility and sustainability:

> Several Southern partners are concerned about the situation
> and feel that the established partnerships are too unsymmet-
> rical and that this may be caused by lack of trust. There is
> little doubt that a further delegation of responsibility to
> partners in the South may help foster an important feeling of
> ownership. It should not be overlooked that a feeling of
> responsibility is among the strongest motivating factors for
> hard and efficient work. (COWI AS 2009: 40)

The NOMA/NUFU evaluation was quite vehement about the negative
impacts that inbuilt asymmetry can have on programmes. Its authors
noted that some donors, such as the Dutch and the Swedish, are already
redesigning programmes to transfer greater responsibilities to the
Southern partners. Their conclusion was that 'maintaining asymmetric
relations North–South is counterproductive and a thing of the past'
(COWI AS 2009: 65). They also pointed out that a stronger focus on
demands and ownership in the South is also more in line with the
intentions of the 2005 Paris Declaration on Aid Effectiveness and the
subsequent Accra Agenda for Action of 2008.

At the same time, and despite the pervasiveness of asymmetric
models, long-term relationships built on mutual respect and interest,
and based on personal and professional relationships, do exist. Visitors
to any of the key partner institutions with which Norwegian universities have worked over the years, inevitably gather multiple stories of
profound encounters shaped by North–South collaborations that have
engendered lasting mutual respect and ongoing friendships. The value
and impact of these long-standing relations, and what they lead to in
terms of knowledge, understanding and knowledge diplomacy, is worth
exploring further.

Several Norwegian universities have been in partnerships with
Ethiopian higher education institutions for decades. Based on their
mutual interests in agriculture, drought mitigation, forestry, etc. strong
relationships have been built. In January 2016, this collaboration celebrated its twenty-fifth anniversary. The Norwegian ambassador to
Ethiopia summarised the partnership as follows:

Many are the Ethiopian scholars that have been trained in different universities in Norway – for them to return to Ethiopia and set their competence to the best use for the development of their country. This was the aim – and it has been a major success. And many are the professors and teachers and doctors from Norway that have contributed their expertise to the higher education sector in Ethiopia.

Clarifying why the Norwegian approach has been particularly appreciated, a former university vice-chancellor from Ethiopia said, 'The Norwegians came to collaborate. The others came to dominate.'

## Gradual shifts

Norway's approach to capacity development in higher education and research changed gradually throughout the years in which NOMA and NUFU operated. More drastic shifts coincided with the establishment of NORHED. One major change was a shift in the partnership model away from one in which the Norwegian university was the main agreement holder, received all the funding, and was responsible for programme delivery, budgeting, reporting and the publishing of results. The opposite now applies. The Southern university signs the agreement with NORAD and takes responsibility for the whole project, including any aspects that may happen in Norway.

Such shifts are in line with the key principles of the Paris Declaration on Aid Effectiveness, the Accra Agenda for Action and the Busan Partnership for Effective Development Co-operation. These changes add new dimensions that will be of interest to researchers in this field – new power structures, different negotiating positions and different dynamics. This is true not only of Southern and Norwegian partners, but also between partners within the same region. NORHED has a strong regional focus, with numerous programmes that involve partners in neighbouring countries, such as Ethiopa, South Sudan and Tanzania, or Nepal, Bangladesh and Pakistan. Discussions around the table when it comes to budget allocations, research agendas, curriculum development and supervision arrangements are numerous, and the potential for conflict is clear. Debates about whose initiatives and priorities are given weight, and who carries the responsibility for budgets, are key. In the arrangement between Uganda and South Sudan, for example, Uganda has so far taken the lead in projects that aim to strengthen capacity at universities in South Sudan.

In general, this shift has received positive responses, both within and beyond NORHED's partner institutions. As highlighted by Damtew Teferra (2016), a professor of higher education and a leader in training and development at the University of KwaZulu-Natal in South Africa:

> It is refreshing that Norway has made a decision that explicitly and directly encourages Southern institutions to lead and manage joint international projects. It also encourages multi-institutional and multi-country partnerships, South–South–North. This indeed is a progressive policy in the North–South partnerships in which the South is encouraged to lead the partnerships as well as utilize the majority of the joint resources.

Another professor I interviewed, who has been involved in North–South projects for years, commented: 'I was very sceptical to changing the main partner to a Southern-based university, but I have completely changed my mind. This is about time, and it goes in the right direction.'

Denmark took a new direction in their Building Stronger Universities programme, which ran from January 2014 to November 2016, and was worth DKK 100 million (approximately US$12 million). In the programme, needs and priorities identified by Southern partners in terms of developing their institutional and research capacity were addressed by matching them with Danish universities, which had the skills and capacities to meet their needs in the areas identified. The latter were selected through a match-making process where consortia of Danish universities were invited to express interest in particular programmes.

Finland's Higher Education Institution adopted a similar approach in its Institutional Co-operation Instrument. To obtain support, all projects are designed to reflect each individual country's specific development aims, and must be based on the needs identified by the local higher education institutions.

With the focus on building stronger universities that are more adapted to local contexts and needs, there is another important dimension that must not be neglected. Universities in Africa are not only African; they are also international. Africa's universities are debating Africanisation versus universalism, which might be linked to demands for internationalisation versus demands for local relevance. In response to a question about this, Mamdani made the following comment, 'We cannot become chauvinist, and contribute to 'us and them'. Then we will have failed' (interview, February 2016).

## Conflicting ideologies

How will the ideas, motives and results of inter-university collaborations change when they are managed from the South? And how will small versus large countries, well-established universities versus smaller or less prestigious institutions, influence this process?

Meanwhile, Norwegian academics also face pressure from the global system and are often offered incentives that do not favour collaborations with universities in Africa, no matter how strong their partnerships with these institutions may be. Collaborations with institutions in low-income countries do not always have a place in the reward system, and tend to fit poorly within university strategies that focus on becoming bigger and better in terms of what the Western world sees as worthwhile knowledge. As one professor at the University of Bergen observed in an interview, 'The whole system is built on the idea that we should aim at partnering with the so-called strongest.' And the internationally accepted indicators for 'the strongest' seldom point towards any of the African countries. This means that researchers will struggle to achieve high visibility in prestigious journals or academic networks. In this context, it can be helpful to remember that these indicators seldom point towards Norway either. The kinds of knowledge that are emerging from NORHED's programmes and networks, therefore, need to find a place despite, and sometimes in contradiction to, the existing system's 'politics of knowledge'. Different attitudes and interests motivate these collaborations and, as emphasised in the SDGs communication across academic and spatial divides is crucial if humanity is to address the challenges we all face.

## No low-hanging fruit

Development co-operation initiatives have always needed to balance competing priorities: dealing with humanitarian crises versus the pressure to deliver longer-term economic development, for example. Too often, development workers are encouraged to grab the 'low-hanging fruit' and push ahead with what are seen as the 'sexy' projects. It is difficult to see university collaborations as either of those things. As noted by one of the participants at a NORAD seminar in 2013, 'Supporting higher education is not for sprinters, it is for stayers.' And, as Göran Hydén notes in his chapter in this book, 'Higher education is not for those who are fans of measuring results'. Of course, university collaboration is difficult to defend in the face of children dying, streams of refugees or sudden humanitarian crises. Against these competing priorities, higher education can only lose. The challenge, therefore, is to identify, document and communicate the real value of higher education and research. In so doing, to echo the words of Nkosazana Dlamini-Zuma quoted at the start of this chapter, it is about time Africa developed its own knowledge, 'only then can Africa be completely free'.

## Notes

1   Opinions expressed in this chapter are those of the author, and do not necessarily represent the views or policies of NORAD.

2   Higher education is directly linked to SDG 4, which is about education, but the expansion of this sector is also acknowledged as crucial to the realisation of several of the other SDGs.

# References

Adriansen, Hanne Kirstine, Lene Møller Madsen and Stig Jensen (eds) (2016) *Higher Education and Capacity Building in Africa: The Geography and Power of Knowledge Under Changing Conditions*. Oxford and New York: Routledge

Anan, Kofi (2015) Keynote address at the African Higher Education Summit. Dakar, Senegal, 10–12 March

COWI AS (2009) *Evaluation of the Norwegian Programme for Development, Research and Education (NUFU) and of NORAD's Programme for Master Studies (NOMA)*. Oslo: NORAD

Dlamini-Zuma, Nkosazana (2015) Keynote address at the African Higher Education Summit. Dakar, Senegal, 10–12 March

DPMG (Development Portfolio Management Group, University of Southern California) (2014) *Evaluation Series of NORHED, Higher Education and Research for Development: Theory of Change and Evaluation Methods*. Oslo: NORAD

Mamdani, Mahmood (2016) Keynote speech at the NORAD 'Knowledge for Development' conference. Oslo, Norway, 6–7 June

Martel, Mirka (2016) Can individual outcomes lead to communal impacts? Measuring social change using longitudinal studies: A challenge and an opportunity. Posted on the Association of Commonwealth Universities' blog, *Measuring Success*. Updated 23 May. Available online

Ndaruhutse, Susy and Stephen Thompson (2016) Literature Review: Higher Education and Development. A paper by the Education Development Trust commissioned for the NORHED Conference on 'Knowledge for Development', Oslo, Norway, 6–7 June. Available online

OECD (2006): *Glossary of Statistical Terms*. Paris. Available online

SIU (2015) *NOMA/NUFU Tracer Study*. Bergen. Available online

Teferra, Damtew (2016) Shifting grounds in higher education partnerships. Posted on *The World View*, a blog by the Center for International Higher Education, 19 June. Available online

World Bank (2000) *Higher Education in Developing Countries: Peril and Promise*. Washington, DC

CHAPTER

# 12

# International co-operation and the democratisation of knowledge

*Tor Halvorsen*

During the 1990s, 'internationalisation' became a hot topic in higher education and research. By the early 2000s, internationalisation had become a separate research specialty and the primary focus of entire units or individual staff members in the administrative and finance offices at many universities. Meanwhile, multiple conferences and organisations promote internationalisation – the oldest being the International Association for Universities (IAU) (Halvorsen and Vale 2012). Judging from the findings of various higher education rating systems, institutions without clear internationalisation policies and strategies don't quite make the grade. Internationalisation strategies can also be interesting in that they tend to reflect the degree of organisational autonomy enjoyed by universities, but more importantly, what values the institution seeks to promote, and from what sectors of society, nationally and internationally, it obtains (or wishes to obtain) support.

In this chapter, I discuss internationalisation as practiced in four 'ideal types' of universities. Each type has emerged and risen to prominence at different points in the history of modern universities, but aspects of each one still strongly influence contemporary tertiary education models and understandings of the role of internationalisation.

Before describing the four ideal types in more detail, I explore some of the cracks in the system, and highlight emerging alternatives.

## Internationalisation and the paradox of competition

University internationalisation strategies have always expressed the ambitions of university leaders. In the contemporary era, in particular, they indicate where institutional managers seek to co-operate with other institutions to sharpen their own organisation's competitive edge. Although these strategies are ostensibly about collaboration, paradoxically their collective effect has been to intensify the competition between institutions. Almost all universities are now seeking to co-operate with a relatively small group of supposedly 'superior' universities to help them improve their positions in the global institutional ranking system. Universities expect that by improving their reputations and rankings, they will attract better students, better professors and more rewarding research projects, as well as more funding and more public support, etc. What happens, however, is that all universities end up competing to collaborate with the most highly ranked institutions. This competition has tended to strengthen the links between some universities and exclude many others. Those left behind tend to be left out.

In addition, cross-institutional competition has led to an increase in standardisation, uniformity and disciplinary specialisation, as well as augmenting managerial control over research agendas. Universities caught up in this system seem highly unlikely to be able to step away from its competitive and standardising imperatives for long enough to fully comprehend, never mind begin to tackle, the challenges of climate change, poverty and rising inequality that are facing us all. Yet, if these issues remain unaddressed, they have the potential to wipe humanity off the face of the planet.

For academics, the strategic shift towards institutional competitiveness has had serious consequences. For most of us, *academic* competition – that is, the ability to compete academically, to propose innovative theories, offer fresh insights, or reveal unexplored aspects of established truths – is far more important than *institutional* competition. Academic competition is often inspired by novelty, and relies on imagination and creativity. In this sense, academic competition knows no borders and cannot be framed hierarchically, socially, spatially, politically or in terms of discipline. In fact, working with the 'not so good' can be as rewarding as working with the best.

Since the establishment of the first modern universities, many academics have sought collaboration wherever they could find like-minded colleagues. That is, in the past, research interests, not organisational strategy, inspired academic networking and motivated all manner of border crossings. In this context, motives for internationalisation were epistemological, and entirely unrelated to strategic alignment with externally imposed criteria for institutional achievement.

## Neoliberalism and institutional competition

The transformation of universities into strategically oriented competitive actors occurred in response to the general shift in society (including 'the public sector') towards making competition a primary instrument of governance (Berndt and Boeckler 2009). No matter which version of neoliberalism we choose to highlight (Schmidt and Thatcher 2013), competition has become key to the governance of individuals and organisations.

As competition becomes global and 'post-national', internationalisation is beginning to dissolve national systems of higher education and research. That is, the need for evaluation initially gave rise to appraisals of institutions within nation-states. From the 1990s, a global evaluation industry emerged. Spawning a whole industry of evaluation instruments, rankings systems turned into measures of organisational success, linking academic quality not to academic content but to the 'production' or output achieved by single universities, which are now expected to compete internationally for resources, students, professors, etc. In this process, the ways in which academic knowledge is valued, and how academics work, has changed radically

(Matthies and Simon 2007; Power 1997, 2007). In essence, internationalisation now presupposes competition.

Ideally, universities should be driven by a search for knowledge (episteme), in which nothing is more relevant than a good theory. In reality, universities now face many pressing external demands that their work be 'relevant'. These are invariably linked to particular social interests that often legitimise their interventions as being of 'service to society'.

In addition, universities need administration; that is, they need to have, but not *be*, bureaucracies. However, when 'relevance' and 'management' combine to promote competition, as they have done in the neoliberal era, academic independence has been thoroughly undermined and epistemology completely undervalued. Essentially, universities are combining epistemology, relevance and management, such that many are turning into 'knowledge factories' (Bok 2004; Mamdani 2007).

## Global challenges

This focus on competition between higher education institutions and their managements has been a dangerously destructive phase in the evolution of universities. In my view, we are entering a new and fundamentally different period in which co-operation between *academics* is again becoming crucial. As we confront the stark and global challenges of our epoch, co-operation between academics seems far more likely to contribute to new knowledge production than the pursuits of institutional reputation-building (Halvorsen 2015).

The challenges facing humanity cannot be solved by the kinds of competitive strategies that are making 'internationalisation' into a tool for ramping up organisational reputations. Instead, co-operation across the globe, *including* with institutions that are rated poorly in existing ranking systems, holds the potential to open up and renew global knowledge systems. Rather than increasing standardisation and uniformity, we need to harness the creativity to which a multitude of experiences allows us access. We must acknowledge the possibility that many of the world's most creative academics might well be of little value in terms of organisational competition but of immense value to sparking our imagination. In the period we are now are entering, academic (as opposed to strategic) co-operation is likely to be crucial for our future.

The stark reality is that humanity must either transform or become extinct after experiencing catastrophe on an unprecedented scale. If we fail to transform, the consequences will initially be toughest for the least affluent countries and communities, but ultimately humans, along with millions of human and plant species, will be destroyed. The Sustainable Development Goals (UN 2015), the Paris Declaration on the Environment (UNFCC 2015), and several documents published by the International Labour Organization (ILO)[1] reflect an acknowledge-ment of how this transformation might begin. Academics must now show their ability to drive big projects and respond to great challenges.

The many scientists who created the atomic bomb worked together for disastrous ends. However, precisely that scale and intensity of co-operation is now needed for more noble goals. In fact, the quality of such co-operation, designed and carried out according to epistemic (and therefore internally defined) criteria, is what all the instruments of grading, rating and ranking should be trying to measure. If this were the case, knowledge that emerges from collaborations with those who have the fewest resources and also face the most severe challenges could well become the most highly valued, even in those universities that are already high up in the rankings.

Let me hasten to add, however, that such co-operation is only likely to be successful if it occurs through networks of academic co-operation that systematically prioritise and reflect on the challenges facing humanity. Our situation demands that we restore the ways in which academics and academic knowledge used to be valued in the past. Linking relevance and epistemology to the global challenges we face has the potential to give rise to a kind of university governance that counters the current drive to reproduce the neoliberal order and endorse academic capitalism (Münch 2007, 2011).

## Contemporary universities and their Western hegemonic histories

Like all organisations, universities have institutionalised behaviours that operate according to norms, values and regulations devised within a variety of material constraints. Universities also change in relation to their interactions with their environments.

Just as there are different roads to modernity, there have been different kinds of universities within the broadly Western model that has spread globally. The varieties most widely adopted, often simultaneously within one institution, are:

- the French system of professional schools (Shinn 1980);
- British notions of liberal education;
- the German (Humboldtian) concepts of 'Bildung' and the freedom to learn and to teach (Bildung durch Wissen); and
- the US version (although only partially applied in their vast higher education system), which combines the German, British and French models (Brandser 2006).[2]

Japan's copying of German technical education (after 1870), and the many Americans who attended German universities from the 1880s, until they themselves became the hegemonic force (see Brandser 2006), are just two examples of Germany's early influence.

Less edifying is how the colonial powers imposed poor replicas of their universities on their colonies, without providing the autonomy or the resources they needed to build up research-based knowledge driven by local needs and perceptions of their own burning issues. Activated by the global challenges facing the world, reactions to these bleak Western-imposed models are now helping to initiate a revisioning of knowledge and disciplinary fields.

Universities in the BRICS countries (Brazil, Russia, India, China and South Africa) are attempting to develop alternatives to Western hegemony, and seem to be achieving a degree of regional influence, even if their global impact remains limited (Halvorsen 2016). Their model of collaboration is state-driven in the sense that political processes have encouraged networking activities between particular centres of excellence creating a network of think-tanks. Although still embryonic, the BRICS initiative, and similar projects within its member countries, indicate the growth of a new type of internationalisation within the global knowledge community.

Of course, India's co-operation with the West and South extends well beyond the BRICS programme, and seems to be driven by academics and their knowledge interests, as much as by universities. Meanwhile, Tjomsland reminds us that, unlike in much of Europe, where the link between nation state and university tends to be dominant, 'the picture of the Arab regional landscape is quite the opposite of the European. It has as a point of departure a strong regional Arab identity that outweighed the national identities of the newly created Arab states at independence and has constituted a challenge to the legitimacy of Arab regimes ever since' (2005: 133).

A new hegemony may emerge from the new linkages and relationships that are being constructed across previous chasms and cleavages from parts of the world that are outside both BRICS and the OECD. It remains to be seen how such networks will respond to the global challenges, and if an alternative to Western hegemony really is in the making.

Given the extent of the global challenges we face, the question is, who or what should be the new external legitimising forces for universities, and for the changes they will have to implement to remain relevant? New types of alliances – particularly across the North–South divide, are not only sensible, but crucial. The question therefore remains: how do we analyse the relations between epistemology, relevance and organisational governance as the universities evolve and are transformed in space and time (Adriansen et al 2016)?[3]


## Our multidisciplinary task

The growth of subject disciplines and increasing specialisation have history on their side. Reason and rationality follows 'discipline', and discipline is needed to make academic progress within ever-growing fields of researched knowledge. The debate about relevance calls this into question, however, in that not all disciplines are necessarily relevant for the problems the world is facing at present. In addition, disciplinary boundaries might be preventing researchers from asking some of the most relevant questions – what falls between (or beyond) these boundaries might be key. Ideally, researchers should not be limited by specialist networks or blinded by successes in any narrow field of knowledge. The paradox is that, to succeed, such initiatives are often required to take the shape of a discipline. That is, to survive over time, and establish a knowledge field that is accessible to others, its disciplining into a discipline is a necessity.

The internationalisation of academic work has been important in raising awareness of the limits of specialisation. Similar disciplines can be constructed very differently depending on local circumstances, and meetings between international representatives of disciplines often quickly remind us that disciplines are social constructs that are held together as such, not by common theory, common methodologies or common 'topics', as is often argued when disciplines are defined (Eigen et al. 1988).

This understanding of disciplines as social constructs opens up space for multi-disciplinary work. This allows for explorations of how gaps between existing disciplines, and the creation of dialogue between disciplines, might help us cope with the challenges of our time. In the long run, this process will probably inspire entirely new disciplines, but the hope is that these arise in a context of stronger epistemic autonomy. In other words, the awareness that knowledge is socially constructed, and that economic and political interests frame all knowledge-creating processes, implies that academics should retain more control over knowledge creation with a new focus on cross-border co-operation and how it can work. Less competition and more imagination is necessary in North–South linkages if we are to deconstruct the old world of imperialist knowledge with its myopic worldview (see the debates around the Rhodes Must Fall movement in South Africa, for example).

How to balance academic specialisation with the views of other social actors about what is relevant, is a crucial issue. Global warming, poverty and social injustice seem impossible to address using the approaches humanity has relied on thus far. The question is, can we change fast enough?

There are some grounds for optimism. Universities do seem to be trying to prove their relevance. In addition, many universities are promoting internationalisation and cross-border networking, and some have already developed international associations and networks. The November 2016 conference of the International Association of Universities (IAU)[4] was one important expression of this; gatherings of European universities that have taken place since the Southern African-Nordic Centre's conference in Namibia in December 2015 are another. Such associations have to come to the fore, not only as epistemic communities, but also as voices that are relevant to the pressing issues of our time. The question is, will this also lead to the transformation of the relations between knowledge and power that is necessary to make new knowledge relevant to the global challenges we face?

## Learning from history

In this section, I examine in a little more detail the history of different kinds of universities, or ideal types, whose 'existence' has had its time, is presently hegemonic, or is just emerging. The analysis is not linear, however. How the old and new are combined varies between regions and countries, and even within countries, thus creating differing motives for, and types of, collaboration between and within institutions. My hypothesis is that, due to the global challenges we are facing, epistemic identities that developed in the first period of modern universities are reappearing again and will become stronger in the phase we are entering now.

My analysis covers four periods as shown in Figure 12.1. The first is strongly related to the spread of the Prussian culture of learning from about 1810 to the late 1930s. It has been referred to as the Humboldtian university, or the *university of culture* (Readings 1996). After the Second World War, the *university of governance* emerged, characterised by an increase in numbers of students, disciplines and thus academics who became involved in the governing of society, state and the economy, as

**Figure 12.1:** A timeline of university development in the West

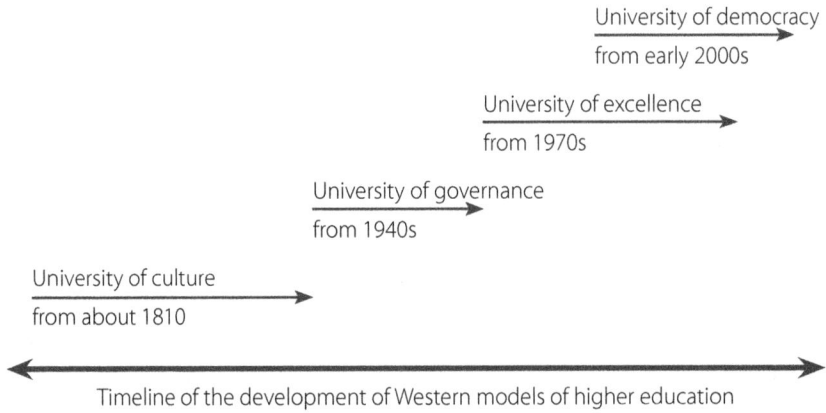

University of democracy
from early 2000s

University of excellence
from 1970s

University of governance
from 1940s

University of culture
from about 1810

Timeline of the development of Western models of higher education

well as the universities themselves. At the same time, hegemony shifted from Germany to the US. In the third period, still led by US universities, but extended globally, the *university of excellence* (a characteristic first suggested by Readings 1996) became dominant. This type of university is best known for its contribution to academic capitalism, underwriting notions such as the 'knowledge economy' and 'innovation societies'. The fourth period, and the one we are just entering, still lacks a name. My suggestion is that we call it the *university of democracy*.

We are all, if not yet to an equal degree, at risk because of our inability to control modernity; all life, and human life in particular, is facing extinction. In my view, humanity will develop solutions to this only if we also deepen and strengthen democracy. Democracy can remind us that the situation we are in is a consequence of knowledge development of the most destructive kind, and to which universities have been central contributors. These include nuclear weapons, all the technologies that are destroying the environment, farming methods that ruin the soil and poison our food, technologies and trade agreements that ensure the continued economic exploitation of low- and middle-income countries, to name just a few.

As indicated, my periodisation focuses less on tracing chronological development and more on highlighting dominant traits and ideal types.

In reality, most universities still try to live up to the ideals of the university of culture, while simultaneously acting as universities of excellence within the framework of academic capitalism. Similarly, a range of values, motivations and knowledge interests can act together to drive academic collaboration programmes.[5] In general, however, the notion of 'relevance', in alliance with management values, has gained the upper hand in most academic institutions. This means that many university management teams not only promote certain disciplines above others (Higgins 2013), they also discern what new combinations of knowledge best serve the social division of labour, and can therefore be accepted as 'disciplines'.

We are entering a period that puts particular demands on academics. Environmental disaster, intertwined with the challenges of 'green' economic growth, dwindling job opportunities, as well as growing poverty and inequality, raises new kinds of knowledge demands. Academics have to reconsider who we want to collaborate with, for what purpose, and within what kinds of disciplinary – and more so – cross-disciplinary contexts. This implies a return to greater academic control of epistemic communities, more emphasis on originality of knowledge, and a far stronger influence on what academics consider relevant.

Journals such as *Ecological Economics*, a transdisciplinary journal of the International Society for Ecological Economics for 'non-commercial research and educational usage', is but one example of how new kinds of knowledge battles are emerging. Economics, as a discipline, is facing the emergence of de-growth theories, arguing for the prioritisation of human relations above market relations, a deepening of democracy, the preservation of ecosystems and a more equal distribution of wealth (Järvensivu 2013). Other disciplines and professions, from farming to pharmaceuticals, are facing similar kinds of questions about their commitment to basic social and political agendas.

Generally, new kinds of knowledge networks are emerging, and the global challenges are transforming how academics choose (or, equally importantly, choose not) to collaborate. In an analysis of the growth of international science organisations in the twentieth century, Schofer (1999) not only described their rapid growth from the 1950s, but also the parallel and (again) exponential growth of socially committed science organisations. The escalation has been particularly marked since the era of the 'university of excellence' began, as academics have tried to counter the hegemonic transition to academic capitalism. The subsequent growth of NGOs dedicated to environmental issues shows that much of this commitment is being carried forward into the coming period (Fink et al. 1996).

## The university of democracy

So let me start with the present. It seems we are at the beginning of a period of radical change with far-reaching consequences for all social institutions, including universities. We must therefore ask anew, why should academics collaborate and what for?

In geological time, the period we are in has been termed the Anthropocene: acknowledging that virtually all of nature is now social-ised (affected by human activity), and that this will have a lasting effect on the earth, even after humans have left it for good. Perhaps more important than this renaming of our age, is the acceptance, as expressed in the 2015 Paris Declaration on Climate Change, that humans are reaching the limits of our existence on earth if we do not end our car-bon dependency by or before 2050 (UNFCC 2015).

While some city dwellers might have difficulty remembering this, nature has the upper hand. We cannot geo-engineer ourselves out of that fact. We need planning and co-ordination, as well as shared (there-fore democratic and binding) decision-making to regulate the world's economic and political actors, so that we harness them into bringing about change. To put it in philosophical terms, the whole is bigger than the parts and, if left unregulated, the parts add up to a self-destructive whole. The need for planning and regulation at the post-national level therefore requires that we revitalise questions of how to expand democ-racy beyond the level of the nation-state, and also how to establish democracy in countries with anti-democratic regimes.

The characteristic feature of the new period, to which universities will have to justify their existence and adjust their institutional values, is the strengthening of democracy such that it becomes a force that enables humanity to transition beyond carbon-dependent economies and infrastructure. Democracy is key because the planning and centralisation of power that will be required to facilitate rapid change will have to be democratically delegated so that entrenched social and economic inequalities do not incite individuals and communities to scupper or sabotage change and jeopardise our future. Universities and academics will therefore have to contribute to producing the knowledge required for a global shift in energy use *and* the widening of democratic influence so that this shift occurs globally. Without the confluence of these two kinds of knowledge, the effects of climate change will be catastrophic for all.

The 2015 Paris Agreement contains a strong appeal to universities to collaborate globally, rather than be part of the competition driven by global capital that generally escalates rather than addresses global problems. By aligning themselves with democratic values and practices, universities could help to counter the values of global capitalism. That is, universities could become the counter-movement that social scientist Wolfgang Streeck was searching for, but could not see, when he asked what actors and institutions will secure the collective good of liveable environment in a world of competitive production and consumption. Quoting Canadian political scientist CB Macpherson, Streeck (2014: 52) argued that capitalism will undermine itself from within, but asked, how the enormous collective resources required for preventing and repairing environmental damage will ever be mobilised in societies governed by 'possessive individualism'.

'Possessive individualism' is precisely what universities of excellence have promoted and shaped through their focus on human-resource (and human-capital) development. The challenges we face as we exit this era seem to demand that the academic world makes its most abrupt shift since Humboldt's era. The character and type of future academic collaborations and networks must be determined by how they address the issues surrounding global warming. As Naomi Klein (2015) put it: 'this changes everything', including who should decide what knowledge is valuable and relevant.

## The university of excellence

Neoliberalism, of which universities of excellence are a by-product, is primarily a political project of the Western world, that challenges basic ideas about liberty, solidarity, justice, individuality and the role of academia (Boldizzoni 2013; Fourcade-Gourinchas and Babb 2002; Mjøset 2011; Peck 2008). From this project, flows a particular understanding of what knowledge is, how to create it and how it should be valued.

The university of excellence is a product of, and is therefore tailored to, the neoliberal policies of the OECD, but it does, of course, also hold sway outside the OECD's member states, and particularly in the post-colonial countries, both in terms of practice and as a political-rhetorical tool of governance. As Streeck (2014) argued, in this era, universities have been transformed from critical institutions into tools of the global economy. They have thus, paradoxically, also been deprived of the reflective role necessary for the reproduction of capitalism itself. Even 'human capital' needs creativity to evolve!

To different degrees, the university of excellence tends to detach itself from the cultural context of the nation-state or region in which it is located. However, 'excellence' as a concept or category is basically empty; it gains meaning only through actors who operationalise it and thus determine what it means. Under neoliberalism, a hegemony related to the valuation of knowledge has been established globally among actors whose interests in university-based knowledge were shaped by how knowledge can be used in the production of profits, to service the elites, and to legitimise their hegemonic project. Among others, Mamdani (2007) has clearly described the particular consequences of this for the South. In many ways, the post-colonial world has become a laboratory for World Bank-led policy experiments related to education and research. Perhaps in response to this, actors in this part of the world have been among the first to develop alternative ideas about knowledge.

To be against 'excellence' is obviously absurd. However, processes of democratic deliberation about what knowledge is useful for social (nation-state) development, and what knowledge is good for communities that are seeking to make democracy work, also seem insane from within a neoliberal framework. Instead, excellence is bureaucratically selected. Bureaucracies grew out of the 'politics of large numbers' (Desrosières 2007) that constitute modern nation-states and their related economies (Angermüller 2010). However, under neoliberalism, they have been transformed from agencies that collect statistics to measure progress in a nation-state into systems that encourage competition for resources between individuals and institutions across and beyond national systems.

A prominent example is the OECD's Pisa test, which measures the knowledge of 15-year-olds all over the world and draws conclusions about the quality of schooling they have had. A network of bureaucrats and universities are now using similar kinds of comparisons for higher education institutions and for the implementation of the SDGs.[6] In effect, a neo-numeriocracy is creating the means for measuring academic work in terms of 'multi-governance interactions', thus giving the final word to post-national organisations such as the OECD (Angermüller 2010).[7]

This meant that, in 1992, the founder of the Institute for Scientific Information (ISI), Eugene Garfield, a pioneer and central actor in the neo-numeriocracy, could sell the ISI to Thomson Reuters, a multinational media company that has since made billions of dollars from exploiting academic texts by selling them across several other databases. Academics who produced what should be public knowledge have thus had their works dissected and sold off for profit. Similarly, increasing numbers of academic institutions are governed by number crunchers, who apply the rules of supply and demand, as informed by institutional ratings, to help them determine the relative importance of research agendas and the size of budget allocations.

The academic world that initially produced the data (and the categories necessary for statistical data collection) to help improve the governance of specific sectors of the nation-state, is now itself governed by statistics calculated by global businesses that measure their competitive abilities across borders. According to Angermüller (2010: 178), an annual subscription to the Science and Social Science Citation Indexes (SCI and SSCI) cost US$700 in 2009. The information technology that made this possible soon made ratings and rankings into hotter topics than the research being rated, while on sites such as Google Scholar, the 'number of hits' is often spuriously correlated with academic merit.

This kind of 'governance by numbers' is complemented by the World Trade Organization's General Agreement on Trade in Services, which aims to promote trade in services, including tertiary education. The agreement is constructed to drive a continual expansion of trade such that public universities either have to privatise or act as if they can compete with private institutions. Whatever crosses borders – from professionals to students, knowledge or other tangibles – count as an exchange of educational services, and have to have a market-related price. Ratings and citation indexes, etc. are in place to confer honour and status on universities and the prices of educational services are determined by the system.

The push to make higher education part of a service economy, and universities into marketplaces for the sale of educational services, has escalated rapidly. In relation to teaching students (as customers), standardised curricula using teaching technologies owned by big media firms are growing. University management experts, and techniques that promise improved rankings, ratings and citation indices, are all beginning to circulate according to a market value, while branding agencies target universities promising to promote their images as knowledge providers in a competitive market. The academic 'economy of honour' has thus been transformed into a monetary economy, on which bureaucratised universities have become dependent.

In terms of research, the transformation is primarily linked to the growing ownership of knowledge that the patent system and the Trade-Related Aspects of Intellectual Property Rights (TRIPS) Agreement allows.[8] As Braithwaite and Drahos (2000: 75) argued, 'intellectual property is perhaps our most spectacular example of economic coercion ... What is clear is that global property rights set strong limits on a state's capacity to define territorial property rights in ways that enhance national welfare'. Altogether, the globalisation of intellectual property rights is fraught with dangers for citizens and state sovereignty (animal patents being just one example of the moral-sovereignty costs inherent in the system). Braithwaite and Drahos did not explicitly explore the impact of this system of global ownership on the universities, but implicit in their argument is the notion that university-developed knowledge has been drawn into the battle in support of capitalist hegemony.[9]

Within this paradigm, the role of universities is to develop competitive 'human capital', while the notion of 'intellectual property' presupposes that prosperity for individuals and organisations involves transforming knowledge into assets that support economic growth and create financial rewards.

As Gorz (2003) pointed out, the so-called knowledge economy is characterised by a conflict between the total instrumentalisation of 'human capital' and the need to make space for human creativity.[10] Human creativity cannot be *directed* by managerial concerns. Ideas of how to work on your 'personal brand', or contribute to intellectual property by putting 'human capital' to work might have evolved from notions of individual freedom, but they have turned into a straitjacket, leading to a growing need for psychological services and the emergence of quasi-psychological services such as 'life-coaching' (Honneth 2012). Within this framework, education is little more than a tool for the formation of a 'subject's' employability. Being self-employed, or making strategic educational and work choices, becomes 'an ideal', in line with what is seen as the ideal future for this neoliberal epoch: the end of wage-related labour and growing numbers of self-employed contractors whose individual identity is subsumed into the category of human capital (Gorz 2003: 27).

In a university of culture, knowledge is not a 'product' but something indefinable, its value indeterminable as part of culture and the public commons. The university of culture promoted the value of creativity for the sake of truth-telling (within the elitist limits of its time). The advent of digital data storage and cyberspace has undermined this aspect of knowledge. Knowledge is everywhere and potentially accessible to anyone who seeks it out. However, to have value in the contemporary market economy, some knowledge has to be limited to create a demand for knowledge services (King, n.d.).[11] The university of excellence therefore became concerned with knowledge as a production value.

With the help of TRIPS, some of the world's wealthiest capitalists made fortunes by creating artificial markets. The individuals involved are lauded as examples of how entrepreneurship leads to success. But at the same time, hackers – the antiheroes of our time – have shown that networking for problem-solving where profit motives and 'human-capital profiling' are not present, often produces superior knowledge and solutions. In cyberspace, the hackers' collective efforts are still ahead – something democrats should be thankful for. At the same time, however, the growth of commissioned research as a source of income for universities is transforming what was once a public research space into a sphere in which private wheeling and dealing is increasingly possible.

Neoliberalism supports this transformation, because it links the university of excellence to 'the politics of large numbers', and this, in turn, is linked to how knowledge is valued in the market economy. Judgement about what knowledge is valuable is shifted to knowledge users, and linked to external criteria for relevance. Users communicate their needs through the neo-numeriocracy, and particularly through knowledge brokers such as ratings agencies and research councils. The criteria for excellence are thus created by a mix of bureaucratic interests, user interests and academic interests, in which the academy and epistemology has the weakest voice.

The aim of research collaboration in this context is primarily to promote competitiveness within and between units of excellence. Their central question is, 'what's in it for us?'

### The university of governance

The inauguration of the university of governance was the final shift away from 'knowledge for the sake of enlightenment' towards 'knowledge for society'. The arrangement of universities into faculties was, of course, linked to Kant and the Enlightenment. The belief was that experts with specialist skills would make more effective interventions in governing society. The further growth of disciplines and specialisations underlined the role of universities in training elites to take up positions in public and private governance.

What is now a widely accepted belief in the value of rationality in the form of 'knowledge for development' came to the fore from the end of the Second World War and remained dominant until the early 1980s. In this period, public and private bureaucracies (as well as academic services – the so-called liberal professions) co-evolved with the massification of higher education within a framework of governance and organisation. The shift in the West from elite to mass (and even universal) access to tertiary education also transformed the universities and how those educated in them became linked to the world of work; the term 'knowledge worker' entered common usage.

In terms of the labour market, the belief in rationality was, above all, a belief in the division of labour with ever-increasing levels of specialisation. In the mid 1980s, Kocka (1987) estimated that about 4 000 disciplines existed. Today that number is probably closer to 6 000. In addition, knowledge that used to reflect on and give meaning to the interaction between disciplines – namely, philosophy in Germany and the liberal arts in the Anglo-American world – became just another 'specialty' alongside and equal to other disciplines, and has never regained its privileged position. Instead, centres for advanced or interdisciplinary research have become arenas in which universities and academics reflect on the accumulated value of all their specialist knowledge and on their roles as social institutions with growing influence, but diminishing power.

A hyper-belief in the value of science drove the growth of disciplines and specialisation to a point where proper dialogue between them in daily practice became almost impossible, even within the same faculties. In this period, academics became (through their specialisations) experts who conquered political and economic administrations. Lawyers had been numerous before, but now other professionals joined government as specialists in different sectors. The realm of governance and of state bureaucracies (as well as the bureaucracies within big companies) grew as new expertise was deployed. In field after field, academics conquered government offices: departments of health, social welfare, industrial policy, economic policy, etc. These are just the prime examples of this new kind of knowledge-based rule. The academic community expanded with (and within) the state, until eventually the state grew into so-called fiscal crisis.

During this period, not academic reflection, but functionality dominated university policy-making. The question that emerged was: does everyone need to professionalise around specialised work roles? In response, Jürgen Habermas (1981) pointed out that the world of 'systems', governed by the language and power of experts, suppressed what he called the 'life world'. By extension, concerns emerged that the debate about experts was also suppressing (democratic) politics. As the realm of expert knowledge grew, anxiety about how experts were shaping politics and influencing the decisions of politicians – essentially, the relationship between politics and knowledge – became acute. As Luhmann (1992) observed, without knowledge it did not work, but with knowledge alone, it cannot work either.

An important perception, which led universities into the next period, was that state expansion exhausted the tax-base. It was clear that further taxation would threaten accumulation and competition, thus undermining the foundations of the state in the long run. This fiscal crisis, together with a shift in popular faith in knowledge as always neutral and technical, and therefore beneficial,[12] transformed ideas about the state, and about the relationship between knowledge and politics. From this point on, limiting the growth of the state became a key element of neoliberalism. The self-governance of institutions was touted as an alternative to state governance, and again the notion of competition came to the fore.

As noted, the number of higher education and science organisations has grown globally during the neoliberal era. What grew even faster were different types of neoliberal regulations and regulatory bodies: quality-assurance agencies, research-funding units, etc. This stands in stark contrast to the university of culture, but also to the university of governance when academics (as professionals) were trusted to develop knowledge and make sure it was relevant. In these models, academic actors earned their autonomy, freedom and creativity in exchange for rationality and responsibility in relation to state and business organisations alike. International co-operation stemmed from the same autonomous academic interests, and could thus flow in all directions wherever cross-national collegial networks were worth pursuing.

The transition from the university of governance to the neoliberal university of excellence was a dramatic shift that introduced competition into the field of knowledge itself, regulated by neo-numeriocratic control mechanisms (again, through the politics of large numbers, and linked to the OECD's means of blaming and shaming via ranking and rating). The contract between academic organisations and the professionals they educate was also terminated, with academic freedom being exchanged for rationality and responsibility. Academia and its professions are more easily controlled by being forced to compete. Crucially, this shaped new ways of valuing knowledge according to its contribution and relevance to private accumulation.

The university of governance and the university of excellence agree on one point however: unlike the university of culture, they both value knowledge products (outcomes) more highly than the process of knowledge creation or the formation of scholars.

## The university of culture

The university of culture can be traced back to the establishment of the Humboldt University of Berlin in 1810, and the intense debates that took place about how it should be organised. Although these debates deserve more discussion, I will limit myself to observations about how this model contrasts with those that prevail today.

Within German Idealism, the movement in German philosophy that began in the 1780s and prevailed in parts of Europe until the late 1800s, the ideal university is strongly linked to Wilhelm von Humboldt's ideas about:

- the indivisibility of research and teaching;
- the 'Bildung' of self-reflexive citizens who think independently;
- universities being funded and protected by, but independent of, the state; and
- universities as spaces for the development of a 'unity of knowledge' (with the help of philosophers).

Humboldt's aim was to create a sense of cultural unity through which, with the help of a common language, *Wissenschaft* could be expressed.[13] The process of research, through which teaching evolves, was seen as far more important than the product of knowledge. It was acknowledged that the process of doing research is what 'builds the person' whose academic leadership then contributes to shaping the nation.

Of course, other models of the university of culture could be highlighted – the English, or Scottish or later the hegemonic American, where 'the liberal arts' served as a unifier of knowledge. For many US universities, Humboldt, and the University of Berlin that he helped establish, was a vital inspiration, with several US institutions seeing themselves as having implemented Humboldt's ideas (Brandser 2006). The point here is more general, however: the period in which the university of culture held sway lasted all the way up to the start of the Second World War.

The model was not static, however, and shifts occurred as Humboldt's ideas were implemented. For example, the Technische Hochschulen in Germany were upgraded to universities around 1900. Later, the model changed again, opening up to professional disciplines whose character was defined by what can be called an 'engineering epistemology'; that is, by an interest in *what works* more than in *what is true*. Humboldt's existential questions about why we do what we do with the help of knowledge began to take a back seat. What was later analysed in England as a conflict between two cultures (as part of the transition from the cultural university to the university of governance) was, in Humboldtian terms, perhaps more a competition between types of '*Wissenschaften*' within the same culture.

## The ideal types and internationalisation

So how do the four types impact on academic collaboration across borders and across regions? Table 12.1 provides a summary of the four typologies of universities in terms of their relationships with other universities and academics around the world.

**Table 12.1: Characteristics of the four university types in relation to international collaboration**

| The university of democracy | The university of excellence |
|---|---|
| New alliances are forged around the globe to develop disciplines relevant to addressing 'global challenges' including social injustice. A growing division between academics working towards zero carbon growth, and those who argue that 'technology and the free market will rescue us'. A growing emphasis on ethical substantive rationality and behaviour with global networking guided by values of democracy and cross-disciplinarity. Allied with post-colonial deconstruction and reconstruction movements to oppose Western hegemony. | Networking and internationalisation is seen as a tool for self-promotion. University leadership guides internationalisation strategies to promote their institutions in competition with others in the so-called free market for educational and research services. 'Human capital development' and 'research output' are the focus of organisational efforts in a global competition. Downgrading of institutions and networks who can't or won't compete. |
| **The (rational) university of governance** | **The cultural university** |
| Collaboration between academics and states to source relevant knowledge for nation-state development and economic growth, with the intention of making state policy scientific (based on empirical evidence). Focus on organisation, rationalism and goal-oriented behaviour, with internationalisation driven by efforts to increase specialised knowledge at home. | Attempts to adapt universal principles of knowledge to local contexts in meaningful ways, and to develop a common language through which these can be expressed. Focus on identity formation using self-awareness as a model for collective culturally embedded behaviour; internationalisation is learning about oneself through the reflections of others. |

Various motives for internationalisation continue to inspire academics, but there has been a discernable shift towards the kind of motives outlined in Table 12.1 under 'the university of democracy'. Historical experience of similar kinds of change indicates that this means there is increasing awareness of the ways in which power shapes academic behaviour.

Each of the university types discussed have been marked by particular kinds of struggles between social actors and universities over the nature and extent of academic freedom. These include debates about degrees of state and religious control, and in the era of the university of excellence, the issue has been how 'knowledge for innovation' or supporting the 'knowledge economy' has conflated the role of universities with that of drivers of 'economic growth'.

If we are entering a new era of democratisation as I suggest, relations between knowledge and politics must and will change too. More importantly, how academics can take responsibility for the ways in which the knowledge they produce is used, and whether they should make their research broadly accessible, is being questioned. Within these debates is a growing awareness of how scientific knowledge is shaped by the powers that determine the contexts within which researchers and professors work. The ways in which Western and colonial knowledge still dominate the curricula of universities in former colonies is just one example. Western knowledge does not clarify its presuppositions and, by imposing its implicit values, this now-hegemonic knowledge system systematically represses other forms of knowledge and other value systems (Habermas 1981). Academics in the post-colonial world must therefore be more explicit about formulating and articulating their worldviews, so that they understand and explore how this shapes their research priorities and practices.

A lack of contextualisation implies a failure to consider or take responsibility for the consequences of one's work, and can easily lead to unethical behaviour. This is as true for academics as it is for anyone else. The need to both contextualise and to take more responsibility for the intended and non-intended consequences of how scientific knowledge is used is a challenge often directed at the academic community. This is where the university of democracy has the potential to stand out as an arena that welcomes new alliances across the previous colonial divides, and around substantial and consequential questions of ethics.

So far, the modern era has given rise to many tragedies and, with the universities co-opted into the 'knowledge economy', this trend is growing (Rudy et al. 2007). A substantial body of research records how academics use 'scientific objectivity' to avoid taking responsibility for the consequences of the knowledge they produce, while also avoiding being critical of the regimes that have long directed and funded knowledge production. After fifty years of silence, information about how the academic community served the Nazi regime, and even used the Nazis to promote their own 'scientific interests' is being exposed, but hardly reflected on (Fløgstad 2016). That there were more Nazi lawyers in the German government *after* the war than there were under Hitler is but one indication of how both universities and professional associations managed to neutralise their role during this period. Hiding beneath the convenient illusion that knowledge is 'objective', they convinced themselves that how knowledge is used is 'political' and that politics lies beyond the responsibility of both the academic profession and the university management (Jarausch 1990).

The same story can be told about apartheid. Many of those who drafted, and thereby helped to justify, apartheid legislation, have unashamedly continued to practise their profession under the new regime, making the necessary adjustments to hide their past, and create continuity within the country's legal institutions.

With hindsight, it seems clear that the atomic bomb was dropped more to announce the arrival of the world's new superpower than to stop the Second World War. Out of protests against nuclear weapons (including by those responsible for inventing them) a movement of scientists evolved who have stood up against weapon production. Admittedly, no network of scientists has had less success. In fact, without the weapons industry, America's elite universities would not enjoy the levels of affluence that they are now using to help them conquer the academic world. Gradually, scientists have given up working against the use of nuclear energy. South Africa's nuclear energy programme met little opposition in the apartheid years; today, plans for its expansion are on the table, although there is no solution to the nuclear waste problem. Again, the continuity is evident, and the protests have so far been too miniscule to make any impact on the state or its foreign allies. Similarly, numerous scientists continue researching and promoting the oil industry, even though the SDGs demand that the sector be scaled down and dismantled.

Economists, lawyers and accountants, particularly those that move in international circles, often with degrees from the most prestigious universities, make their fortunes by finding loopholes in tax laws, creating avenues for tax evasion and helping to create tax havens for multinational corporations and their tycoons. The universities that educate them boast of their candidates' abilities as proof of the outstanding quality of the education they received.

University ranking systems include 'labour market success' as a criterion, and the ratings (at the international level) go up, no matter who their graduates end up working for. A high number of the companies that currently offer the most rewarding and prestigious jobs are in industries that generate massive amounts of carbon emissions daily, regardless of the Paris Agreement. Thus, thanks to post-national academic networks, tax havens protect the global industries most responsible for global warming. Many critics of 'Western knowledge' from the post-colonial and other countries on the periphery condemn these kinds of alliances between knowledge, power and economics, pointing out that global capitalism's tax-evasions undermine the least developed countries even more.

The alternatives are growing, however, both within the universities and between the professionals they educate. Concerned scientists try to make colleagues aware of the consequences of their work, and develop an awareness that knowledge production has political consequences that scientists and academics must take responsibility for.

In the democratic university, which I believe is beginning to emerge, academic co-operation across borders will have to be politically responsible for its knowledge networks. Transcending the interests of individual universities with their logos and marketing departments, academics, whose aims are primarily epistemological, must drive post-national co-operation. This is necessary, both to renew scholarly disciplines and to strengthen the roles that academics play. However, as debates about how to escape the iron cage of neocolonial Western knowledge domination have shown, reforming curricula and knowledge institutions is not easy. Academics will need to ally themselves with and support other social forces that cut across national borders, to ensure that changes occur, making use of what can perhaps be called 'oppositional internationalisation' to supersede competition-based processes. International networks will be faced with the dilemma of how to take ethical and political responsibility for what knowledge to produce (while respecting academic freedom) and for how it gets shared and used. This includes reversing the TRIPS agreement and dismantling the patent system. Both what research is done and how findings must be shared is both a research and a political issue. The academic profession must regain control over its own work. Given the urgency of both reducing global warming and getting rid of poverty, this process must begin immediately.

For a start, the academic profession must rid itself once and for all of the notion that knowledge is invariably 'positive', that every question has one correct answer (the truth), and that this is to be obtained through one correct method. Rather, those seeking knowledge try to tell the truth, but acknowledge that any truth is relative to the social and political environment it reproduces.

Until now, far too many excellent academics and innovative researchers with great qualifications from prestigious institutions have devoted their time and energy to inventing products and processes that increase carbon consumption and/or help businesses improve their profit margins by laying off their workers and poisoning our planet. In the period of democratisation, the question is: can academics be persuaded to take responsibility for the consequences of their research and innovations? Can we regain control over the means of our own knowledge production, and commit ourselves to at least meeting the SDGs and the requirements of the 2015 Paris Declaration on Climate Change?

## Notes

1   On the ILO, see Stokke's (2015) broad analysis that seems to support the view that ILO was weakened during the neoliberal epoch. Stokke also noted that the adoption of the SDGs means that the ILO must play a more important role, and that it is likely to have the space to do so.

2   Interestingly, by establishing departments of like-minded professors, the US democratised the German model, and introduced academic competition within universities and its departments, not only between the holders of chairs at different institutions (as was the case in Germany). See Brandser (2006: 343), who attempts 'to describe how the Humboldt-university had a great impact on American education in the early and mid-nineteenth century'. He also tries to show 'how the ideas gradually were brought into disrepute, first because they were considered old-fashioned and residues of pre-modern social order, later because they were assumed to be dangerous and a potential threat to democracy'.

3    The time–space dimension is discussed in an exceptional book titled *Higher Education and Capacity Building in Africa* (Adriansen et al. 2016). The contributors bear witness to the tragedies of academic imperialism, arguing that the main struggles related to universities' European heritage 'is that what counts as legitimate, relevant and valuable knowledge on these campuses is measured by the same standards as in the Global North – a standard presented as universal when in fact it is shaped in a particular context, historically in a Western European context, and currently most often in an Anglo-American context' (p. 31).

4    The IAU planned to focus on how universities can contribute to the SDGs at their World Conference in Bangkok in mid November 2016. Before that, European universities gathered in October to discuss collaboration as well as the Higher Education Sustainability Initiative (HESI), which was established to influence the 2012 UN Conference on Sustainable Development (Rio+20). With a membership comprising almost 300 universities from around the world, HESI took responsibility for more than a third of all the voluntary commitments that came out of the Rio+20 conference (see https://sustainabledevelopment.un.org/index.php?menu=1073). In addition, masters degrees in sustainable development are springing up worldwide, showing universities' willingness to certify cross-disciplinary knowledge.

5    For a periodisation driven by a focus on power in and between societies, and which explains some of the environments within which universities institutionalise, see Mann (2013).

6    See http://www.oecd.org/edu/skills-beyond-school/higher-education.htm for more information on the OECD's schemes for 'enhancing higher education system performance'.

7    The numeriocratic period (without the neo) was between about 1945 and 1980 and was linked to state control.

8    Braithwaite and Drahos (2000: 62) called the TRIPS agreement 'a classic case of legal entrepreneurship'. According to them, the US's political and business communities combined their efforts (following the US mode of governance), and worked through the Advisory Committee for Trade Negotiations. They were joined by the major OECD countries, and then managed to link intellectual property issues to trade, thus profiting from the kinds of control and systems of punishment developed within what

became the World Trade Organisation (WTO). In the run-up to the formation of the WTO, the TRIPS agreement became part of the domain of that organisation. The US business community thus managed to initiate a new global epoch – the beginning of 'intellectual property globalisation' (p.63), with an organisation to oversee and manage the agreement. The consequences for the cyberspace and of course for the pharmaceutical companies, who were the first to push for the General Agreement on Trade in Services, have been enormous.

9      As Braithwaite and Drahos have shown, the hegemonic powers have secured control over the raw materials, the sources of capital, the markets and all the competitive advantages involved in the production of highly valued goods. This includes control of 'knowledge inputs' and 'abstract objects', such as 'algorithms implemented in software, the genetic information of plants and animals, chemical compounds and structures' (2000: 84).

10     In their book on the tragedies of academic capitalism, Rudy et al. (2007: 4) note that 'there are arguably three central principles and associated practices that must stand at the center of the world of higher education ... creativity, autonomy and diversity ... [and creativity is perhaps] the central principle'. What might be more important is to acknowledge that diversity is often a precondition for creativity. And diversity is precisely what the world stands to gain from new kinds of North–South relationships that are based on equity and respect.

11     King (n.d.: 5) noted that 'only by making intellectual resources scarce can capital profit from it; but only against a background of non-scarce, culturally common resources can it market its products and be sure to have new products to market'. Alerting us to the dawning of the epoch of the university of democracy, King showed that the privatisation of knowledge in the software-development and pharmaceutical industries has been outcompeted by communal knowledge networks. He observed that 'the fact that free peer co-operation can work and work well, makes the deliberate manipulation of knowledge for accumulation intolerable.' Observing that groups across the political spectrum are agreeing that 'concentrated ownership and control of knowledge, technology, biological resources and culture should be resisted by any means possible', King argues that 'the rights and identities underlying this ownership are contingent' and that 'new modes of co-operation are emerging on capital's own network infrastructure' (n.d.: 12).

12    Debates about positivism were also an important part of this shift.

13    Readings (1996: 65) defined *Wissenschaft* as 'the unity of knowledge that marks a cultured people'.

# References

Adriansen, Hanne Kristine, Lene Møller Madsen and Stig Jensen (eds) (2016) *Higher Education and Capacity Building in Africa: The Geography and Power of Knowledge under Changing Conditions*. London and New York: Routledge

Angermüller, Johannes (2010) Wissenschaft als Zälen. Regieren im digitalen Panoticon. In: Leon Hempel, Susanne Krasmann und Ulrich Bröckling (Hrsg) *Sichtbarkeitsregime: Überwachung, Sicherheit und Privatheit im 21. Jahrhundert* (Leviathan Sonderhefte). Berlin: VS Verlag

Berndt, Christian and Marc Boeckler (2009) Geographies of circulation and exchange: Constructions of markets. *Progress in Human Geography* 33(4): 535–551

Bok, Derek (2004) *Universities in the Marketplace. The Commercialization of Higher Education*. New Jersey: Princeton University Press

Boldizzoni, Francesco (2013) *On History and Policy: Time in the Age of Neoliberalism*. MPIfG Discussion Paper. Max Planck Institute for the Study of Societies, Cologne

Braithwaite, John and Peter Drahos (2000) *Global Business Regulations*. Cambridge: Cambridge University Press

Brandser, Gry Cathrin (2006) *Humboldt Revisited. The Institutional Drama of Academic Identity*. Bergen: University of Bergen Publications

Desrosiéres, Allain (2007) Quality and statistics: Origin of the movement and reflection on the criteria. In Tor Halvorsen and Atle Nyhagen (eds) *Towards a New Contract Between Universities and Society*. Bergen: University of Bergen Publications

Eigen, M, HG Gadamer, J Habermas, W Lepenies, H Lübbe and KM Meyer-Abich (1988) *Die Idee der Universität: Versuch einer Standortbestimmung*. Berlin: Springer

Fink, Leon, Stephen T Leonard and Donald M Reid (eds) (1996) *Intellectuals and Public Life: Between Radicalism and Reform*. Ithaca, NY: Cornell University Press

Fløgstad, Kjartan (2016) *Etter i saumane*. Oslo: Samlaget Gyldendal

Fourcade-Gourinchas, Marion and Sarah L Babb (2002) The rebirth of the liberal creed: Paths to neoliberalism in four countries. *American Journal of Sociology* 108(3): 533–579

Gorz, André (2003) *Wissen, Wert und Kapital: Zur Kritik der Wissensökonomie*. Zürisch: Rotpunktverlag

Habermas, Jürgen (1981) *Theorie des kommunikativen Handelns. Band 1: Handlungsrationalität und gesellschaftliche Rationalisierung*. Franfurt am Main: Suhrkamp

Halvorsen, Tor (2015) Introduction. In: Tor Halvorsen, Hilde Ibsen and Vyvienne M'kumbuzi (eds) *Knowledge for a Sustainable World: A Southern African–Nordic Contribution*. Cape Town: African Minds

Halvorsen, Tor (2016) South Africa, the OECD and BRICS. In: Einar Braathen, Julian May, Marianne Ulriksen and Gemma Wright (eds) *Poverty and Inequality in Middle-income Countries: Policy Achievements, Political Obstacles*. London: Zed

Halvorsen, Tor and Atle Nyhagen (eds) (2005) *The Bologna Process and the Shaping of the Future Knowledge Societies*. Bergen: University of Bergen Publications

Halvorsen, Tor and Atle Nyhagen (eds) (2007) *Towards a New Contract Between Universities and Society*. Bergen: University of Bergen Publications

Halvorsen, Tor and Peter Vale (eds) (2012) *One World, Many Knowledges: Regional Experiences and Cross-Regional Links in Higher Education*. Cape Town: SANORD

Heilbron, Johan (1995) *The Rise of Social Theory*. Cambridge: Polity Press

Higgins, John (2013) *Academic Freedom in a Democratic South Africa: Essays and Interviews on Higher Education and the Humanities*. Johannesburg: Wits University Press

Honneth, Axel (2012) *The I in We: Studies in the Theory of Recognition*. Cambridge: Polity

Jarausch, Konrad (1990) *The Unfree Professions. German Lawyers, Teachers, and Engineers, 1900–1950*. Oxford: Oxford University Press

Järvensivu, Paavo (2013) Transforming market-nature relations through an investigative practice. *Ecological Economics* 95: 197–205

King, Jamie (n.d.) The dissolving fortress. Available online

Klein, Naomi (2015) *This Changes Everything*. New York: Penguin

Kocka, Jürgen (ed.) (1987) *Interdisziplinarità: Praxis-Herausforderung-Ideologie*. Frankfurt am Main: Suhrkamp

Luhmann, Niklas (1992) *Die Wissenschaft der Gesellschaft*. Frankfurt am Main: Suhrkamp

Mamdani, Mahmood (2007) *Scholars in the Marketplace*. Dakar: CODESRIA

Mann, Michael (2005) *The Dark Side of Democracy. Explaining Ethnic Cleansing*. Cambridge: Cambridge University Press

Matthies, Hildegard and Simon Dagmar (Hrsg.) (2007) *Wissenschaft unter Beobarchtung. Effekte und Defekte von Evaluationen* (Leivathan Sonderheft). Berlin: VS Verlag für Sozialwissenschaften

Mjøset, Lars (ed.) (2011) *The Nordic Varieties of Capitalism* (Comparative Social Research, Vol. 28). Bingley: Emerald Group

Münch, Richard (2007) *Die akademische Elite*. Franfurt am Main: Suhrkamp

Münch, Richard (2011) *Akademischer Kapitalismus*. Berlin: Suhrkamp

OECD (1981) *The Future of University Research*. Paris

OECD (2016) *Measuring Distance to the SDGs Targets: A Pilot Assessment of Where OECD Countries Stand* (July). Available online

OECD (n.d.) *The Sustainable Development Goals: An Overview of Relevant OECD Analysis, Tools and Approaches* (September). Available online

Peck, Jamie (2008) Remaking laissez-faire. *Progress in Human Geography* 32(3): 3–43

Power, Michel (1997) *The Audit Society: Rituals of Verification*. Oxford: Oxford University Press

Power, Michel (2007) Research evaluation in the audit society. In: Hildegard Mathies und Simon Dagmar (eds) *Wissenschaft unter Beobarchtung. Effekte und Defekte von Evaluationen* (Leivathan Sonderheft). Berlin: VS Verlag für Sozialwissenschaften

Readings, Bill (1996) *The University in Ruins*. Cambridge, MA: Harvard University Press

Rudy, Alan P, Dawn Coppin, Jason Konefal, Bradley T Shaw, Toby ten Eyck, Craig Harris and Lawrence Busch (2007) *Universities in the Age of Corporate Science: The UC Berkeley–Novartis Controversy*. Philadelphia: Temple University Press

Schafer, Evan (1999) Science associations in the international sphere, 1875-1990: The rationalisation of science and that scientization of society. In J Boli and GM Thomas (eds) Constructing World Culture: International Nongovernmental Organizations Since 1875. Stanford, CA: Stanford University Press

Schmidt, Vivien A and Mark Thatcher (2013) *Resilient Liberalism in Europe's Political Economy*. Cambridge: Cambridge University Press

Shinn, Terry (1980) *Savoir scientifique et pouvoir social. L'École polytechnique 1794–1914.* Paris: Les Presses de Sciences Po

Stokke, Hugo (2015) *Decent Work: Principles, Policies and Programmes of the International Labour Organisation.* Bergen: University of Bergen Publications

Streeck, Wolfgang (2014) How will capitalism end? *New Left Review* 87: 35–64

Tjomsland, Marit (2005) Higher education and research in the Arab world: Status and future challenges. In: Tor Halvorsen, Gigliola Mathison and Tom Skauge (eds) *Identity Formation or Knowledge Shopping: Education and Research in the New Globality* (SIU Report). Bergen: NORHED

UN (United Nations) (2015) *Transforming our World: The 2030 Agenda for Sustainable Development.* Resolution adopted by the General Assembly on 25 September. Available online

UNFCC (United Nations Framework Convention on Climate Change) (2015) *Paris Agreement.* Paris. Available online

# About the authors

**Anders Bjørkelo** is a professor at the University of Bergen, Norway.

**Tor Halvorsen** is a senior researcher at the University of Bergen Global, and an associate professor in the Department of Administration and Organisation Science at the University of Bergen, Norway.

**Sk Tawfique M Haque** is a professor at North South University in Dhaka, Bangladesh.

**John Higgins** is the Arderne Chair of Literature at the University of Cape Town, South Africa.

**Johnson Muchunguzi Ishengoma** is a senior lecturer and head of the Department of Educational Foundations, Management and Lifelong Learning at the University of Dar es Salaam's School of Education, Tanzania.

**Ishtiaq Jamil** is an associate professor at the University of Bergen, Norway.

**ABK Kasozi** is a research associate at the Makerere Institute of Social Research in Kampala, Uganda.

**Ane Landøy** is head of the libraries at the University of Bergen, Norway.

**Mahmood Mamdani** is director of the Makerere Institute of Social Research in Kampala, Uganda, and Herbert Lehman Professor of Government at Columbia University, USA.

**Joe Mlenga** is a lecturer in the Department of Journalism and Media Studies at University of Malawi Polytechnic in Blantyre, Malawi.

**Maria GN Musoke** is professor of information science at the College of Computing and Information Sciences, Makerere University, Kampala, Uganda.

**Jorun Nossum** is a senior adviser at NORAD and the programme co-ordinator for the NORHED programme.

**Fadwa Taha** is a professor at the University of Hafr Al-Batin in Saudi Arabia and at the University of Khartoum, Sudan.

**Eren Zink** is a senior researcher in the Department of Cultural Anthropology and Ethnology at Uppsala University in Sweden.

www.ingramcontent.com/pod-product-compliance
Lightning Source LLC
Chambersburg PA
CBHW081736270326
41932CB00020B/3289